HISTORY OF THE PORTUGUESE IN BENGAL

Agud do Gange, esa terra de Bengala,
Ferti de sorte que outra nao lhe iguala.
Camões, *Lasiadas*, Canto VII, Stanza xx.

Here by the mouths, where hallowed Ganges ends,
Bengala's beauteous Eden wide extends.
Mickle's *Trans.*

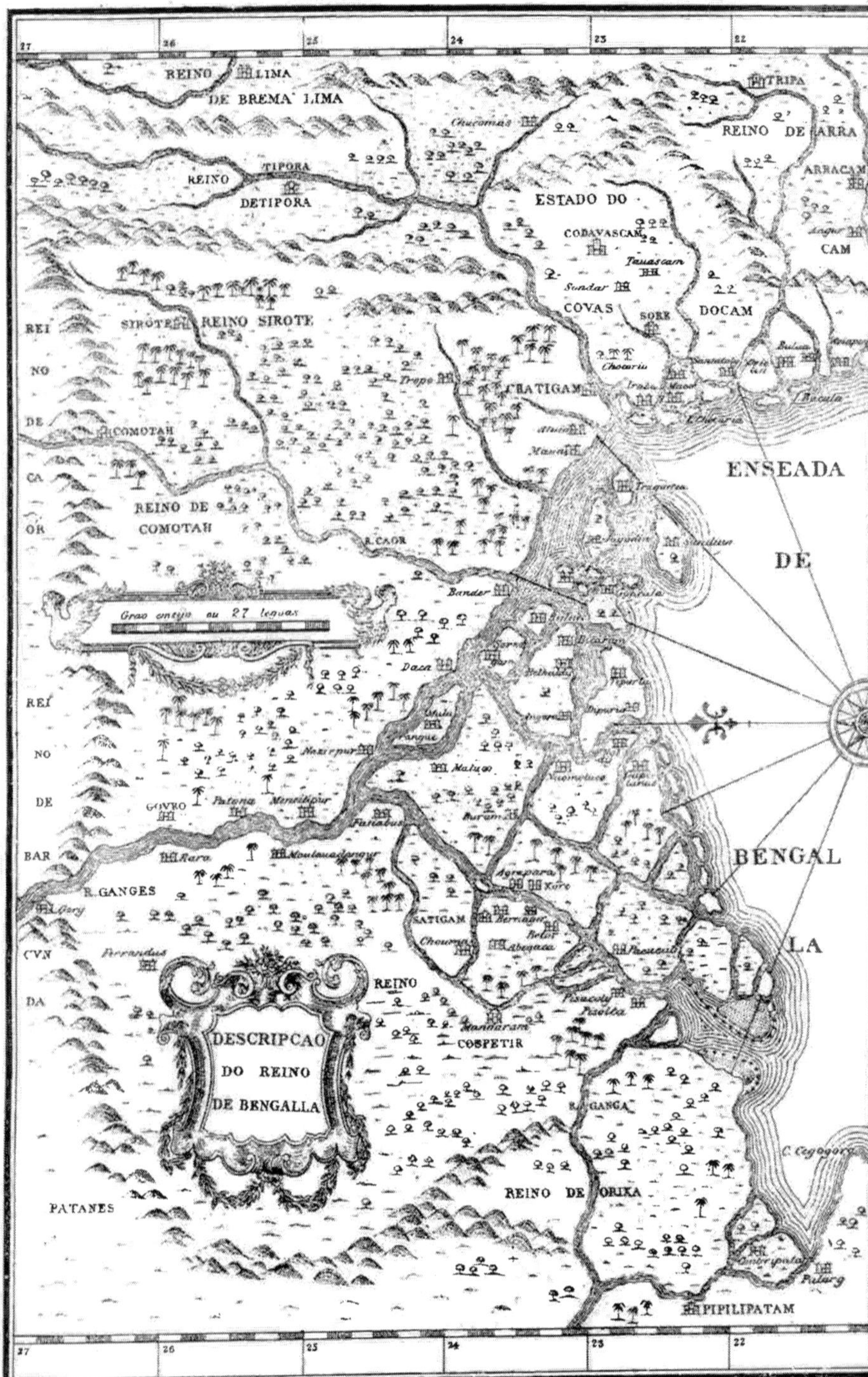

DE BARROS' MAP OF BENGAL (1550 *circa*)—*Asia, Dec. IV, Pt. II, page 451.*

History of the Portuguese in Bengal

J. J. A. CAMPOS

WITH AN INTRODUCTION BY
F. J. MONAHAN

MANOHAR
2026

Due to the academic and scholarly importance of this volume, we are reprinting/republishing it from the original source without any modifications or changes. Therefore, some misprints and errors may occur.

First published 1919
Reprinted 2025, 2026
First eBook edition 2025

ISBN 978-93-6080-698-9 (Hb)
ISBN 978-93-6080-944-7 (eBook)

Published by
Ajay Kumar Jain *for*
Manohar Publishers & Distributors
4753/23 Ansari Road, Daryaganj
New Delhi 110 002

Printed and bound in India

HISTORY OF THE

PORTUGUESE IN BENGAL

WITH MAPS AND ILLUSTRATIONS

BY

J. J. A. CAMPOS

JOINT EDITOR, THE CENTURY REVIEW,
MEMBER, ASIATIC SOCIETY OF BENGAL,
ETC. ETC.

WITH AN INTRODUCTION BY

THE HON'BLE MR. F. J. MONAHAN, I.C.S.

PRESIDENCY COMMISSIONER OF BENGAL.

CALCUTTA:

BUTTERWORTH & CO. (INDIA), LTD., 6, HASTINGS ST.

WINNIPEG: BUTTERWORTH & CO. (Canada), Ltd. | SYDNEY: BUTTERWORTH & Co. (Australia), Ltd.

LONDON:

BUTTERWORTH & CO., BELL YARD, TEMPLE BAR,

Medical Publishers

1919

INTRODUCTION

Mr. Campos has collected some interesting facts relative to the commercial, political and religious enterprises of the Portuguese in Bengal. The work done by the Portuguese as pioneers of European commerce in this part of India has not, perhaps, been sufficiently recognized, for it may truly be said that they paved the way for the commercial ventures of the Dutch, the English and other European nations. Mr. Campos quotes an array of authorities in support of his account, which shows that the Portuguese, at the beginning of the seventeenth century, occupied a position in Bengal comparable to that of the British in the middle of the eighteenth, with their settlements and factories, not only at the principal ports, Hughli and Chittagong, but at many other places in Eastern and Western Bengal, and as far up the Ganges as Patna. The earliest British mercantile adventurers in Bengal and the adjacent countries established themselves, naturally, at places where the Portuguese had already found openings for European commerce. Some of the Portuguese settlements in Bengal became virtually independent of the Mughal rulers of India, being directly subject, for a time, to the jurisdiction of the Portuguese Government of Ceylon.

The causes of the decline of the Portuguese power in the East, and the hostilities between the Portuguese in Bengal and the Mughal Emperor, culminating in the Mughal attack on Hughli, the heroic defence, and the tragic fall of that place, are briefly sketched in this book. There is a striking parallel between the early history of Hughli and that of Calcutta, though the circumstances of the taking of Hughli by Kasim Khan in 1632, differed greatly from those of the capture of Calcutta by Siraj-ud-daula in 1756, which led to the establishment of the British Empire in India.

The Portuguese were the first to introduce Christianity in Bengal, and their Missionaries of different Orders were active at all their settlements. Christian Churches and settlements still existing are the most conspicuous and enduring memorials of Portuguese influence in this province.

The first type-printed works in the Bengali language were a Catechism, a Compendium of the Mysteries of the Faith, and a Vocabulary, published at Lisbon in 1743. It is difficult to realize now, that, at one time, Portuguese was the common language of the important centres of maritime commerce in India, spoken by Europeans of all nations, who came to trade in this country and by the Indians who did business with them. Current Indian languages contain many Portuguese words, most of them connected with trade, or the Christian religion, or names of articles of common use, imported from Europe.

Mr. Campos has evidently devoted much care to the compilation of the book and has drawn on Portuguese sources not often utilized by students in this country. He has been careful to refer to the authorities for statements made by him and his work is, I think, an useful contribution to the history of Bengal and bibliography of the subject with which it deals.

CALCUTTA, 9-1-19. F. MONAHAN

PREFACE

This work has grown out of a series of lectures delivered on the "History of the Portuguese in Bengal," in commemoration of the fourth centenary of the advent of the Portuguese in the Bay of Bengal.* It is scarcely necessary to explain the *raison d'être* of the book for, in spite of the existence of vast stores of material for a history of the Portuguese in Bengal, there is not a single comprehensive work on the subject. Most of the information about the Portuguese, given in modern historical writings and scattered in the Calcutta Journals and in the Bengal District Gazetteers, is fragmentary and often erroneous.

No Portuguese writings, except Captain Stevens' misleading translation of Faria y Souza's *History*, have been generally taken into account, and some errors of Faria y Souza himself, which F. Danvers perpetuated, have gained ground. Considering that the Portuguese were the earliest Europeans to found settlements in Bengal, that other European nations generally established themselves on or near the very places which had grown into centres of trade owing to the Portuguese, and that the influence which the Portuguese once exerted is still working silently in Bengal, a work presenting their history in a correct perspective is evidently a pressing need. The production of this book will, I hope, supply this long-felt need. I am conscious of its many imperfections which were unavoidable owing to the stress of other duties which left me little leisure, but I have spared no effort to sift truth from tradition, to obtain unvarnished historical accuracy,

* The lectures were delivered at the Union Chapel Hall, Calcutta, under the auspices of the *Indo-Portuguese Association* and the *Young Men's Union*, on the 3rd, the 10th, and the 17th April, 1918, the first and the second being presided over by the Hon'ble Mr. Justice W. Greaves, and the third by the Hon'ble Mr. F. J. Monahan, I. C. S. Presidency Commissioner of Bengal.

and to present a connected account of the rise, the fall and the relics of the Portuguese in Bengal.

In the preparation of this work I cannot claim to have exhausted all the sources of information, but I can say I have utilized the chief Portuguese writings and balanced them with contemporary foreign and Indian writings. The importance of the Portuguese writings lies in that they give valuable information not only about the Portuguese doings in Bengal but also about the general history and geography of Bengal. In this work I have, however, confined myself to the essential facts about the Portuguese only, compelled as I was by other duties to set narrow limits to it. In the near future, it is my intention to bring out a contribution to the History and Geography of Bengal, based on Portuguese and other European writings, which have not yet been utilized or exist in scarce and scattered fragmentary studies. The materials for such a work are numerous and should fill volumes.

I must express my gratitude to the Hon'ble Mr. F. J. Monahan, I. C. S. for generously consenting to write an introduction for the work, to Mr. O. Lys, Acting Consul for Portugal for much encouragement and a donation towards the costs of printing, to Dr. H. W. B. Moreno B. A. Ph. D., my learned colleague in *The Century Review*, for many valuable suggestions, to Mr. H. M. Rogers, who has always been my ready helper, to Mr. E. Boxwell and Dr. P. Bragança e Cunha for much kindly assistance, and to Mr. S. P. Banerjee for carefully revising the proof sheets.

My thanks are due in a special measure to the Revd. Fathers of the St. Xavier's College, my old professors, for having kindly placed at my disposal, their "Count Gœthals Indian Library," which contains valuable Portuguese works and also to the Revd. Vicars of the Portuguese Churches in Bengal, who very kindly furnished me with information regarding the Churches entrusted to their care.

I owe a debt of gratitude to the management of *The Bengal Past and Present,* for their courtesy in lending for this book, the blocks of the illustrations facing pages, 58, 108, and 149.

The orthography followed in the book is that of the Bengal Gazetteers, but the Portuguese proper names, with a few exceptions, have been spelt as in the Portuguese language.

J. J. A. CAMPOS

CONTENTS

PAGES

CHAPTER IV

PORTUGUESE SETTLEMENTS IN THE HOOGHLY DISTRICT

CHAPTER V

THE GROWTH OF THE SETTLEMENT OF HOOGHLY

CHAPTER VI

PORTUGUESE SETTLEMENTS IN EASTERN BENGAL

CHAPTER VII

THE RISE OF SEBASTIAO GONSALVES TIBAU

CHAPTER XVII

PORTUGUESE LANGUAGE

CHAPTER XVIII

PORTUGUESE CHURCHES

PAGES

ADDENDA

MAPS AND ILLUSTRATIONS

CORRIGENDA

Page	Line	
22	2	for "joins it higher up" read "flowing southwards joins the Hooghly above Sankrail."
43	3	for "condutced" read "conducted"
52	17	for "wife" read "wife's name."
54	8	for "be" read "he"
"	note 1	for "Akbarnama" read "History of India"
90	note 1	for "Pilgrimes" read "Pilgrimes, Vol. X."
93	19	for "wreek" read "wreck"
94	11	for "the earliest settlement" read "one of the earliest settlements"
"	15	for "was referred" read "referred"
102	4	for "church*" read "church"
105	2	for "Nicote" read "Nicote's"
"	23	for "1622" read "1632"
107	6	for "280" read "380"
110	9 and 10	for "The Marquis...premier" read "the Portuguese government"
115	8	for "cinammon" read "cinnamon"
118	7	for "unstincted read "unstinted"
130	8	for "intervened" read "interviewed.
132	10	for "his" read "her"
148	13	for "historian" read "historic"
"	15	for "seige" read "siege"
"	18	for "280" read "380"
150	note †	for "elsewhere" read "in the Addenda"
205	23	for "Quaterly" read "Quarterly"
206	18	for "the some" read "some"
227	1	for "Bengali" read "Hindustani"
244	12	for "Jesoph" read "Joseph"

The references to the pages of *The Bengal Past and Present* relating to the quotations from Manrique's *Itinerario* are not correct as the pagination of the reprints, which were consulted, did not correspond to the original pagination of the *The Bengal Past and Present.* But there will be no difficulty in finding the correct page, when the No. of the Journal is known.

BIBLIOGRAPHY

Aīn-i-Akbarī, The, by Abul Fazl 'Allami. Translated from the original Persian in 3 Vols. ; Vol. I by H. Blochmann, Calcutta, 1873 ; Vols. II and III by H. S. Jarret, Calcutta 1891-94 ; Printed by the Asiatic Society of Bengal.

——Translation by F. Gladwin, 3 Vols., Calcutta 1783-86.

Albuquerque, Braz de—*Commentarios de Affonso Dalbuquerque.* These Commentaries of the great Albuquerque were published in Lisbon by his son Braz de Albuquerque in 1557 ; were re-printed by him in 1576 and republished in 1774 in four Vols. They have been Englished by W. de Gray Birch and published by the Hakluyt Society in four Vols., (1875-1884). There are some misunderstandings in the translation of Birch, which A. C. Burnell puts down to the translator's want of acquaintance with Indian matters.

Archivo Nacional da Torre do Tombo, Alguns Documentos de—Lisboa, 1872. This work contains documents dating from the time of Prince Henry upto the year 1529, and includes many Albuquerque's dispatches.

Asiaticus—*Ecclesiastical Chronology and Historical Sketches respecting Bengal,* Calcutta, 1803.

Barbosa, Duarte—*Liuro em que da relação do que viu e ouviu no Oriente.* The author was the cousin of Magellan and it is possible Magellan himself wrote parts of it. The author gives one of the earliest Portuguese accounts, geographical and historical, of the lands he visited in the Indies, not ommitting Bengal. Barbosa knew well the Indian languages, and Gaspar Correa has great praise for him. A translation of the work from a Spanish MS. by the Hon. Henry E. T. Stanley was published by the Hakluyt Society in 1866 under the heading "*A Description of the Coasts of East Africa ana Malabar.*

Barros, Joao de (1496-1570)—*Asia* : *dos Feitos que os Portugueses fizeram no Descobrimento e Conquista dos Mares e Terras do Oriente.* The author was Treasurer and Factor at the India House (*Casa da India*) and made use of all the documents at his disposal. Though he never came to India he is a valuable and recognized authority on Portuguese affairs in India. He wrote the work in four Decades in imitation of Livy. The first Decade was published in 1552, the second in 1555, the third in 1563, and the fourth was left in disorder at the time of the author's death. As arranged and completed by Lavanha it was published in 1613. The whole history deals with the affairs up to 1539. The best edition is the one published along with Couto in 1777-78 in 24 volumes. The fourth Decade contains a chapter especially devoted to the history of Bengal and an invaluable Map which though published in 1613 is based on the author's drawings. Its date may be roughly set down to 1550, and as such it is the earliest Map of Bengal.

Bartoli—*Missione al Gran Mogor del Padre Ridolfo Acquaviva*, Rome, 1714.

Bernier, Francois—*Travels in the Mogul Empire*, (1656—1668) translated by A. Constable and revised by V. Smith. Second edition, 1914.

Beveridge, H.—*The District of Bákarganj, its History and Statistics*, London, 1876.

Bicker, J. F. J.—*Collecção de Tratados e Concertos de Pazes*, 14 vols., Lisboa, 1881-1887. The twelfth volume contains two valuable documents regarding the Bandel Church.

Blochmann, H.—*Contributions to the Geography and History of Bengal*, Calcutta 1873, reprinted from the *Journal of the Asiatic Society of Bengal*. The work relates to the Muhammadan Period A. D. 1203 to 1538.

——*Aīn-i-Akbarī*, Vol. I, *vide* s.v. Aīn-i-Akbarī.

Bocarro, Antonio(+1628)—*Decada XIII da Historia da India*, (1612—1617). Lisboa, 1876. The author was the successor of Couto in Goa. He continued the decades of Couto, as the latter continued those of de Barros. The work of Bocarro is not, however, a real continuation of Couto as between the chronicles of the two authors there is a lapse of twelve years during which five Governors ruled Portuguese India.

Bowrey, Thomas—*A Geographical Account of Countries Round the Bay of Bengal* (1669—1679), Edited by Sir R. C. Temple and published by the Hakluyt Society, 1905.

Bradley-Birt, F. B.—*The Romance of an Eastern Capital*, London, 1906.

Burnell, A. C.—*vide* Yule

Cabral, Fr. Joao, (S. J.)—*The Fall of Hooghly.* This is a letter written from Ceylon on November 14, 1633. Fr. Cabral was an eye-witness of the siege of Hooghly. Its translation by the Rev. Fr. L. Besse has been published in the *Catholic Herald of India*, Calcutta, January, the 30th, 1918 and succeeding Nos.

Cacegas, Fr. Luis—*Historia de San Domingos, reformada e amplificada por Souza*, 4 vols., 1767.

Camoes, Luis de—*Os Lusiadas*, first published in Lisbon 1572. Besides being one of the greatest Epics of the world, the *Lusiadas*, is a valuable history and contains graphic descriptions of Indian scenes, places, customs and manners. The two complete translations of the poem are those of Mickle and Burton.

Careri, Gemelli—*A Voyage Round the World*, in Churchill's *Collection of Voyages* Vol., IV. Third Ed., London, 1745.

Castanheda, Fernao Lopes de (+**1559**)—*Historia do Descobrimento e Conquista da India pelos Portuguezes*, 8 books. Coimbra 1551—1561. The author came especially to, and travelled much, in India in order to write his history. In date of publication the first book of this history is anterior to that of de Barros's. It covers the period from 1497 to 1549. The accuracy of Castanheda's history is unquestionable. There were ten books written but the last two were destroyed by the King as they contäined unvarnished truth, not complimentary to Portugal. Faria y Souza, however, finds fault with Castanheda's style and wlth his Geography but gives him the credit of the accuray of his statements. A translation into English by N. L [itchfield] was published in 1582, but as Burnell points out it differs from both the first and second Portuguese editions.

Catrou, Fr. F. F.—*A History of the Mogul Dynasty in India*, London 1826.

Census Reports—Birch's *Census of Calcutta* of 1876, Beverley's *Census of Calcutta and Suburbs* of 1881, O'Malley's *Census of Bengal and Calcutta* of 1911

Chronista de Tissuari, O,—*vide* Cunha Rivara

Correa, Gaspar—*Lendas da India*, 4 vols., Lisboa, 1858—64. The author came fo India in 1514 and was secretary to Albuquerque. This very trustworthy history covers the period between 1497 and 1550. It was published for the first time in 1858—64, three centuries after the author's death. The first volume is legendary but the other three, beginning with Albuquerque, are of great value. His chronology, which differs from that of de Barros, is more accurate and has been followed in this work. Correa's account of the three voyages of Vasco de Gama have been translated by Lord Stanley of Alderley for the Hakluyt Society, 1869

Cossigny, Charpentier—*Voyage au Bengale*, 2 vols., Paris, An 7 de la Republique Françoise

Couto, Diogo de(+1616)—*Asia, Decadas IV—XII.* The author was for a long time employed at Goa. He wrote nine decades in continuation of de Barros treating of the history of the Portuguese from 1526 to 1600. The first decade of de Couto overlaps the last decade of de Barros. The eleventh decade is lost. The sixth decade was touched up by Adeodato, Couto's brother-in-law, and is not of much value The edition consulted is of Lisbon 1778—1788.

Crawford, Lt. Col. D. G.—*A Brief History of the Hughly District*, Calcutta, 1903.

Cros, Fr. J, (S. J.)—*Lettres de S. François Xavier*, 2 vols. Toulouse 1900.

Cunha Rivara, Joaquim Heliodoro—*Archivo Português Oriental.* Nova—Goa, 6 fasciculos, 1857—1876. This extinct perodical, contains valuable documents found in the government Archives of Portuguese India.

——*O Chronista de Tissuari* 1866. In this monthly periodical edited by Cunha Rivara are to be found valuable historical and political documents relating to the Portuguese in India. Cunha Rivara was the worthy successor of de Barros, Couto and Bocarro.

Dalgado, S. Rodolfo (Monsenhor)—*Influencia do vocabulario Português em Linguas Asiáticas*, Coimbra, 1913. This is a learned work on the influence of the Portuguese language on the Asiatic languages, and contains lists of Portuguese words in no less than fifty-two Asiatic languages

Dalrymple, A—*The Oriental Repertory*, 2 vols. 1808. Printed by the E. I. Co., Originally published in numbers, 1791—97.

Danvers, F. C.—*The Portuguese in India*, 2 vols., London, 1894. This work is very disappointing, in as much as it is no more than a new version of Faria y Souza. It contains the errors of Faria y Souza, does not take into account the Indian historians and is not written in relation to the general history of India.

——*Report on the Portuguese Records relating to the East Indies*, etc., London, 1892. The author was commissioned by the English Government to examine and report on the Portuguese records in the public libraries of Portugal and the work contains extracts from some documents examined by the author.

Diaries—*Vide* Hedges and Master.

Documentos Remettidos da India—These documents taken from Goa to Portugal have been published by the Royal Academy of Lisbon. 3 vols. 1880-1883. These volumes form the VII, and IX Tomos of the

Collecção de Monumentos ineditos para Historia das Conquistas dos Portugueses em Africa, Asia and America.

Elliot, Sir H. M.—*The History of India as told by its own historians*, 8 Vols., London 1867-1877.

Ennes—*Historia de Portugal.*

Encyclopedia, The Catholic, New York, 1907-14. Contains an historical article by Fr. L. Delaunoit S. J. on Catholicism in Bengal s. v. Calcutta.

Faria y Souza, Manoel de (1581-1649)—*Asia Portuguesa*, 3 Vols., Lisbon, 1616-75. The author never came to India but made use of many unedited MSS. On the whole this history is only a summary of de Barros. A very unfortunate translation of the work by Captain Stevens was published in London, 1694-95, some passages being mistranslated, others badly summarized and many omitted altogether. Unfortunately this bad rendering of a Portuguese history has served as an authority for for most writers on Bengal and Burma.

Federici, C. de.—*Viaggio de M. Caesare de Federici nell India Orientale etc.* Venice 1587. In Purchas, *Pilgrimes*, Glasgow 1905, Vol. X, there are "Extracts of Master Cæsar Frederike, his eighteene yeares Indian observations", to which references have been made.

Fitch, Ralph—*Voyages to Ormuz and so to Goa etc.* (1583-1891). Also in Hakluyt, in Purchas and in Pinkerton. The text consulted in this work is Horton Ryley's *Ralph Fitch*, London, 1899.

Foster, William—*The English Factories in India*, 9 Vols. Oxford 1986-1915. This work is a Calendar of documents in the India office, British Museum and Public Records Office, ranging from 1618 to 1654. These are printed as a continuation of *Letters received by the East India Company from its servants in the East, 1602-17*, published in 1896-1902.

Gazetteers, Bengal District.—*Hooghly*, 1912, by L. S. S. O'Malley and Monmohan Chakravarti ; *Chittagong*, 1908, by L. S. S. O'Malley ; *Dacca*, 1912, by B. C. Allen ; *Noakhali* 1911 by J. E. Webster ; and other volumes.

Gladwin, F.—*Vide* Āin-i-Akbarī.

Glanius—*A Relation of an Unfortunate Voyage to the Kingdom of Bengal*, London 1682. It was first published at Amsterdam.

Goes, Damiao de.—*Commentarii rerum gestarum in India circa Gangem a Lusitanis anno 1538*, Lonvain 1544.

Guerreiro, Fr. Fernao—*Relaçam Annual das Cousas que fizeram os Padres da Companhia de Jesus nas partes da India Oriental* etc. Lisboa 1605, second edition. The Relation on Bengal, Arakan and Pegu in Book III, foll. 41r-49v refers to the years 1602 and 1603. Du Jarric follows him closely.

Hamilton, Captain Alexander—*A new Account of the East Indies*, 2 vols., London, 1739, second edition.

Heber, Bishop R.—*Narrative of a Journey through the Upper Provinces of India* etc. 2 vols., London 1828.

Hedges, William.—*The Diary of Hedges*, 3 vols, Hakluyt Edition, 1887-89.

Hill, S. C.—*Bengal in 1756-1757*, 3 vols., London, 1905, Published in the India Record Series. Contains a selection of papers and documents, regarding the affairs of the English during the reign of Sirāj-ud-daulā in Bengal and an author's summary of events at this time.

Hunter, W. W.—*Orissa*, 2 vols. 1872.

Hyde, Henry Barry.—*Parochial Annals of Bengal*, Calcutta 1901.

Jarret, H. S.—Vide Aīn-i-Akbarī.

Jarric, Pierre de (S. J.) 1566-1616—*Histoire des choses Plus Memorables* etc. 3 vols., Bordeaux 1608-1614. Part IV, Book VI contains an account of missionary work in Bengal and Arakan, based on Pimenta, or more probably on Fr. Fernão Guerreiro, who utilized the letters in Pimenta.

Kloguen, Fr. Cottineau de.—*An Historical Sketch of Goa*, Madras 1831. Reprinted by the *Catholic Examiner*, Bombay.

Laet, John de.—*De Imperio Magni Mogolis sive Indica Vera, Commentarius*, Leyden 1631. Partly translated and annotated by E. Lethbridge in the *Calcutta Review*, October 1870—January 1871.

Lafiteau, P. Pierre Francois.—*Histoire des Decouvertes des Portugais dans le Noveau Monde*, 2 vols. Paris 1733.

Laval, Francois Pyrard de—*The Voyage of François Pyrard* Translation by Albert Gray for Hakluyt Society, 2 vols., 1887-90.

Linschoten, J. H. Van (1563-1633)—*The voyage of John Huyghen van Linschoten to the East Indies.* Edited by A. C. Burnell and P. A. Tiele for Hakluyt Society, 2 vols. 1885.

Manucci, N.—*Storia do Mogor*, Irvine's translation, London 4 vols. 1907.

Manrique, Sebastiao (+1669)—*Itinerario de las Missiones, Que hizo el P. Maestro Seb. Manrique* etc. etc. Rome 1649 and 1653. Manrique, though a Portuguese, wrote in Spanish like Faria Y. Souza. The *Itinerario* of Manrique covers the period between 1628 and 1641 and deals with his travels and experiences in Bengal,

Arakan, Cochin, Goa, Malacca Macao, Cochin China, Macassar, Masulipatam Punjab, Kandahar etc. It contains a valuable account of Shāh Jahān, his government, his treasures and his dominions. Father Cardon S. J. has translated chapters 1—9 dealing with Bengal, (*Bengal Past and Present Vol. XII 1916*) ; F. Cotta chapters 10—16 dealing with Arakan (*ibid.* Vol., XIII., *1916*) ; Sir Edward Maclagan Chapters 1-72 (*Journal of the Punjab Historical Society, Vol. I. 1911-12.*) ; Fr. H. Hosten chapters 78-82 dealing with the Fall of Hooghly, (*The Catholic Herald of India*, 17th April 1918 to 12th June 1918 Calcutta).

Marshman, John Clark—*The Life and Time of Carey, Marshman and Ward*, embracing the History of the Serampore Mission, 2 Vols. London 1859. This work is quoted as *History of Cri Ramapur Mission.*

Master, Streynsham—*Diaries of Streynsham Master 2* Vols., London 1911. These Diaries relating to the period 1675-1680, are edited by Sir Richard C. Temple and published in the Indian Record Series.

Mc. Crindle, J. W.—*The Commerce and Navigation of the Erythræn Sea*, Calcutta, 1879. This work is a translation of the *Periplus Mari Erythræi* and of Arrian's account of the Voyage of Nearkhos.

Monseratte, Fr. A. (S. J.)—*Mongolicae Legationis Commentarius*, translated by Fr. Hosten S. J. and published in the *Memoirs of the Asiatic Society of Bengal* Vol. III.

Murray, Hugh—*Historical Account of Discoveries and Travels in Asia*, 3 vols., Edinburgh, 1820.

Nunes, A.—*Livro dos Pesos da Ymdia e assy Medidas e Mohedas,s* 1554. Published in the *Subsidios para a Historia da India Portuguesa*, by the Royal Academy of Lisbon, 1868.

Oliveira Martins—*Historia de Portugal.*

Oriente Portugues, vide under Periodicals.

Orme, Robert—*History of...Hindustan*, 2 Vols. London, 1778, 1780.

Orta, Garcia de—*Colloquios dos simples e Drogas e Cousas Medicinaes da India* etc. Originally printed in Goa in 1563 and re-printed in Lisbon in 1872. Though the title of the book suggests it is a Pharmacographical work, it contains much valuable information on other matters respecting India and is characterized by a sound sense.

Ovington, Rev. F.—*A Voyage to Suratt in the year 1689*, London, 1696.

Phayre, Sir Arthur P.—*History of Burma* etc. London 1883.

Pimenta, Fr. Nicolau (1546-1614)—*Carta que o P. N. Pimenta... escreveu ao Geral a 26 de Novembro de 1599 e ao 10 de Dezembro de 1600.* This letter of Pimenta which includes the letters of other Missionaries describe the Missionary work in Bengal during 1599 and 1600 and throw much light on the conditions of Bengal at the time. The letter was originally written in Latin. A Portuguese version of the letter was pnblished in 1602. There are German, Latin and French Versions. Du Jarric utilized it freely.

Purchas, Samuel—*Hakluytus Posthumus, His Pilgrimes* etc. 20 Vols. Glasgow 1905. Purchas was assisting Hakluyt to collect the materials which the latter did not live to publish. At his death in 1616, Hakluyt left the pa pers for Purchas.

——*His pilgrimage, or Relations of the World* etc. 1614. This is really a separate work from the above one, though usually bound in continuation with it. The edition of 1614 is consulted in the book,

Roteiro da Viagem, de Vasco da Gama—First edition was published in Lisbon in 1838 and the second in 1861.

Salim, Ghulam Husain—*The Riyazu-s-Salatin*, Calcutta 1902. The work is translated from the original Persian by Maulvi Abdus Salam and published by the Asiatic Society of Bengal.

Santa Maria, A. de—*Information de un Indio de Bengala que vivio 400 annos*, Salamaanca 1609. I have not been able to find this book, which it appears, throws much light on the history of the Portuguese in Bengal. It is mentioned by Ternaux-Compans in the "*Bibliotheque Asiatique*" and afterwards by A. C. Burnell in his *Tentative List of Books and some MSS relating to the History of the Portuguese etc.*

Sen, Dinesh Chandra—*History of Bengali Literature and Language*, Calcutta, 1911..

Smith, George—*Life of William Carey*, London, 1885.

Souza, Fr. Francisco de, (S. J.) + 1713—*Oriente Conquistado a Jesu Christo pelos Padres da Companhia de Jesus etc.* Vols. 2, Lisbon 1710. A new edition published by the Examiner Press in Bomhay in 1886, has been consulted in this work,

Stavorinus—*Voyage to East Indies*, translated from the Dutch by S. H. Wilcoke, 3 Vols. 1798.

Stewart, C.—*History of Bengal*, Calcutta 1910, Second edition. The original edition was published in.

Stirling, A.—*An Account of Orissa*, Calcutta 1904, reprinted from the original edition of 1882.

Talish, Shiāb-ud-dīn—*Fathiyah-i-Ibriyah* and its *Continuation* (Bodleian Library M S. Bod. No. 589). Talish was in the service of Mir Jumla and accompanied him in the invasion of Cooch 'Behar and Assam. H. Blochmann gave a long abstract of the *Fathiyah-i-Ibriiah* in the *Journal of the Asiatic Society of Bengal* 1872, Part 1, No. 1 pp. 64-96 and Jadunath Sarkar has translated the parts relating to the *Conquest of Chittagong* and to the *Pirates of Chittagong* in the same *Journal*, 1906 Vol. II. No. 6 [N.S.]

Tavernier, J. B.—*Travels in India*, 2 Vols. London 1889, translated and annotated by V. Ball.

Tennent, Sir J. E.—*Ceylon, an account of the Island*, 2 Vols. 1859.

Thevenot, M. de—*Relation de divers voyages curieux* etc. Paris Paris 1696. The second volume contains a valuable Portuguese Map.

Tieffenthaler, J. Fr. and others—*Description Historique et Geographique de L'Inde*, 3 Vols., Berlin 1786-88. Vol. 1 contains Fr. Tieffenthaler's description.

Toynbee, G.—*Sketch of the Administration of the Hooghly District from 1795 to 1845*, Calcutta 1888.

Valentyn, Francois—*Ond en Nienw Oost Indien*, Amsterdam, 5 Vols. Fifth Volume (5 de Deel) contains *Keurlyke Beschryving van Choromandel, Pegu, Arracan Bengale* etc. The Map of Bengal and Arakan faces p. 146 of Bk. IV. 5 de Deel.

Valle, Pietro del—*Voyages* etc. 8 Vols. Paris 1745.

Varthema, Ludovico de.—*Itnerario de Ludovico de Varthema etc.*, 1570. The translation by Dr. G. P. Badger was published by the Hakluyt society in 1863. Purchas gives an abridgment. Though Varthema relates his travels in Egypt Syria Arakan Persia etc, Garcia de Orta (*Colloquios* f. 29 v and f. 30) denies Varthema's having ever gone beyond Calicut and Cochin, a thesis which, Yule aptly says, would not be difficult to demonstrate out of the very narrative.

Westland, J.—*A Report on the District of Jessore*, Second edition, Calcutta 1874.

Whiteaway, R. S.—*The Rise of Portuguese Power in India* (1497-1550), Westminster, 1899. This history though incomplete, is, indeed, of great merit as the author has consulted all Portuguese historians and has connected his history with the general history of India.

Wilson, C. R.—*Early Annals of the English in Bengal*, 2 Vols. 1895-1911. The second volume is in two parts.

Yule, Henry, and Burnell, Arther Coke—*Hobson-Jobson, A Glossary of Colloquial Anglo-Indian Words, etc.* London, 1903.

PERIODICALS

Bengal Catholic Herald, Calcutta (extinct).

Bengal Past and Present, Calcutta.

Calcutta Gazette, The, Calcutta.

Calcutta Review, The, Calcutta.

Catholic Herald of India, The, Calcutta.

Indo-European Correspondence, Calcutta (merged into *the Catholic Herald of India*).

Journal of the Asiatic Society of Bengal, Calcutta.

Missions Belges de la Compagnie de Jesus, Bruxelles. This is a monthly periodical, published from 1899, and its collection contains some articles on Portuguese Missionary work in Bengal.

Oriente Português, O, Nova-Goa. This monthly periodical, founded in 1904, is devoted to historical and archæological studies regarding the Portuguese in the East. It is a worthy continuation of the *O Chronista de Tissuari* and of the *Archivo Português Oriental*.

PART I

THE RISE

OF THE

PORTUGUESE IN BENGAL

HISTORY

OF THE

PORTUGUESE IN BENGAL

CHAPTER I

THE PORTUGUESE EPIC PERIOD

Cesse tudo o que a Musa antigua canta,
Que outro valor mais alto se alevanta.*
Camões, Lusiadas Cant. I St. iii.

A General Outline

Four centuries have sped since the Portuguese first drank of the waters of the Ganges. It was 1517. King Manoel, the fortunate (*o venturoso*), whose reign was immortalized by the discovery of the sea-route to India, was on the throne of Portugal. Queen Elizabeth was not yet born and over eighty years were yet to elapse before she was destined to sign the memorable charter which originated the East India Company. Baber had not come down from the heights of Kabul to found the Mughal Empire. The Portuguese had, however, already established the foundation of an Eastern Empire and were already pushing their power to Bengal.

* Cease, ye heavenly Muses, songs of ancient lore,
A greater star now rises on Creation's shore.
Trans. J. C.

D. João de Silveira was the first Portuguese commander* of an expedition to come to Bengal. In 1517 he landed on the coast of Arakan whence he steered towards Chittagong staying in the Bay for a considerable portion of the year 1518. He had come to Bengal not as an itinerant foreigner like the Venetian Nicolo Conti or the Bolognese Ludovico Di Varthema. Like the ancient Megasthenes, who was perhaps the first European to behold the Ganges, Silveira came to Bengal as the envoy of a European nation—of that small nation, shot into the western corner of Europe, geographically occupying an area of barely 34,000 square miles but historically great in civic feats and martial triumphs. He belonged to that race that had scurried the Moors out of Portugal and had hotly pursued them into Africa, conquering such possessions as Ceuta, Fez, Morroco, Macau, Mozambique, Congo, and Guinea ; that had even penetrated into their stronghold in Asia establishing their supremacy in such rich Eastern centres as Goa, Malacca, Ormuz, Cochin and Ceylon. The Portuguese visited Bengal when their long-cherished dreams about the creation of an Empire in the East were about to be realized. The dawn of the sixteenth century had ushered in a period of conquest as the close of the fifteenth century had witnessed the culmination of discovery. As early as 1494 Spain and Portugal, known together as Iberia to Herodotus and the Greeks, and called Hispania by the Romans, had already divided between themselves the eastern and western hemispheres.

A glance on this great movement that revolutionized an age and marked a new era in discovery and geographical expansion, revealing to man "more than half the globe" !

* Silveira commanded the first expedition to Bengal but he was not the first Portuguese to come to Bengal, as stated by modern writers. João Coelho was in Chittagong before Silveira, and many Portuguese, specially from Malacca, had come to Bengal in Moorish ships as roving traders. Besides, the Portuguese who had settled in Piplī (Orissa) in 1514 had visited Hijīlī (Western Bengal) about the same time.

On a July morning in the year 1415 the waters of the Tagus witnessed the departure of an esquadron of 59 galleons, 63 transports and 120 various kinds of vessels carrying 20,000 soldiers and 30,000 sailors against the Moorish stronghold of Ceuta*. On the 21st of the next month Ceuta passed into the hands of the Portuguese after a glorious and well-contested fight with the Moorish Chiefs. Overwhelmed with joy the King of Portugal knighted on the battlefield his three sons, one of whom was the renowned Prince Henry the Navigator, and the other Dom Pedro, the first foreigner to be elected Knight of the Garter. It was the first conquest, the first firm foothold on the coast of Africa. The effect of the conquest was magical. The whole nation rose as one man in a burst of enthusiasm. The spirit of discovery and conquest was kindled and Portugal dreamt of greatness at the cost of the vast, unknown lands where a legend placed a Prester John† and of a boundless sea that extended from her shores to—where?

The Taking of Ceuta, 1415

The national sentiment would have, however, been strangled and all aspirations suffocated unless a master-hand had guided the energies of the Portuguese people. With the times arose the man. This genius was the Prince, known to immortality as Infante Henrique. Strong, daring, and determined, his one ardent desire was to rescue from the oblivious empire of the sea, lands that were unknown or else indifferently regarded by the rest of the civilized world. But the task was not easy. The current opinion was that Africa was not circumnavigable. Hipparchus had

Prince Henry, the Navigator

* Ceuta, situated on the African side of the Straits of Gibraltar, was strongly fortified and defended by the bravest portion of the Muhammadan population.

† Prester John, a semi-mythical Asiatic potentate of the Middle Ages, was supposed to be both king and priest of a Christian country between Persia and Armenia. Modern scholars identify him with Gur Khan founder of the Black Cathay Empire in the XII. century.

stated that Africa was a big continent extending to the South Pole and that there was no sea but was shut up by land. Ptolemy had adopted his opinions and the Greek geographers had mapped out about the equator of the earth an uninhabitable land which they fancied as being surrounded by a torrid zone of fiery heat, where life would be scorched by the blazing sun. The Prince, however, was convinced of the error of these views by the power of inspiration which is the gift of genius. In the twilight age of geographical knowledge he fought, with the firmness of his conviction, the geographers and the existing beliefs. He vowed to show that Africa was circumnavigable and that in all probability there existed a maritime route to India.* He found heroes equal to the task. It is difficult to say whether the people made the man or the man the people. A race Celtic in origin but mixed with Roman, Carthaginian, Gothic and lastly Semitic blood had developed into heroes and sages. When Prince Henry proposed the conquest of Ceuta the whole nation rose to the call. Even the dying queen† was foretelling days of grandeur on her death-bed, and when consoled that she would yet see Portugal emerge glorious was murmuring with lips that were soon to close for ever :—

"No....................yes, from above. My death will not, however, detain you a moment. In a week, for the feast of San Thiago.........................." She had breathed her last.

It is interesting to note that in the expedition to Ceuta

* It is not certain whether Prince Henry was fully convinced of the existence of a sea-route to India, but he had hopes of reaching India by rounding the southern point of Africa.

† Queen Phillipa, wife of Dom João I, and mother of Prince Henry was an English Princess being the daughter of John of Ghaunt, Duke of Lancaster. She was so high-souled that on her death-bed she gave a sword to each of her five sons in order to wield it in defence of the country, widows, orphans and especially against infidels.

England sent some help to Portugal and encouraged a wealthy Englishman to take with him four ships laden with provisions. There had been amicable relations between England and Portugal since King João, the father of Prince Henry had signed with Richard II of England the Treaty of Windsor in 1386 and had tightened the bond of alliance by his marriage with Phillipa of Lancaster. Prince Henry the Navigator was, therefore, the nephew of Henry IV of England and great-grandson of Edward III.

England, an Ally

The whole of Europe was so astounded at the conquest of Ceuta that Prince Henry was invited by the Pope of Rome, by the Kings of England and Castille and by the Emperor of Germany to take command of their forces on land and sea. His dreams were however different. He had bridged over the Atlantic and had united Portugal and Africa. He would not rest satisfied until the whole continent of Africa was explored and, if possible, the maritime route to India discovered. He erected an observatory and established a naval school on the promontory of Sagres in Algarve where he collected the best geographers and mathematicians. It was in this school that Columbus learnt the first principles of navigation. Absorbed in his sea-problems he discussed here the probability of the existence of new worlds and investigated the secrets of the sea and the winds. Here he built those small barques of one mast, or two in the case of long voyages, with which the first Portuguese argonauts braved the fury of the sea. It was here that for the first time the possibility of sailing round the continent of Africa and ultimately reaching India was established.

It was the time when sailing a few degrees beyond the Straits of Gibraltar was considered to be a wonderful feat. The last limit of Spanish exploration was Cape Non, (*No*) and as its name indicates it was thought to be impossible to double its rocky point where the winds and waves beat furiously. Prince Henry, however,

First Discoveries

knew no impossibilities. Year after year he sent expeditions till at last Cape Non was passed. Zarco at the head of an expedition landed about 1418 in the Island of Madeira. This discovery was the first result of Prince Henry's explorations. Another expedition driven eastward by the winds discovered Porto Santo. In 1433 Gonçallo Velho discovered the Azores; In 1434 Gil Eannes at last doubled Cape Bojador and dispelled the age-long superstitious belief, that none would return who rounded it.

However successful the Prince may have been there were not wanting captious minds who questioned what was, barring an empty glory, the material benefit of these discoveries. He was too far in advance of his age and had to battle with ignorance and blind prejudice. The geographers still ridiculed the belief in the existence of a sea route to India. The enormous cost of the expeditions was not worth incurring for the barren gain of a cape or a coast land. But the Prince was inflexible and the nation stood by him. He was conscious, however, that a small country like Portugal could not fit out so many expeditions without risking financial ruin. He was sure on the other hand that there would finally grow up between Portugal and the discovered lands a trade which would enrich her beyond measure. He, thereupon, prevailed on the Pope to concede to the crown of Portugal the perpetuity of all lands beyond Cape Bojador including the Indies, on the ground that he had to contend at an enormous expense against the infidels of the African coast. The vast revenues of the Order of Christ at first provided him with necessary resources for his daring plans of conquest and discovery.

The Dawn of Trade

What the Prince anticipated was at last realized. In 1439 one of his expeditions entered Porto Cavalleiro and for the first time brought gold and slaves to Portugal. Here at last was the material advantage of the discoveries clearly demonstrated. Gold quickened the desire for more gold. The very same critics who had tried to convince the nation that the cost of the Prince's expeditions was more than she could bear, laid down their pens and flocked to the Bay of Lagos. Not only in Portugal but all over Europe there was a feverish excitement to navigate under the Portuguese flag. Success followed success. One expedition explored the coast as far as Cape Blanco and another going beyond Cape Blanco discovered Arguin in 1445. Thus regions lying 300 leagues distant from the continent were revealed to the knowledge of man. The sea was dark no more.

Prince Henry's Last Successes

In 1447, a new fleet was in preparation. To bring rich cargoes of merchandise, gold and slaves small boats were no longer serviceable. They now built caravels with two to four masts, weighing 50 to 150 tons. This was the type of ships which made the fifteenth and the sixteenth centuries notable for a wonderful geographical expansion. The next year a fleet of these caravels entered the Gulf of Arguin and laid the foundations of the first military fortress. In 1455-56 Luigi Cadamosto, a Venetian gentleman who commanded the Navigator's expeditions, not only discovered Cape Verde Islands but cruised along the Senegal, the Gambia and the Rio Grande. Prince Henry was not unfortunately destined to live long to see the fruit of his enterprises. Death came to claim him in 1460 amidst his plans still unfructified and maps still incomplete. He left, however, in the hearts of his people the love of discovery and conquest. The motto which graces his statue to-day—"*Talent de bien faire*"—is a striking testimony to his genius and his greatness.

Dom Affonso V 1438-1481

Dom Affonso V, who was on the throne of Portugal at this time had the enterprising spirit of his uncle Prince Henry but did not possess his energy. Moreover in the latter part of his reign his attention was directed towards his war with Spain for the succession of Queen Joana to the crown of

Castille. He entrusted all the maps, which his uncle had not lived to complete, to a Venetian in the Convent of San Miguel of Murano. The completion of the new map took three years to accomplish. In this map, *Cavo Di Diab* (Cape of Good Hope) was distinctly laid down as the southern-most extremity of Africa and to the north-east of it, *Sofala* and *Xengibar* (Zanzibar) were correctly marked, 30 years before Dias doubled the Cape of Good Hope or Covilhão landed in Sofala from a Moorish ship. In 1461, a year after the Prince's death Pedro de Cintra, who was entrusted by the king with two caravels, discovered Sierra Leone and went some miles southwards. Fernão Gomes, on the other side, who had bought the monopoly of trade with the African coast went for the first time two degrees south of the equinoctial line and woe to the geographers ! he was not scorched by the fancied fire of the sun. A period of inactivity followed, synchronous with the war with Spain. The kingdom of Prester John was still obscure ; there was not the faintest sign of the gorgeous and mysterious land of India. After half a century of voyages Portugal had only collected a little gold and a few slaves. The national sentiment was growing cold.

Dom Affonso's son, João II, now ascended the throne and a new era dawned. He set to work with all the energy of

Dom João II
1481-1495

Prince Henry but was unfortunate, however, in that he treated Columbus as a visionary when he submitted to him his schemes of a wonderful discovery.* He sent an expedition under Diogo Cão, who in 1484 went up to the Zairie and discoverd Congo, sailing 200 leagues beyond. On his voyage back, Diogo Cão brought with him an ambassador of the King of Benin who requested the King of Portugal to send

---

* It must be said to the credit of Dom João II that he himself was ready enough to accept the proposals of Columbus, but he was overruled by his Council.

missionaries to his kingdom in order to establish there the Christian religion. He also spoke of a powerful king named Ogane, who wielded temporal as well as spiritual power over a large number of people dwelling 350 leagues in the interior of Benin. Could he be the Prester John of the legend? The description tallied. The time was opportune for the propagation of the Christian religion and for commercial expansion.

Peres de Covilhão and Paiva Affonso

He lost no time in despatching in search of Prester John, Peres de Covilhão and Paiva Affonso whom he knew to be the fittest men as they had been in Barbary before and knew Arabic well. They started in May 1487, went to Naples, thence to Rhodes, Alexandria and Cairo. In Cairo they joined a company of Moors who were going to Aden, where they learned of the profits that could be derived from the trade with Calicut. They parted at Aden and agreed to meet again in Cairo. Paiva went to Ethiopia, Covilhão bent his way towards India. With his good knowledge of Arabic and fascinating manners he made friends with the Moorish traders he came across. In their ships he travelled to Cananor, to Calicut, to Goa, to Ormuz and even to Sofala. His object was to observe and draw a map of his travels for his king. He saw at Calicut an enormous trade of ginger, pepper, cloves and cinnamon. In Sofala he gained the valuable information that all along the west, the coast may be sailed and that not far off lay the Island of the Moon (*Lua*) now known as Madagascar. He immediately communicated to the King all he had seen and learned, assuring him that if he sent an expedition to sail along the coast of Sofala the vast Island of the Moon would be in his hands. He also suggested the possibility of crossing the eastern seas and reaching Calicut. He at last returned to Cairo in order to meet his friend Paiva, only to find that he had died some time before. Here ended all that Covilhão did for the Portuguese Empire. His future career was quite singular. He went to Ethiopia and penetrating near Zeila at last reached the court of Prester John whom the Portuguese people were determined to reveal for almost a century. The legend was not wholly a myth. The discovery was memorable. Covilhão was however a changed man. He renounced the west for the luxuries and gorgeousness of the East. He did not even care to give an account of his discovery to the King. Neither did he see Portugal any more. He spent 33 years of his life in the court of Abyssinia, where he was the leading spirit. It is worthy of note that to Covilhão belongs the honour of having been the first to mark the itinerary of the voyage to India showing that the East might be reached by cruising round the south of Africa.

Bartholomeu Dias 1486

King João not hearing anything from Covilhão, prepared another expedition under command of the renowned navigator Bartholomeu Dias. This memorable expedition consisted only of one tender and two ships weighing 50 tons each. With the object of reaching India he sailed southwards along the route which Diogo Cão had traced and reached the bay named Dias Point. Against rough weather he persisted in a southerly direction until he reached the southern point of the Orange River. He called it *Angra das Voltas* or Cape of Turns. The storm increased in fury. With ragged sails and battered ships the crew were driven mercilessly along the coast. But Dias did not flinch. Suddenly the weather changed. Why was it so terribly cold? Dias guessed the position of land was some geographical landmark. With the skill of a navigator he turned in an easterly direction and then steered northwards. He had achieved a feat of far-reaching importance and he knew it not. He had rounded the Cape. He continued his course and endeavoured to ascertain where he really was. He reached a small island, where he planted a pillar with a cross on a rock which still survives. This island is known as Santa

Cruz. He hardly realized still that he was treading the land beyond the Cape where no European had yet ventured to appear. He had braved fierce winds. His crew clamoured for return. He turned west and the reality dawned upon him. He sighted the Cape and found to his surprise that he had rounded the southernmost point of Africa. He called the cape *Cabo Tormentoso,* (Stormy Cape) in memory of the tempests and high winds that assailed this vast promontory.

When Dias returned to Portugal the people were in raptures. The passage to India which haunted the dreams of Prince Henry was now within reach. Amidst the acclamation of the people, the King, buoyant with hopes of reaching India, changed the name of the Cape into *Cabo de Boa Esperança* (Cape of Good Hope.) This was the last discovery which King João II rejoiced over, before his death.

The era of navigation saw its climax in the reign of King Manoel who ascended the throne in 1495. Two years later the

Vasco da Gama 1497-1498

new monarch with Bartholomeu Dias, was occupied in presiding over ship-building works and the construction of a new fleet. This fleet consisted of only four ships of 100 to 200 tons each. Why, then, this great sensation on the shores of Belem? The King was sending Vasco da Gama to discover the sea-route to India. After attending Mass in the chapel of Santa Maria de Belem in the midst of the nobility of Portugal, da Gama sailed out from the Tagus, on the 8th of July 1497* with the fleet which was destined to lay open the gates of the mysterious East. He passed the Canaries, Cape Verde Islands, San Thiago, St. Helena, and then turned towards the Cape of Good Hope. He sailed to Mombassa, Mozambique and Melinde where there were already a handful of Portuguese. At Melinde they took a pilot and sailing northwards reached the coast of

* This date is the one given by de Barros. Correa fixes the date on the 25th March, Osorio on the 9th July.

Calicut in August 1498.* The riddle of centuries was solved. East and West had met.

When da Gama allowed a Portuguese convict to land in Calicut a Moor from Tunis asked in Castilian "*Al diablo que te doy, quiem te trouxe aqua?*" †

The Moor, the Moor again—in Portugal itself, on the coast of Africa and now again in India. What was the reply?

"*Viemos buscar Cristãos e speciarias*". ‡

Christians first and then spices. The incident shows that the object of the Portuguese discoveries was more to convert new people to Christianity than to establish commercial relations.

Portugal did not still rest satisfied. In 1500 Alvares Cabral set out with an imposing fleet from the shores of Portugal, commissioned by the King to establish commercial relations with India. He had, however, his own ideas. Steering eastwards in the Atlantic he asked himself—what lay to the west? In the northern hemisphere Columbus had discovered the Indies. Were there no Indies in the southern hemisphere? He determined to explore. The result was the discovery of Brazil.§ Within the next five years Ascension Island (1501) St. Helena (1502) and Ceylon (1505) were discovered. In 1506 Tristão da Cunha explored in the Atlantic, the Islands known by his name and in the same year the veil which covered the Island of the Moon or Madagascar was lifted. In 1507 the Maldive Islands, in 1509 Malacca and Sumatra, in

* It is not quite correct to suppose that da Gama *first* landed in Calicut. He first landed in Pantalani and not in modern Calicut. As to the exact date of da Gama's arrival there are quite a dozen different versions. De Barros and Goes give 29th August, Correa 18th September, Castanheda beginning of September.

† "May the devil take you, what brought you here?"

‡ "We have come to seek Christians and spices."

§ De Barros, Goes and Osorio state that Cabral was driven westwards by the gales ascribing the discovery of Brazil to chance. The author of the *Lendas* has another story. However, recent researches based on the letters written to Dom Manoel show that Cabral deliberately bent his way westwards in the Atlantic.

1512 the Moluccas and China were explored. In 1519-22 Magellan at last penetrated the portentous Pacific, landed in the Philipines and for the first time in the history of mankind sailed round the world.

The Period of Conquests

The discovery of the sea-route to India! What was its meaning for the world? When the Moorish sword was hanging over the fate of Europe, the discovery struck a blow to the Moorish power in Asia checking its onward advance. It gave the deathblow to the trade of three continents that passed through the Arab gates, the Red Sea and the Persian Gulf,—to this trade that had made the East proverbial for wealth and embellished the dreams of the Arabian Nights. Portugal was now no longer the *discoverer*. She was the *conqueror*. Early in the sixteenth century the entire trade of Europe, Asia and Africa was by force of arms wrested from Moorish hands by the bold Portuguese. Albuquerque that astute and far-seeing administrator, the first European after Alexander the Great to dream of an Eastern Empire and the first European who actually held sway in the East, since the Tartars had driven out the last of the Greeks from Bactria, had already achieved his memorable conquests by 1515. He had secured in safety three most important centres on the Eastern coasts: Malacca, commanding the straits through which the trade of India and China passed; Ormuz that commanded the other channel through which the traffic of the east was forced to pass on its way through Persia and thence to Europe; and Goa, on the Malabar Coast, which eventually became the Portuguese metropolis in the east where flocked the traders from Arabia, Melinde, Sofala, Cambay, Bengal, Pegu; merchants from Siam, Java, Malacca, Persia, China and even America. Every vessel that passed the Persian Gulf had to first pay the Portuguese toll at Ormuz; and even the African vessels that crossed the Red Sea paid their toll at Muscat. The

Portuguese commercial supremacy was now firmly established in the East and her flag waved triumphantly on an almost unbroken coast from Gibraltar to Abyssinia and from Ormuz to Malacca.

In the reign of King Manoel, the reign immortalized by the discovery of the sea-route to India, factories were established

King Manoel
1495-1521

in Calicut, Cananore and Cochin, (1500). The Kings of Quiloa* and Baticola were forced into submission (1502). In 1503 the first Portuguese fortress in India was erected at Cochin. Mombassa was occupied in 1505 and in the same year forts were erected at Quiloa, Angedive† and Sofala. The fortress of Socotra was captured (1506) and a settlement established there and in Ormuz. In 1510 Goa was finally conquered. Malacca (1511) and Ormuz (1515) the two keys to the main Arab channels of commerce passed into the Portuguese hands. In 1517 the Portuguese penetrating into China settled at Canton establishing factories at Shangch'wan and Ningpo. In the same year the Portuguese began to visit Bengal. A fort was erected in Ceylon, in 1518, and treaties of peace were signed with the Kings of Siam (1518) and Pegu (1515). In 1521 the Portuguese supremacy was firmly established in the Malay Archipelago and forts were erected at Pacem (Sumatra) and Ternate (Moluccas).

The reign of Dom João III, which followed, marked a period of the foundation of towns and the establishing of

Dom João III
1521-1557

settlements. On the Coromandel coast were founded the cities of St. Thomé of Mylapore, of Negapatam and of Jafnapatam. In the Moluccas, Tidore was made tributary to the crown of Portugal.

---

* Quiloa is not the same as Quilon. The former is an island off the coast of Zanzibar, and was a kingdom in Africa. The latter (Coulão of the Portuguese) was a kingdom and a city south of Cochin.

† Angedive is an island two miles off the coast of North Canara.

On the northern coast rose the Portuguese cities of Chaul, Bassein and Damaon and various towns on the coast of Cambay. Forts were built in Diu and Chale. In Ceylon were raised the towns and forts of Galle, Negumbo, Baticola and Trincomali. On the coast of China was founded Macau which still belongs to Portugal.

On King Sebastião ascending the throne, the Portuguese empire in the east flourished for a time but soon after its decadence began. In the earlier part of his reign the conquered foes were pacified and Portugal was reaping the benefits of her former struggles. It seemed the new King might easily occupy the throne of the Great Mughals and the destinies of a vast empire pass in his hands. The successes were, however, the last flashes of a flickering flame, about to be extinguished. Mombassa was secured and a fort erected; more forts were raised in Mangalore, Barielore and Onore (Canara province), in Siriam (Pegu) and in Sena and Jete on the rivers of Cuama. And then the town of Hooghly was about to be founded in Bengal. The Moorish vessels were swept from the Indian Ocean while the Portuguese vessels sailed with safety in the eastern seas commanding all the principal sea-routes.

Dom Sebastião 1557-1578

Well may Faria y Souza be stirred to ecstasy when he speaks that his country's power extended from the Cape of Good Hope to the frontiers of China embracing a coast line of not less than 12,000 miles.

The riches which the Portuguese commercial enterprises brought to the nation are inconceivable. From Japan came fleets laden with silver. China furnished gold, silks and musks. Cloves were shipped from Moluccas; spices and nutmegs from Sunda, cinnamon from Ceylon, wood from Solor, camphor from Borneo. From Bengal came rich varieties of cloth; from Pegu the finest rubies; from Masulipatam valuable diamonds;

The Extent of Trade

from Manar pearls and seed-pearls. The Maldives were explored for amber; Cochin was sought for raw hides; Malabar for pepper and ginger; Canara for all sorts of provisions; Cambay for indigo and cloth. Linseed was conveyed from Chaul, incense from Casem; horses from Arabia; elephants from Jafnapatam; carpets and silks from Persia, aloes from Socotra; gold from Sofala; and ivory, ebony and amber from Mozambique. Above all vast sums of money came from the gateways of commerce—Ormuz, Goa and Malacca, and from the tributes paid by the kings under Portuguese suzerainty.

One can scarcely imagine this violent superhuman impulse which led a small nation to immortalize two centuries of discovery and conquest. To say that a fort was built in Ormuz or that Malacca and Goa were captured is easy enough. It is difficult, however, to realize what sacrifices it entailed. The East which the Portuguese found was far, far different from the East which the English and Dutch found when they sought for facilities of trade. The Portuguese had to overthrow the influence of the Moors when their avalanche was threatening to sweep through the whole of Europe and make the way easy for themselves and, incidentally so, for other European nations. They succeeded, but the nation small as it was, and is, soon exhausted itself in the attempt. When the Portuguese came to India they had not to deal with savage tribes as the Spaniards and the English found in America, but they were confronted with a civilization much older than that of Europe and with theological and philosophical speculations whose antiquity extended far beyond the times of Greek and Roman legends.

The Epic

Fortunately the soul of the nation found expression in an epic—the sublime epic of Camões in which as Montesquieu says* the poet combines the charm of the Odyssey with the magnificence of the Æneid. Though the golden age of the Portuguese has

* *Spirit of Laws* (Nugent) xxi, 21.

departed, the song that the poet sang still burns bright immortalizing the flame of Portuguese genius. By a strange irony of fate the *Lusiadas*, "that Homeric apotheosis of a great, heroic people" was voiced forth at the hour of their fall. Were Camões to add any more strophes to the *Lusiadas* they would constitute an elegy, not an epic.

Fallen, as is the Portuguese Empire in the East, it may be well to quote the verdict pronounced on the Portuguese by the *Historians' History of the World.** "If the Portuguese had been as skilful speculators as they were intrepid sailors and distinguished warriors, Henry the Navigator, who set the example of maritime conquest, Dias, Vasco Da Gama, Cabral Albuquerque, valiant captains identified with all the glories of the Aviz dynasty, would have imitated the speculative prudence of the Dutch, their rivals. And if, when the illustrious house of Braganza opened the era of national liberties, the people had had in their heads less of poetic imagination, and more power of reason; if, courageous and adventurous as they were, they had shown themselves more positive, the French, at first, and then the English, would never have invaded their treasury, exploited their soil, and paralyzed their industries. Truly a child-like nation, satisfied with little, pursuing the ideal, economical without avarice, pure in morals, sober, generous, hospitable, the Portuguese have bred heroes in place of diplomats, poets in place of capitalists."

The Verdict

In the glowing picture of the heroic age of the Portuguese one cannot fail to discern the shadow of crime that followed in the wake of their triumphs; but which nation has been spotless? Portugal abused her power; but when was not abuse the curse of mankind? The Portuguese efforts for dominion in the East have been attended with much violence

* *Historians' History of the World* Vol. X p. 425.

and bloodshed but one cannot help gazing in wonder on the enterprise and valour of a small nation that taught the world a new geography and opened the gates of the East to the West.

CHAPTER II

BENGAL

"The Paradise of India"*

Bengal at the time of the Advent of the Portuguese

When in quest of new horizons and a wider scope of activities the first Portuguese bent their way to the shores of Bengal the reigning dynasty was that of the Lodi independent kings who had thrown off the yoke of Bakhtiyār Khiljī's successors in 1338. Syūd Husain Shāh, known as the most powerful of the independent kings of Bengal, was on the throne and held his court in historic Gaur, which was, it is computed, a magnificent city five or six centuries before Christ. Gaur was to Bengal what Delhi was to Hindusthan. It was still magnificent and opulent, seat as it was of a thousand kings, though Husain Shāh in a freak of fancy had allowed his soldiers to plunder it on his ascending the throne. The dynasty of the independent Kings lasted only up to 1538 when Sher Shāh, the Tiger, made himself master of Bengal. In the beginning the Portuguese had, therefore, to contend with the Muhammadan chiefs and only a few years after, with the successors of Sher Shāh. Neither the Lodi rulers nor the Afghāns were so liberal-minded as the Mughals proved to be when after the fall of Daūd Khān in 1576 they wrested the kingdom of Bengal from the Afghān chiefs.

---

* A Memoir by Monsieur Jean Law, Chief of the French Factory at Cossimbazar says: "In all the official papers, *firmans, parwanas* of the Moghal Empire, when there is question of Bengal, it is never named without adding these words "Paradise of India", an epithet given to it *par excellence*". Cf. Hill's *Bengal in 1756-57*. Vol. III p. 160. Aurangzeb is said to have styled Bengal, "the Paradise of nations."

The Portuguese found a vast majority of Hindus in Bengal ruled by a minority of Muhammadans for more than 300 years, that is, since the defeat of the last Hindu King Lukshmanya and the taking of Nadiā in 1203. Until the battle of Plassey in 1757, that is, for more than five centuries and a half, Bengal was practically in the hands of the Muhammadan chiefs, strangers to Bengal by race and custom if not by birth. Hindu principalities flourished for a time but seldom exerted any considerable influence on the government of Bengal as a whole. Peaceful by disposition, docile and easy going, the people of Bengal were submissive to this foreign rule and apparently content with seeing their liberties not trampled upon and the virtue of their wives protected from force in their cloistered seclusion. But given the opportunity, the Bengalees were ready to rise against the Muhammadans and join with the new European comers as they did when Sebastião Gonsalves conquered Sandwīp and ordered the Hindus to deliver up to him every Moor in the land.

The "Bengalas"

The Portuguese historians dwell much on the wickedness of the "Bengalas". De Barros remarks: "the people natural to the land of Bengal, are mostly Hindu, weak in fighting but the most malicious and treacherous in the whole East; so that to injure a man anywhere (*sic*) it is enough to say he is a Bengala".* The Portuguese historian seems to have erred in the application of the word "Bengalas", whom the Portuguese in India referred to as treacherous in the reports sent to Portugal. By "Bengalas" the Portuguese in India did not only mean the Hindus but the Muhammadan rulers of Bengal who were indeed most malicious and treacherous especially towards the Portu-

* De Barros, Dec. IV. Liv. IX Cap. I p. 457.

Whiteaway says in his *History of Rise of Portuguese Power in India*, that a Portuguese description of the Bengalis calls them "False and thieves, people who get up quarrels as an excuse for robbery" See p. 233, n. 1.

guese whose earliest expeditions they had either treacherously put an end to or tried their best to do so in every covert manner. Hence de Barros who had never come to India probably confounded "Bengalas" with the "native people of Bengal" and ascribed to the latter the character which the rulers of Bengal possessed.

Geography of Bengal

The geography of Bengal was not exactly what it is to-day. It was an irony of fate that in India towns and cities should have risen and fallen, depending as they did on the fickleness of a river that shifted its course here and there ; or on the whims of a ruler who fixed his heart on a newer spot ; or still more on the grim destinies which in every age create kingdoms and as quickly destroy them.

Chittagong

When the Portuguese came to Bengal, Chittagong was its chief port, and the main gateway to the royal capital Gaur. Its geographical position lent it importance. Situated as it is at the mouth of the Meghna, this port was most convenient for navigation. The Meghna was the principal route to Gaur, the other being up the Hooghly. With the fall of Gaur, Chittagong began to decline, and trade was diverted to Sātgāon, which in its turn was supplanted by Hooghly. Chittagong was always a bone of contention between the Rajas of Bengal, Arakan and Tippera, who strove for supremacy over the seaport until the Mughal conquest of Bengal. All the Portuguese commanders that came to Bengal first entered Chittagong. In fact to go to Bengal meant to go to Chittagong. It is the "city of Bengala" referred to in the early Portuguese writings. They named it *Porto Grande* (great port) in contradistinction to their *Porto Pequeno* (small port) in Sātgāon. Hooghly eventually came to be known as *Porto Pequeno.*

From ancient times the chief port and emporium of trade on the Western side of Bengal, was Sātgāon, situated on the river Saraswatī, which branches off from the Hooghly below Tribeni and joins it higher up. The main current of the Hooghly till the middle of the sixteenth century streamed through the Saraswatī; hence the importance of Sātgāon which was more accessible to larger ships. The town of Hooghly was then a mere collection of huts. Sātgāon was the Saptagrama that figures so prominently in the ancient Puranas. It was so called because it consisted of seven villages on the banks of the river Saraswatī, each of which was occupied by one of the seven sons of the Rishi King Pryavanta. This district undoubtedly played an important part in the Mauryan civilization. It is Sātgāon (*Gangé*) that is probably described by Ptolemy as the capital of the *Gangaridæ*, Saraswatī being the *Ganges Regia.** The unknown author of the "Periplus of the Erythræan Sea" who wrote in the first century A. D. speaks of Sātgāon thus: "There is on it (Ganges) a mart called after it *Gangé* through which passes a considerable traffic consisting of betel, the Gangetic spikenard, pearl and the finest of muslins, those called the Gangetic".† There were times when the muslins of Dacca shipped from Sātgāon clad the Roman ladies and when spices and other goods of Bengal that used to find their way to Rome through Egypt were very much appreciated there and fetched fabulous prices. Till the middle of the 16th century large vessels sailed up to Sātgāon with merchandise. In the reign of Akbar it brought an income of 12,00,000 *dams* or 30,000 rupees.‡ This historic port was, however, destined to decline on the advent of the Portuguese, chiefly because the river Hooghly diverted its current through the main channel, and caused the silting up of the Saraswatī which became unsuitable for naviga-

Sātgāon

* Wilford's *Asiatic Researches*, Vol. V., p. 278.

† McCrindle's *Commerce and Navigation of the Erythræan Sea* p. 146.

‡ Gladwin's *Ayin Akbari* pt. II, p. 472.

tion. Fifty years ago the Saraswatī was a dead river, with its bed traversed by a few chains of pools. To-day, however, it is a running stream even in summer as water is let into it from the Kala Nadā in connection with the Eden Canal Scheme. The Portuguese called it *Porto Pequeno* (small port) as it was of lesser importance than the port of Chittagong.

De Läet who in his *India Vera* (1630) described Sātgāon as a beautiful town drew largely upon his imagination. In 1660 Van den Broucke called it a village and by 1870 the proud name of Sātgāon, the *Gangé* of Ptolemy, was applied to a collection of eleven huts. A ruined mosque can be seen at Sātgāon even to this day attesting to its former glory.

Topography of the Hooghly

The river Hooghly was not navigable for larger vessels higher up than the Adhi-Ganga (Tolly's Nollah) but lighter craft could transport to Sātgāon and other places on either bank of the river the goods which the Portuguese disembarked at Garden Reach. The topography of the Hooghly river was not very different from what it is to-day. Kalikatta (Calcutta) was an insignificant village on the left bank. The towns of Hooghly, Chandernagore, Chinsura, Serampore and Barrackpore did not even exist in name. They flourished only as European settlements. An idea of the villages on the banks of the Hooghly can be well formed by the following description of the voyage of Kabi Kankan who wrote the famous Chandi in 1577 (1499 of the Saka Era). Going down the Hooghly from Burdwan to the Sea, the poet passed or touched at the following places :—

" Floating down the river Ajai the boats came to Indrani. Further down they passed Bhrigu Sinha's Ghat on the right and Materi Ghat on the left. Then they passed Chandi Gach ; Balanpur Ghat ; Puravastali ; Navadip ; Parpur ; Mirzapur ; Ambua on the right side, Santipur on the left, Guptepara on the right ; Oola Kismar Fula, Joshepur Kodal Ghat, Halishahar on the left side, and Tribeni on the right ; Saptagramma (Sātgāon), Garefa (Gouripur), Andalpara, Jagathal, Nowpara, Teliapur, Nunai Ghat, Mahesh on the right side and Kurdaha, Konnagar, Kotrung, Kuchinan, Chitpur, Sulkhia, Kalikatta (Calcutta) Bithoor (Betor or modern Howrah). Leaving on the right, the way to Hijuji (Hījīlī) they turned to the left, passed Balughata, Kali Ghat, Mirnagar, Nachangacha, Vaisnav Ghata, Barasat, Chatra Bhuj, Ambri Bhuj, Hithagar and then came to Mogara."* How many of these places are not familiar to us to-day, and with a slight change in the orthography, do appear in our most modern guide-books?

Bengal, an Attraction for Pirates

The geographical position of Bengal has considerably influenced its history. Away from the heart of India, Bengal was a refuge for fugitive princes who like Humāyūn, Sher Shāh and Shāh Jahān made it the scene of their bloody exploits. Southern Bengal, woven as it is by a network of rivers as no other part of India, was calculated to offer the sea-faring people like the Portuguese the greatest scope for their instincts of navigation and love for adventure. Unfortunately this very geographical character of Bengal, fostered a greed for piracy and plunder, the terrors of which still form the darkest themes of popular tradition. In a labyrinth of rivers, the adventurers could dive and dart, appear and disappear, ravage the country and escape with impunity. Hence Bengal has been the victim of exploits and depredations of foreign and native adventurers alike,† who inclined by temperament or driven by circumstances looked to privateering as the best and most convenient method of making a bid for wealth. Before the Sundarbans became a nest of pirates, this unfortunate part of Bengal, a prey to the wickedness of men and no less to the whims of the rivers was not in such a flourishing condition as some writers have made

---

* *Calcutta Review* No. 186. Oct. 1891, p. 373.

† The Portuguese were not the only nor the worst offenders. Cf. Chap. XIV.

it out to be. The ruins of the villages and towns marked by de Barros and Van den Broucke in their maps and overspread to-day by thick jungles, indicate according to Blochmann* mere attempts at civilization. Westland† has moreover shown that the desolation of the Sundarbans is due to the changes of the river system of the Delta, and Beveridge‡ in his enquiry, "*Were the Sundarbans inhabited in ancient times?*" comes to the conclusion that it is very doubtful indeed that the Sundarbans were ever largely peopled, and still more so that their inhabitants lived in cities or were, otherwise civilized.

Bengal Trade

Regarding the trade and wealth of Bengal, the Portuguese had the most sanguine expectations which did not, indeed, prove to be far from true. Vasco da Gama had already in 1498 taken to Portugal the following information: "*Benguala* has a Moorish King and a mixed population of Christians and Moors. Its army may be about twenty-four thousand strong, ten thousand being cavalry, and the rest infantry, with four hundred war elephants. The country could export quantities of wheat and very valuable cotton goods. Cloths which sell on the spot for twenty-two shillings and six pence fetch ninety shillings in Calicut. It abounds in silver."§ From time to time Albuquerque had written to King Manoel about the vast possibilities of trade and commerce in Bengal. When the Portuguese actually established commercial relations in Bengal, they realized to their satisfaction what a mine of wealth they had found. Very appropriately, indeed, did the Mughals style Bengal, "the Paradise of India".

---

* H. Blochmann, *Contributions to the Geography and History of Bengal*, p. 23, reprinted from J. A. S. B. 1823, pt. I.

† *Report on the District of Jessore.*

‡ *History of The District of Bákarganj*, p. 169.

§ Appendix to the *Roteiro of Vasco de Gama.*

CHAPTER III

EARLY EXPEDITIONS TO BENGAL

For almost twenty years after Vasco da Gama discovered the sea-route to India, the Portuguese had no definite commerce with Bengal. The goods of Bengal, indeed, found their way in native crafts to Goa, Malacca and other Portuguese ports. As evident from the letters sent from Malacca to Portugal, the Portuguese had visited Bengal in these crafts even before D. João de Silveira, who came with the first expedition to Bengal, but these were passing tradesmen who sold or exchanged their goods at the first port in Bengal they touched at, and then availed themselves of any vessels to repair to their own havens.

The First Traders

Albuquerque who with a lynx-eye had surveyed the whole map of the East had not left Bengal out of his reckoning; but his attention was absorbed with affairs on the other side of India. Besides, he had only a limited number of ships and with those that he had, he preferred to consolidate the conquests he had already made, rather than embark on new ventures in trying to secure the trade of Bengal and China. He, however, informed King Manoel* about the possibilities of trade in Bengal, and probably acting upon his injunctions the King sent in 1517 Fernão Peres d'Andrade with four ships particularly to open a trade with Bengal and China. This captain sailed towards Sumatra, took Pacem, filled his ships with chillies and other commodities and learning that the goods would fetch a higher price in China, sailed towards the Chinese coast thinking

---

* On Dec. 1513 Albuquerque wrote to King Manoel "Bengal requires all our merchandise and is in need of it." Cf. *Doc. de Arch. Nacional da Torre do Tombo* p. 300.

of returning to Bengal at a later date. But a candle flame by an accident set fire to his largest ship and he was forced to return to Malacca where he hoped to replace the lost vessel. On his way back he sent a messenger to Bengal in a Moorish ship as an advance agent to announce his arrival. This man was João Coelho who had arrived at Chittagong before Silveira. Fernão Peres, however, explored the coast of China, secured its trade, returned laden with riches, but never realized his hopes of coming to Bengal.

D. João, de Silveira 1517-1518

D. João de Silveira* was sent to Bengal from the Maldives with an expedition by Lopo Soares de Albergaria, the Governor of the Portuguese possessions in the East, who had succeeded Albuquerque. The Governor sent three other expeditions at the same time to Malacca under D. Aleixo de Menezes; to Diu under Manoel de Lacerda; and to the coast of Arabia under Antonio de Saldanha. The Governor himself went with an expedition to Ceylon and on account of some commercial disputes compelled the King to become a vassal of the King of Portugal, and to pay a yearly tribute of 12,000 *Quintals*† of cinnamon, twelve rings of rubies and sapphires, and six elephants. To ensure the Portuguese interests, he built a fort thus laying the foundation for the conquest of Ceylon, which proved to be one of the richest Portuguese possessions in the East. All the expeditions that had sailed at this time were successful but the one that came to Bengal. Silveira landed in a port situated, according to de Barros, at the mouth of the river Arakan that flowed from the country called Arakan itself ‡ and where the King of the place resided. As Chittagong

* For an account of Silveira's expedition see de Barros Dec. III. pt. I. Chap. III. p. 135 *et seq* There were at least four Portuguese captains by the same name João de Silveira. The one that came to Bengal was the nephew of the Governor Lopo Vaz de Sampayo according to Correa.

† Each *quintal* was equivalent to 128 lbs.

‡ At present, Arakan is the most westerly division of Lower Burma

was at this time the chief port in the whole of Bengal Silveira moored there and found that João Coelho whom Fernão Peres d'Andrade had sent in order to announce his arrival had already arrived at Chittagong in a Moorish vessel, by a curious coincidence belonging to Gromalle himself. Silveira sent with a messenger his compliments to the King of Bengal* asking in the name of the King of Portugal for facilities of trade and for permission to erect a factory where the Portuguese merchants could rest during their voyages and exchange goods with other parts of India; but the messengers were never received. During Silveira's voyage to the Maldives an event had occurred which influenced the fate of this expedition to a great extent. He had captured two ships that were going from Bengal to Cambay and sent them to Cochin. These ships belonged to a Moor named Gromalle who was related to the Governor of Chittagong. Silveira took over in his own ship the pilot of the captured ships and his nephew who were from Bengal. The latter pretended to be a great friend of the Portuguese and even informed Silveira about some of the plans of the country; but no sooner did he land in Bengal than he related to the Governor at Chittagong all that had happened. The Governor covertly made preparations for a fight taking Silveira for a corsair, though Silveira had no intentions what-

---

consisting of a narrow tract which extends from Chittagong Division to within 90 miles of Cape Negrais. The old kingdom of Arakan was practically the same in boundaries as the present Division. The capital of Arakan was Myo-haung and this is the City of Arakan referred to by Portuguese writers.

* It is doubtful who this king was. Husain Shāh was at this time King of Bengal but according to the *Rājmālā*, the King of Tippera conquered Chittagong from him in 1512. O'Malley, *Chittagong Gazetteer* p. 22, says, "in 1517, when, as mentioned later it was visited by John de Silveira it was a port held by the Kings of Arakan." For a statement like this there is no evidence in the Portuguese historians. On the contrary de Barros says, Dec. III. pt. I. p. 142, that at this time the King of Arakan was a vassal of the King of Bengal. Any way, it is related that Nasīr-ud-din Nasrat Shāh, the son of Husain Shāh reconquered Chittagong from the King of Arakan.

soever but those of commercial interests. The suspicious and unfriendly manner in which the early European merchants were received by the Indian rulers, impelled them in a large measure to constitute themselves into a military power. The Portuguese originally came only for purposes of trade and evangelization. From the difficulties that were put in their way and from the consequent commercial disputes, arose the necessity of defence by arms, and from this grew up the idea of conquests.

Suspecting nothing of the attack that was about to be made against him, Silveira was waiting still to open negotiations. The Governor was, however, well disposed towards Coelho, as the Moors who had come from Pacem along with him and who had received good treatment from Fernão Peres, gave favourable reports about Coelho to the Governor, who naturally thought that while Coelho was the real messenger of the King of Portugal, Silveira was actually a corsair. Silveira, knowing nothing about what was passing, would not allow João Coelho to arrange the trade matters preferring to do so himself as he was the real ambassador sent by the Portuguese Governor. Meanwhile food ran out and Silveira found himself in the necessity of capturing a boat full of rice. This pretext served the Governor's intentions. He suddenly opened fire from land and Silveira had to defend himself with great difficulty. He did not give in, however, though his men were about to die of starvation and spent the whole of winter in the Bay of Bengal as he could not return during the rains.

The only revenge Silveira could take, was to paralyze the whole sea-trade of the Governor's ports. He must have, indeed, stopped all shipping in the Bay, because the Governor who was expecting the arrival of some ships which he knew very well Silveira would capture, made overtures of peace. During these negotiations Silveira learnt how well disposed the Governor was towards Coelho. Coelho being allowed to land, arranged the terms of peace with the Governor and sent food stuffs to Silveira. But the Governor never really meant to stand by the treaty. As soon as the Governor's ships landed unmolested by the Portuguese, he made war again on Silveira. Coelho was meanwhile on land. The Moors who had come in the new ships, also knew well João Coelho and Fernão Peres d'Andrade and confirmed the earlier reports as to how favourable these two captains had been to the Moorish people. Coelho used all his influence in favour of Silveira but the Governor* was obstinate in his hostility towards Silveira. Coelho, thereupon, sailed to China, and Silveira bent his way towards the coast of Arakan, where he had first touched. The King of Arakan was at this time subject to the King of Bengal, and his city, called Arakan itself was, according to de Barros, 35 leagues from Chittagong. On opening negotiations, the King sent a messenger with a precious present of a ruby ring assuring Silveira that though he was not well received in Chittagong he would be pleased to be friends with the Portuguese. Silveira however came to know in time that the offer was part of a treacherous plot that was laid in order to capture him just after landing. Unsuccessful and disappointed, he sailed to Ceylon and was given the command of the Fort of Ceylon which Lopo Soares had built sometime before.

Ruy Vaz Pereira 1526

Although Silveira had achieved nothing, it became an established custom from the time of Silveira's visit to Bengal to send annually to Bengal a Portuguese ship with merchandise. According to this yearly custom of sending ships, the Governor Lopo Vaz de Sampayo chose Ruy Vaz Pereira† to command the ship going to Bengal in 1526. Having entered Chittagong with his merchandise, Ruy Vaz Pereira saw in the

* Though the Governors of Chittagong were subject to the authority of the Kings of Bengal or of Arakan, they seem to have acted largely on their own.

† De Barros, Dec. IV. pt II. pp. 466-7.

port a galleot belonging to one Khājeh Shihāb-ud-dīn (Coge Sabadim), a rich Persian merchant, built after the Portuguese fashion in order to plunder merchant ships and ascribe the crime to the Portuguese. Ruy Vaz Pereira immediately captured this galleot and took it along with him with all its merchandise. It was this event, as it will be seen, that eventually contributed to the liberty of Martim Affonso de Mello, after two years of captivity.

Martim Affonso de Mello Juzarte, 1528

In 1528 an expedition commanded by Martim Affonso de Mello* landed by a curious chance on the coast of Bengal. This Captain had built a fort in Sunda where he had gone with eight ships and four hundred men. He then sailed to Colombo and put to flight *Pate Marcar*, the captain of the King of Calicut, who was coming to attack King Cotta of Ceylon, the Portuguese ally. Proceeding on his voyage he was overtaken by a storm, and his ships being driven adrift he was left stranded on a sandy bank near the island of Negamale opposite the city of Sodoé.† Some fishermen promised to guide him to Chittagong but they played him false and took him to Chakariā ‡ which was under the Governorship of Khudā Baksh Khān (Codovascam), a vassal of King Mahmūd Shāh III, the last independent ruler of Bengal. This King kept a gay and rich court at Gaur, his women alone, according to Faria y Souza, amounting to ten thousand. As Khudā Baksh Khān had a feud with a neighbouring chief, he employed the Portuguese to fight for him promising to give them liberty and leave to go to their destinations. They won for him the victory but far

---

* De Barros Dec. IV. pt. I. p. 171 *et. seq.*

† Neither Negamale nor Sodoé has been marked by de Barros in his Map of Bengal, *Da Asia, Dec. IV.* The city of Sodoé referred to is obviously the town of Sandoway in Burma (Arakan).

‡ Chakariā is a police division of the Chittagong District containing at present a thana and a subregistry. De Barros speaks of it as "the city called Chacuriá".

from keeping his promises he imprisoned them in his city of Soré* situated on a river which emptied in the sea eight miles away. This was the second instance of treachery the Portuguese met with in Bengal.

Two of the ships of Affonso de Mello that had gone adrift during the storm reached Chakariā under Duarte Mendes Vasconcellos and João Coelho, probably the same Coelho who had joined Silveira in Chittagong. These captains tried to ransom Affonso de Mello with all the goods they had brought in their ships but Khudā Baksh Khān demanded more. As a last bid for safety, Martim Affonso de Mello made an attempt to escape with the co-operation of Coelho and Vasconcellos but it proved unsuccessful. And then followed a tragedy. The Brahmins† had made a vow that if they ever caught hold of the Portuguese they would sacrifice to their gods the most handsome of them. The man sacrificed was the nephew of Affonso de Mello himself, named Gonçalo Vas de Mello, a young man on whose cheeks, as de Barros says, the downy plush of youth had not yet begun to appear—"*Jeune homme d'une figure charmante et d'une trés haute espérance*", as Van der Hoult describes him.

The Ransom of Martim Affonso de Mello, 1529

Nuno da Cunha, the son of the famous Tristão da Cunha whose name is borne by three islands in the Atlantic, was at this time the Governor in Goa. Although he concentrated most of his energies on obtaining fortresses in Bassein and in rocky Diu as defence against the powerful Muhammadans of Gujrāt, his cherished ambition was to secure

---

* Soré is marked by de Barros in his Map of Bengal and also by Van Blaev in his Map in *Theatrum Orbis Terrarum*, Vol. II. It is placed south-east of Chittagong further in the interior.

† The fact that the Brahmins vowed to make sacrifices of foreigners in the face of a Muhammadan Government would show that they had some power in the land. Couto, however, explains that they obtained their victim by bribing the Moors. Dec. IV, Liv. IV, Cap. X. p. 323.

the trade of Bengal and gain a footing on its shores. With this object in view he fitted out many expeditions to Bengal. It happened that Khājeh Shihāb-ud-dīn referred the matter of the capture of his galleot to Nuno da Cunha and agreed to ransom Affonso de Mello for 3000 *cruzados** if he got back his vessel. His vessel, with all its goods, was restored to him and he indeed ransomed Affonso de Mello in 1529 and sent him with his cousin Khājeh Shakr-Ulla (Coge Sukurulá) to Goa. Khājeh Shihāb-ud-dīn became now a great friend of the Portuguese and with their help he determined to free himself from some trouble he had got into with Nasrat Shāh, the Sultan of Bengal, and to escape to Ormuz in a Portuguese vessel. He promised to use his influence with the king to give them great facilities for trade and even to give them permission to build a fort in Chittagong, if they would only send an expedition to help him in his projects.

Second Expedition under Martim Affonso de Mello, 1533

Nuno da Cunha naturally chose Martim Affonso de Mello, the same man whom the Persian had ransomed, to command the expedition. This captain landed in Bengal in 1533 with five ships and two hundred men.† One ship called São Raphael was government property, the other four being the property of private captains. All the cargo belonged to joint stock companies. The object of this expedition was not only to help Khājeh Shiāb-ud-dīn but through his influence to attempt to open commerce with Bengal and choose a suitable site for a factory. When Affonso de Mello reached Chittagong, he sent to Gaur his ambassador, Duarte de Azevedo with twelve men

---

* A *cruzado* was a Portuguese coin, so called from the cross marked on it. It was worth 420 *reis* that is about 9 sh. according to the value attached by Yule to the *reis* in the sixteenth century. Cf. *Hobson-Jobson* s. v. *pardao*. According to Gerson da Cunha a *cruzado* or 420 *reis* would be worth about 2 sh. only. Frei Ambrosio de Santo Agostinho says in 1750 "we spent 1,200 rupees which amount to 1200 Cruzados". Cf. O *Chronista de Tissuary* Vol. II. p. 62.

† Correa gives the date as 1533, de Barros as 1534, Faria y Souza as 1538. I have generally followed the dates of Correa.

among whom was Nuno Fernandes Freire and according to the prevailing custom, he sent presents to the King such as horses, brocades and sundry other things worth in all about £1200. King Mahmūd Shāh was at that time in a sullen and irritable frame of mind, gnawed as he was by the remorse of having ascended the throne by the murder of his nephew Fīruz Shāh III. Moreover, he is said to have been prejudiced against the Portuguese because he recognized among the presents some boxes of rose water which a Portuguese corsair named Damião Bernaldes had seized from a Moorish ship. Highly incensed, the King immediately decided to put to the sword not only the ambassador and his men but, by any form of treachery, all the Portuguese that came in this expedition. A Moor named Alfu Khān* and a Moorish saint, reputed to be a hundred years old, interceded in their favour dissuading him from murder. The King, however, determined to imprison them, and sent a Guazil † to the port of Chittagong where Affonso de Mello was staying, in order to seize him and his men. A dispute had meanwhile arisen between Affonso de Mello and the Moorish custom officers ; and the Guazil took this opportunity to interfere and ultimately invited the Portuguese commander and his men to a dinner. Affonso de Mello and forty other Portuguese suspecting no treachery accepted the invitation while the rest preferred a hog-hunt. The dinner was held in a large courtyard surrounded on all sides by verandahs above. During the dinner the Guazil rose on pretence of illness and immediately a number of Moors came with guns and bows and arrows and began to hurl them against the unfortunate guests. The Portuguese did not, however, give in but tried to defend themselves with their

---

* Blochmann identifies him with Alfā Hussanī of Baghdad. Cf. *Geography and History of Bengal J. A. S. B.* 1873 p. 298 n.

† De Barros defines *Guazil* as a Moorish judicial Officer. Correa, *Lendas*, Vol. III, p. 722, calls Nuno Fernandes Freire *Gozil* of the custom house of Sātgāon in connection with his appointment as chief of the custom house. The word finds no place in *Hobson-Jobson.*

swords. Unable to hold out, they eventually surrendered. Some of those that were on shore were also killed and property valued at £100,000 was confiscated. De Barros dwells at length on this event and his pages read like the description of the Black Hole.* Ten Portuguese were killed including Christovam de Mello, the nephew of the Governor Lopo Vaz de Sampayo. Affonso de Mello himself was wounded. Thirty Portuguese who survived the massacre were tied up and put in a dark room. Their wounds were not attended to for some days and then they were forced to march six leagues during one whole night till they reached a place called Mavá. They were eventually taken to Gaur and were treated not like men but like beasts. Duarte d'Azavedo and his twelve men who had gone to Gaur as envoys were also confined in what de Barros calls a hell (*inferno*).

Antonio da Silva Menezes, 1534

Nuno da Cunha, the Governor, swore revenge when the news of this disaster reached Goa. He prepared in great haste a fleet of nine sail manned by 350 Portuguese. He sent it under the captainship of Antonio da Silva Menezes† instructing him to demand an explanation from the King of Bengal why his ambassador who had gone to establish relations of peace and friendliness was so badly treated. If the King did not return Affonso de Mello and his men, Menezes was ordered to wage war with "fire and blood." As soon as Menezes arrived in Chittagong he sent Jorge Alcocorado to King Mahmūd Shāh with the message of the Portuguese Governor and with the threat that if any harm were done to him or if he were not allowed to return within a month, war would be declared against him. Mahmūd Shāh, as obdurate as ever, would not think of setting free Affonso de Mello and his men but sent a letter to Antonio da

* Couto, Dec. IV. Pt. I. Liv. IV, Cap. X, and Francisco D'Andrade Part II, Chap. 80, 81, describe this episode a little differently.

† De Barros, *Da Asia*, Dec. IV, Pt. II, Liv. IX, Cap. V.

Silva Menezes requesting from the Governor of Goa a number of carpenters, jewellers and other workmen. Before these negotiations were over, a month had elapsed. Menezes thereupon, set fire to a great part of Chittagong and captured and killed a great number of people.* Although Jorge Alcocorado had to stay beyond the limit of his time, he had departed from Gaur only three days before the burning of Chittagong had begun. The King immediately ordered his arrest but Jorge Alcocorado escaped just in time and joined Antonio da Silva Menezes. One would expect that the days of Martim Affonso de Mello and his men were numbered ; but new developments were taking place, and Bengal was soon to become a theatre of war owing to the quarrels between Sher Shāh and Humāyūn in which Affonso de Mello was destined to play an important part.

Sher Shāh, 1535

Sher Shāh,† who was perhaps the greatest and the most treacherous of the Afghāns ; who had introduced himself in the service of Bābar and then sworn to oust the Mughals from India ; who unable to oppose the Lodi King of Bihar had joined him, marched with him to fight against Humāyūn and then deserted him and given the victory over to Mughals, came now to Bengal and determined to make himself master of it whilst Humāyūn was busy in Gujrāt. He began a campaign against Mahmūd Shāh who, now no longer proud and unrelenting, was compelled by circumstances to implore the help of the very man whom he had treated so cruelly. He sought advice from Martim Afonso de Mello as to the plan of defence and decided

---

* Another account differs a little from de Barros and relates that Mahmūd Shāh demanded £15,000 as ransom, which being too exorbitant, Menezes decided upon bombarding Chittagong.

† At the time of Sher Shāh's invasion of Bengal he was known as Sher Khān and hence the Portuguese historians call him *Xercansur*. De Barros, however, calls him *Xerchan*, quite correctly.

to send an ambassador to Nuno da Cunha, the Portuguese Governor in Goa, asking for help.

Diogo Rebello, 1535

At this critical juncture there happened to arrive at Sātgāon, Diogo Rebello, the Portuguese captain and factor of the Coromandel pearl fisheries.* According to Gaspar Correa he came in his own vessel and two foists well armed with guns. Nuno da Cunha had asked him to go to Bengal to see if by any means he could save Martim Affonso de Mello and his men. At this time two big ships laden with merchandise came to Sātgāon from Cambay. Rebello, without molesting these ships, forced them to leave this port and forbade them to carry on any trade. This illustrates the policy which the Portuguese had adopted, in order to destroy the Arab commerce, claiming for themselves alone, the right of trading in the Indian seas. Rebello sent Diogo de Spindola, his own nephew, and Duarte Dias, to the King in Gaur with a message that if he did not liberate the Portuguese prisoners he would seize his ports and repeat in Sātgāon what Menezes had done in Chittagong. This was the first time when a Portuguese captain is recorded to have sailed up to Gaur by the Hooghly, the others having gone to Gaur up the Meghna from Chittagong. As already stated, Mahmūd Shāh was no longer the same as Menezes had found him. He wrote to the Governor in Sātgāon to receive Rebello well, and to inform him that he was sending his ambassador to the Portuguese Governor in Goa as a proof of his friendship. He asked for Portuguese help and in return he promised to grant them land to erect their factories and permission to build fortresses in Chittagong and Sātgāon. The object of Martim Affonso de Mello was gained; he had been in prison for two years before he was liberated, and had undergone captivity again in pursuance of the very object which was now about to be realized. The

* Cf. De Barros, *Da Asia*, Dec. IV, Pt. II, p. 496 *et seq.*, and Correa, *Lendas*, Vol. III, p. 649; also Castanheda, Liv. VIII. Cap. CX. p. 261 *et seq.*

King returned twenty-two prisoners to Diogo Rebello and excused himself for not sending back Martim Affonso de Mello because he needed his advice most of all. Affonso de Mello himself wrote a letter on behalf of Mahmūd Shāh assuring the Governor that the Portuguese would get permission to erect their factories and fortresses. *Sic tempora mutantur et nos in illis.*

Sher Shāh's Invasion and the Portuguese Successes, 1536

Meanwhile Sher Shāh was advancing and decided to enter Gaur by the passes of Teliāgarhi and Sikligali leading to the fortress of Gorij (Garhi).* To defend these passes which were considered to be the gateways to Bengal, troops were sent in two ships, one under the command of João de Villalobos and the other of João Correa. The Portuguese offered a stubborn resistance and prevented Sher Shāh from taking the city of Ferranduz, which was twenty leagues from the city of Gaur. The Portuguese historians say the Portuguese did wonders and captured a particular elephant which King Mahmūd Shāh especially wanted; but Sher Shāh went by another less protected way and entered Gaur with 40,000 cavalry, 1,500 elephants and 200,000 men and with a fleet of 300 boats.† Mahmūd Shāh, unable to offer any resistance paid an enormous sum of money amounting to thirteen lakhs of gold or 525,000 *pardaos* ‡ and made peace with him although Martim Affonso

* These passes, near Colgong, are now traversed by the East Indian Railway. For the position of Ferranduz and fortress of Gorij see Map of de Barros.

† De Barros, *Da Asia*, Dec. IV. Pt. II. Liv. IX, Cap. VII, p. 500.

‡ Castanheda, *Historia*, Liv. VIII, Cap. CXXVIII. The historian is not definite as to in what coins the "thirteen lakhs of gold" were paid. He however gives the equivalent of the sum in *pardaos*. As the Portuguese historians generally speak of money in *pardaos* it is important to ascertain the value of a *pardao*, the value of which has undergone many variations. Originally it was a gold coin of Western India, which was adopted in the Goa currency. Later on a Portuguese silver coin was called a *pardao*. Hence there were two kinds of *pardaos* a gold one (Pardao d'ouro) worth 360 *reis* and a silver one (Pardao de Tanga) worth 300 *reis*. Castanheda obviously attaches to a *pardao* the value which A. Nunes (1554) attached to it, viz. 5 silver *tangas* or 300 *reis* which amount

de Mello advised him to the contrary. The soundness of Affonso de Mello's advice was apparent when Sher Shāh soon after attacked Mahmūd Shāh again, utilizing the latter's money against him.

Though Mahmūd Shāh had not emerged victorious in the campaign, he did not fail the recognize the services of the Portuguese. He gave to Affonso de Mello a present of 45,000 *reis* and alloted to each of the Portuguese a daily sum of money equivalent to ten *cruzados* for food expenses. However, finding himself secure from the menace of Sher Shāh, he changed his mind as to allowing the Portuguese to build fortresses in Chittagong and Sātgāon but he permitted Affonso de Mello to build factories and offered to give them custom-houses. He, indeed, appointed Nuno Fernandez Freire the chief of the custom-house of Chittagong, granted him land with many houses empowering him to realize rent from the Moors and Hindus who lived there, and gave him many other privileges over the people. The custom house of Sātgāon which was less in importance than that of Chittagong, was given to João Correa. The people were indeed surprised to see that the King had given the Portuguese so much power and such a firm footing in Bengal. This was the first establishment of the Portuguese in Bengal, almost simultaneously in Chittagong and Sātgāon.*

First settlements in Chittagong and Sātgāon, 1536-1537

Under conditions so favourable and pregnant with possibilities, Affonso Vaz de Brito† came in a ship to Bengal from

to about 4 sh. 6 d. as the value of a *real* in the 16th century was about one-fourth of a penny while to day it is about one-seventeenth. The value of a *pardao* deteriorated until its worth became 10½ d. Cf. Yule and Burnell, *Hobson-Jobson* s. v. Pardao.

* Castanheda, *Historia*, Liv. VIII, Cap. CXXVIII, 303. For a fuller account of these settlements, *Vide infra*.

† Cf. Correa, *Lendas*, Vol. III, p. 814 and Castanheda, *Hist.* Liv. VIII, Cap. CLXXVII, p. 403 *et seq.* De Barros makes only a passing reference to Affonso Vaz de Brito. *Vide* Dec. IV, pt. II. p. 502.

Cochin with instructions from Nuno da Cunha to bring back Martim Affonso de Mello and carry his letter in reply to Mahmūd Shāh's request about the help that the latter had asked for. He, however, hesitated a good deal to land in Chittagong as there was temporarily a great commotion against the Portuguese arising from a report to the King about the Portuguese Governor having murdered the King of Cambay and ransacked his property. But Antonio Menezes de Crasto having, at this juncture, arrived in Chittagong, with merchandise and a letter from the Portuguese Governor explaining the Cambay affair, there was no more trouble.

Affonso Vaz de Brito, 1538

Affonso Vaz de Brito landed in Chittagong where he met Nuno Fernandes Freire at the Portuguese custom-house. Having, then, gone to the Court of Gaur he requested the King to liberate Affonso de Mello and gave him Nuno da Cunha's letter in which it was stated that he could not send him any help because the wars in Cambay had made a demand on all his available men and that he would assuredly send it the following year. Mahmūd Shāh highly grateful as he was to the Portuguese for the valuable assistance they had rendered in defending the passes permitted Martim Affonso de Mello to leave Bengal with his men. He kept only five Portuguese, including Affonso Vaz de Brito, as hostages for the promised help.

The Campaigns of Sher Shāh and Humāyūn, 1538

After the departure of Affonso de Mello, news arrived in Gaur that Sher Shāh was advancing again with a very powerful force in order to demand another large sum of money which he declared was to be his annual tribute and was now due to him after the lapse of a year. Mahmūd Shāh who had never agreed to such a compact refused to pay the tribute; whereupon, Sher Shāh invaded Gaur, burnt and pillaged the town, and took possession of sixty millions in gold. Mahmūd

Shāh covered with wounds fled to Hazipore and thence to Chunar, where Humāyūn was waiting with a large army to punish the revolt of Sher Shāh. Humāyūn sent one of his captains to Mahmūd Shāh asking him to come to him, but the latter died of his wounds before he could see Humāyūn and was burried by the Mughals with great pomp and ceremony.

Humāyūn advanced against Sher Shāh, attacked Gaur and forced him to retreat to Sasseram, after which he spent three months rioting in Gaur. The rains having set in, Sher Shāh cut off the retreat of Humāyūn, who was forced to ask the Afghān to allow him to return promising to give him Bengal and Bihar. Sher Shāh agreed and swore on the Koran that during the return of Humāyūn's army he would injure no Mughal. But that very night he treacherously put eight thousand Mughals to death and the Emperor himself narrowly escaped with a few friends and fled to Lahore where his brother Kamrān (Camiran Mirza) whom he had recently poisoned and who had not yet recovered from the effects thereof, received him hospitably.* Sher Shāh proclaimed himself Emperor of Bengal in 1538 and the following year marching against Humāyūn at the head of 500,000 Afghāns, fought the great battle of Kanouj, defeated him and ascended the throne of Delhi. Thus he gained the throne for which he had fought for fifteen years and which he after all retained for only five years.† Henceforward till 1576 the Portuguese had to struggle with the successors of Sher Shāh.

The help which Nuno da Cunha had promised Mahmūd

---

* Faria y Souza, *Trans. Stevens*, Vol. I, p. 241.

† The campaigns of Sher Shāh and Humāyūn in Bengal are described in the Portuguese chronicles so minutely, that it is a pity no History of Bengal has taken them into consideration. Even the Muhammadan accounts give a poor and scanty information of this period, a comparitive study of which I reserve for my larger work referred to in the Preface.

Shāh did come indeed, but it was too late. The expedition was commanded by Vasco Peres de Sampayo and consisted of nine vessels.* This captain reached Chittagong when Sher Shāh was already master of Bengal. At this time disputes arose between the generals of Mahmūd Shāh, Khudā Baksh Khān (Codovascão) and Amirza Khān (Amarzacão) regarding the possession of Chittagong. Nuno Fernandes Freire whom Mahmūd Shāh had created chief of the custom-house and who wielded great influence in Chittagong intervened and declared in favour of Amirza Khān. Sher Shāh, however, sent his captain (Nogazil) to Chittagong and he took possession of the town. Finding Chittagong in such a precarious state Nuno Fernandes Freire advised Sampayo to conquer the town which he could easily have done. But whether it was on moral or political grounds, he refused to do so. Meanwhile Amirza Khān collected a force and sent it against Sher Shāh's captain who asked for the help of Nuno Fernandes Freire preferring rather to be a prisoner of the Portuguese than of the "Bengalas". When Fernandes went to the house of Sher Shāh's Nogazil which was now under a siege, the men of Amirza Khān who knew him well gave him a great ovation. He dissuaded them from seizing the Nogazil but, he himself, with fifty Portuguese whom Sampayo had sent ashore, eventually captured the Nogazil and imprisoned him in one of Sampayo's vessels whence after six month's captivity he managed to escape by bribing a subordinate. It happened, however, that a galleot with sixty armed Moors of Raja Suleiman came to Chittagong and engaged some of Sampayo's men; but Sampayo who had behaved cowardly all throughout, would not send any more men for their help nor send a ship to defend a Portuguese merchantman, which

Vasco Peres de Sampayo, 1538

* The account of this expedition is based on Castanheda, *Historia*, Liv. VIII, Cap. CXCVIII.

was in danger, inspite of Fernandes repeatedly asking him to do so. Diogo Rebello and Nuno Fernandes themselves condutced the defence during which the latter was wounded.

Vasco Peres de Sampayo passed the whole of winter in Bengal and then went to Pegu where he died. Castanheda who gives a very full account* of this event concludes that through the folly and indiscretion of Sampayo the King of Portugal lost Chittagong which could easily have been taken possession of, considering that Sher Shāh was busily engaged on the other side of Bengal. Any way, Martim Affonso de Mello's sufferings had not been in vain. The Portuguese had obtained from Mahmūd Shāh a vast establishment and a custom-house in Chittagong and a smaller one in Sātgāon. The latter establishment did not seem to have prospered and gained any importance, as Mahmūd Shāh died and the Afghāns came into power. Most writers on Hooghly have, curiously enough, given Sampayo the credit of having established the first settlement in Sātgāon or rather Hooghly, when the fact is that Sampayo never came to Hooghly.

Many other Portuguese captains came to Bengal besides those mentioned above, but their doings may be passed over in silence as not being of sufficient importance.

* Castanheda, *Historia*, *ut supra*.

CHAPTER IV

PORTUGUESE SETTLEMENTS IN THE HOOGHLY DISTRICT

Hooghly

The history of the Portuguese is not now one of expeditions but of their trade and settlements in Bengal, nay more, of their conquests. The Portuguese, as has been shown, had already come with arms and fought on the fields of Bengal, not so much for themselves as for others, in return for which they obtained a settlement in Sātgāon, in the Hooghly District. In Indo-European history there is not, undoubtedly, a more interesting Indian town than Hooghly because there, within a range of a few miles, seven European nations fought for supremacy: the Portuguese, the Dutch, the English, the Danes, the French, the Flemish, and the Prussians.* Before the Portuguese settlement Hooghly had neither a distinct existence nor history of its own. It was only a small insignificant village consisting of a few huts, while Sātgāon was a great port and a flourishing city whose antiquity extended beyond the times of Ptolemy. The Portuguese, indeed, were founders of the town of Hooghly.

---

* The Dutch settled in Chinsura, with headquarters in Fort Gustavus ; the English first established themselves in the town of Hooghly ; the French in Hooghly, then in Chandernagore ; the Danes in. Gondalpara, south-east of Chandernagore and then in Serampore ; the Flemish in Bankibazar ; and the Prussians or Embdeners in a place a mile south of Fort Orleans in Chandernagore. There is a good deal of confusion about the Prussian and Flemish settlements. O'Malley, *Hooghly Gazetteer*, p. 87-91 understands that Bankibazar was a Flemish and not Prussian settlement and that the Ostend Company which settled there was a Flemish and not Prussian Company. Hill in his *Bengal in 1756-57* enters Bankibazar as a Prussian settlement in the Index, though he says it was held by the Ostend Company. Sir W. Hunter also calls Bankipur (Bankibazar) a Prussian settlement understanding the Ostend Company to have been the Prussian Company. *Vide*, *India of the Queen and other Essays*, pp. 201-2. The real name of the Prussian or Embden Company which was founded by Fredericke the Great in 1753 was *Bengalische Handels-Gessellchaft.*

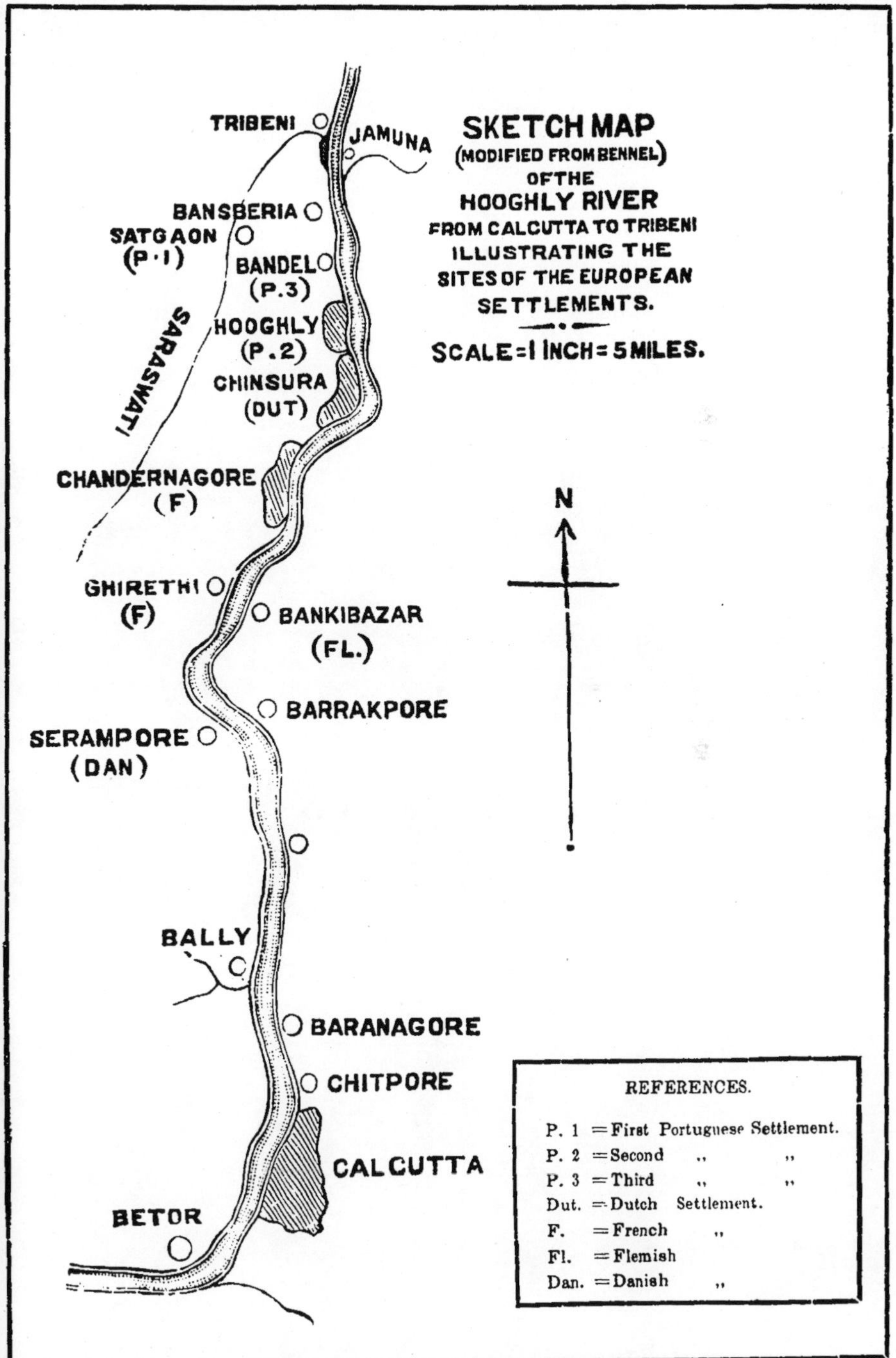
SKETCH MAP
(MODIFIED FROM BENNEL)
OF THE
HOOGHLY RIVER
FROM CALCUTTA TO TRIBENI
ILLUSTRATING THE
SITES OF THE EUROPEAN
SETTLEMENTS.
SCALE = 1 INCH = 5 MILES.
N
TRIBENI
JAMUNA
BANSBERIA
SATGAON
(P·1)
BANDEL
(P.3)
SARASWATI
HOOGHLY
(P.2)
CHINSURA
(DUT)
CHANDERNAGORE
(F)
GHIRETHI
(F)
BANKIBAZAR
(FL.)
BARRAKPORE
SERAMPORE
(DAN)
BALLY
BARANAGORE
CHITPORE
CALCUTTA
BETOR
REFERENCES.
P. 1 = First Portuguese Settlement.
P. 2 = Second ,, ,,
P. 3 = Third ,, ,,
Dut. = Dutch Settlement.
F. = French ,,
Fl. = Flemish
Dan. = Danish ,,

Common Errors about the Portuguese Settlements in the Hooghly District

The account of the foundation of the Portuguese settlement in Hooghly has taxed the imagination of most writers on Hooghly. On this point much has, indeed, been written for which there is absolutely no historical evidence. The Rev. Long * states the Portuguese got Bandel in 1538 and built a fort there in 1599. Others say that Vasco Peres de Sampayo came to Hooghly in 1537-38 and built a fort at Hooghly. Shumbhoo Chunder Dey † doubts its truth and yet Dr. Crawford‡ quotes him as having asserted the fact about Sampayo's building the fort. Succeeding writers have perpetuated and even added to these errors, until they find a place in our most modern Gazetteers. If the original Portuguese sources were consulted many mis-statements would have been avoided.

The fact was that the Portuguese established three settlements in the Hooghly District, each distinct in its origin, time and even place. The confusion about them has obviously arisen from the one being mixed up with the other. The first settlement was made in Sātgaon, not in Hooghly proper, nor in Bandel. It was, moreover, made by Affonso de Mello and not by Vasco Peres de Sampayo, who made a poor display of himself in Chittagong. Neither de Barros nor Correa refers to any of the doings of Sampayo in Bengal, and Castanheda who gives a detailed account of his expedition has nothing to say about his ever being in Hooghly. As Faria y Souza rightly says,§ Sampayo arrived too late to be of any help to Mahmūd Shāh, and in fact he arrived after the latter had died of wounds at Chunar. The second settlement was founded in

* Cal. Rev. Vol. V, 1846, p. 258.

† Cal Rev. Vol. XCV, 1892, p. 259.

‡ *A Brief History of the Hughly Dist.* p. 4.

§ Cf. Faria y Souza, *Trans. of Stevens*, 1695, Ch. IX, pp. 418-20. For further account see Castanheda, *ut supra*.

Hooghly proper by Tavares to whom Akbar granted a *farman* (1579-80). The third settlement was established in Bandel, close to the previous one, under a *farman* of Shāh Jāhān granted in 1633, a year after the Siege of Hooghly. As to the supposed existence of a Portuguese fort in Hooghly, all evidence points to a contrary conclusion.*

The descriptions of the Portuguese settlement in Sātgāon are found in Castanheda and Correa. The following is a literal translation of the passage in Castanheda† a gist of which has already been given :—"and the King after seeing himself free from war, or for some other reason, changed the wish which he had of giving fortresses to the King of Portugal in Chittagong (Chatigão) and Sātgāon (Satigão) but not of giving the custom-houses with houses of factories, and thus he told Martim Affonso who reminded him that he promised fortresses ; and he seeing that the King would not assent to this, did not like to dispute it and told him to give whatever he liked. And at his request the King made Nuno Fernandes Freire the the chief of the custom-house of Chittagong giving him a great circuit of houses in which the Moors and Hindus lived in order that it might bring him rent as also the custom-house of Chittagong (might bring him rent) and gave him many other powers at which all in the land were surprised, as also at the King being such a great friend of the Portuguese whom he wanted to settle (*arreigar*) in the country. And the custom-house of Sātgāon which was smaller he gave to João Correa and soon he and Nuno Fernandes Freire went to these two cities to perform their offices, for which the Guazils of these two cities were very sad because the power that they had was taken, chiefly of Chittagong which was bigger." Castanheda

The First Settlement, Sātgāon 1537-38

* *Vide* Chapter V.

† Cf. Castanheda, Liv. VIII, Cap. CXXVIII, p. 303.

does not, indeed, distinctly say that the Portuguese erected a factory in Sātgāon but it is evident that they did erect a factory or made some sort of establishment from the fact that Mahmūd Shāh did not change his mind as to giving the Portuguese, custom-houses and factories both in Chittagong and Sātgāon and did actually appoint João Correa, the head of the custom-house in Sātgāon. Gaspar Correa* also confirms Castanheda differing only in that he says Nuno Fernandes Freire was given the custom-house with much rent (*sic*) in Sātgāon (Satigão) and that Christovam Correa (not João Correa) was given the custom-house of Chittagong (Chatigão) with much rent and power (*sic*) over the people of the land. As early as 1554 Antonio Nunes† referred to Sātgāon as Porto Pequeno and obviously the Portuguese must have thus named it from the time of their first settlement in 1537-8. When the Portuguese established themselves in the town of Hooghly, and Sātgāon was no longer the great city that it was, they applied the name Porto Pequeno to the port of Hooghly. Yule and Burnell lose sight of this second denomination in their *Hobson-Jobson*, where only Sātgāon is said to have been called Porto Pequeno.

A Muhammadan Account of the Settlement

The Muhammadan historian Abdul Hamīd Lāhorī who died in 1654, also dates the Portuguese settlement earlier than Akbar's time. He says in the *Bādshāhnāmā*‡ :—"Under the rule of the Bengālīs, (*dar' ahd-i-Bāngalīyān*) a party of Frank§ merchants, who are

* Cf. *Lendas*, Vol. III, p. 722. Castanheda certainly deserves more credence than Correa because we find Nuno Fernandes Freire in Chittagong and not in Sātgāon, receiving Portuguese Captains in his custom-house and settling the quarrels between Khudā Baksh Khān and Amirza Khān.

† Nunes, *Livro dos Pesos etc. Subsidios*, p. 37.

‡ Elliot, *Hist. of India*, Vol. VII pp. 31-32.

§ *Frank* is the parent word of *Feringhi* by which name the Indian-born Portuguese are still known. The Arabs and Persians called the French cruzaders *Frank*, *Ferang*, a corruption of France. When the Portuguese and other Europeans came to India the Arabs applied to them the same name *Ferang*, and then *Feringhi*.

inhabitants of Sūndīp came trading to Sātgānw. One *kos* above that place they occupied some ground on the bank of the estuary. Under the pretence that a building was necessary for their transactions in buying and selling, they erected several houses in the Bengalī style. In course of time, through the ignorance or negligence of the rulers of Bengal, these Europeans increased in number, and erected large substantial buildings, which they fortified with cannons, muskets, and other implements of war. In due course a considerable place grew up which was known by the name of the Port of Hūglī. On one side of it was the river, and on the other three sides was a ditch filled from the river. European ships used to go up to the port and a trade was established there. The markets of Sātgānw declined and lost their prosperity. The villages and the district of Hūglī were on both sides of the river and these the Europeans got possession of at a low rent." It is evident from this passage that the Portuguese had some sort of settlement in or above Sātgāon before Akbar's conquest of Bengal in 1576. The question is who these Bengali kings were, during whose reign the Portuguese settled above Sātgāon. The Oriyā Kings possessed the Hooghly district from Tribenī downwards from 1560-1567. From 1568 to 1575 reigned the dynasty of Sulaimān Kararanī (1568-73). O'Malley* suggests that the settlement must have taken place between 1568 and 1573 in the reign of Sulaimān Kararāni. This conjecture has nothing to support it.

It is probable that Abdul Hamīd Lāhorī confirms the Portuguese historians though rather vaguely and that the Bengali rulers referred to were the Lodi Kings, the last of whom granted the Portuguese a settlement in Sātgāon. The Mughal historians actually referred to the earlier Muhammadan rulers of Bengal as *Bengali* kings. It cannot be said

* *Hooghly Gazetteer*, p. 48.

the account of Lāhorī is quite indefinite for while he places the settlement *above* Sātgāon, he says it grew up into what is known as the port of Hooghly, which is really *below* Sātgāon. It is true in a way that he confounds the Portuguese settlement of Sātgāon with that of Hooghly. Yet the fact that he places the first Portuguese settlement *above* Sātgāon has some significance in that he probably means that it was a little above the main Muhammadan city of Sātgāon, whence it extended to Hooghly. Else, Lāhorī's account would be an absurdity.

Other Accounts

In spite of the abundant evidence of Portuguese historians partly corroborated by a Muhammadan account modern writers have not recognized the Portuguese settlement of Sātgāon. Fr. H. Hosten S. J. whose authority is very valuable in Portuguese history asserts*: "The Portuguese first settled at Hugli under a farman from Fatehpur Sikri between 1578 and 1580. Until that time they had not been allowed when coming up the river to do more than build godowns in bamboo and thatch which were burnt down regularly every year when they returned to Goa." Fr. Hosten evidently bases his statement on the account of the traveller Caesar Federici who writing about what he saw in Bengal about 1565 says.† "Every year at Buttor they make and unmake a village with houses and shops made of straw, and with all things necessary to their uses; and this village standeth as long as the ships ride there, and till they depart for the Indies, and when they are departed, every man goeth to his plot of houses and there setteth fire on them which thing made me to marvel. For as I passed upto Satagan, I saw this village standing with a great number of people, with an infinite number of ships and bazars, and at my return coming down with my Captain of the last ship for whom I tarried, I

* *Bengal Past and Present* Jan.—Mar. 1915 pp. 42-43.

† C. Federici. *Purchas* V. 411, 439.

was all amazed to see such a place so soon raised and burnt and nothing left but the sign of burnt houses." Federici, it will be seen, only speaks of the making and unmaking of villages in Betor, (Howrah, near Botanical Gardens) which he saw when going up to Sātgāon. Even though in the rest of his account he does not refer at all to the Portuguese settlement in Sātgāon, it cannot be inferred that the Portuguese never had a settlement in Sāgtāon. By 1565 when Federici visited Sātgāon all traces of the Portuguese settlement might have disappeared and the Afghāns who reigned after Māhmūd Shāh might have taken away from the Portuguese their custom-house and their factory, so that they found it necessary to build many sheds on the banks of the Hooghly to store their goods in. If Castanheda and Correa are to be believed, and there is no reason to doubt them, the Portuguese did something more than "build go-downs in bamboo and thatch" before they founded their great settlement in Hooghly in Akbar's time. Manrique also dates the origin of the city of Ugolim (Hooghly) to the *farman* of Akbar and speaks of the *golas* (store-houses) of the Portuguese.* His evidence does not obviously go against that of Castanheda since he speaks of the Portuguese settlement in Hooghly and not the one in Sātgāon about which he does not seem to have been informed at all. It must be considered that between the date of the settlement in Sātgāon and Manrique's visit to Hooghly almost a century had elapsed.

Second Settlement, Hooghly, 1579-80

Whatever might have been the fate of the first establishment of the Portuguese, they definitely settled in the town of Hooghly about 1580 by virtue of a charter conceded to them by Akbar. Manrique, who was in Bengal (1628-29) gives a pretty detailed account of this settlement, prior to which the Portuguese according to him, did not permanently stay in Bengal. They remained during the

* Manrique, *Bengal Past and Present* Apr.—June 1916, p. 286.

rainy season in Bengal buying and selling goods and went home to Goa when the rains were over. Later on the Portuguese remained for one or two years without going back and the Moorish collector in the district even invited them to bring their Fathers and erect churches. Akbar seeing the precious goods which the Portuguese used to bring to Bengal from Borneo, Malacca and other ports ordered the Nawab of Dacca under whom the Hooghly District then was, to send from Sātgāon two principal Portuguese to his Court in Agra. The Nawab immediately sent a messenger to Sātgāon for this purpose but on account of the delay that occurred on the way he reached Sātgāon after a journey of twenty-eight days and found that the Portuguese had gone, some to Malacca and others to China. However the Mirza assured the Nawab that the Portuguese would come back the next year as they had left behind in the hands of some merchants (Sodagones) goods worth more than two thousand rupees. But Akbar having expressed his indignation at the Nawab's negligence, the latter took it so much to heart that, as Manrique relates, he died shortly after.

Pedro Tavares, the Founder of the Settlement of Hooghly, 1579-80

The following year a Portuguese captain named Pedro Tavares* "a man well versed in politics and state-affairs" arrived in Sātgāon and was received with great joy. On learning that the Emperor Akbar wished that two Portuguese should come to him from Bengal, he gladly accepted the invitation and chosing two Portuguese and many servants went to Agra. Akbar, favourably impressed with the conduct and valour of the Portuguese who with Antonio Cabral had, sometime before, gone to see him at Surat,

* A full account of Pedro Tavares is given by Manrique, *Itinerario* etc. For what relates to Bengal *Vide* Fr. Cardon's Trans. *Bengal Past and Present*, April—June 1916. Bartoli, *Missione al Gran Mogor*, 1819, p. 5. calls Tavares a military servant of Akbar, which is wrong.

took a great liking to Tavares and had several interviews with him. He gave him many valuable presents and a *farman* permitting him to build a city in Bengal wherever he liked. He granted the Portuguese full religious liberty with leave to preach their religion and build Churches and even baptize the gentiles with their consent. Besides, the Mughal officers were ordered to help the Portuguese with all materials necessary for the construction of their houses.

The Akbarnāmā* mentions one Partāb Bār Feringui one of the chief merchants of the port of Bengal who came in 1579† to Akbar's Court at Agra with his wife Basūrbā and won great favour and esteem from the Emperor. As H. Beveridge suggests,‡ this Partāb Bār must have been Pedro Tavares. The name, indeed, approximates very closely, in spite of the mutilation which is very common in the Muhammadan historians. In the different MSS. of the Akbarnāmā there are various forms of the spelling of Partāb Bār's wife, such as Basūrbā, Nashurna, Nasunta, while some MSS. do not refer to her at all. It is only a guess of H. Beveridge or of the lady who told him, that the real name of Tavares's wife might have been Assumpta. Considering the severe mutilation which the Portuguese names have undergone in the Muhamadan histories it is wiser not to hazard groundless conjectures in the attempt to identify them. In the Akbarnāmā§ there is a further reference to Partāb Bār where it is said that Mirza Najat Khān, Akbar's *Faujdar* at Sātgāon, fled to the Portuguese Governor of Hooghly, after being defeated by the King of Orissa. This leads

* Elliot *Hist. of India*, Vol. VI. p. 59.

† Though Tavares was at Akbar's Court in 1579, he must have gone there a year or two before. *Vide infra.*

‡ J. A. S. B. 1888, p. 34 and J. A. S. B. 1904, p. 52.

§ P. 320 of the original.

Blochmann* to identify Partāb Bār with the Portuguese Governor of Hooghly. As Tavares who was at Akbar's Court in 1579 must have been the same as the Portuguese Governor of Hooghly in 1580, the account of the Akbarnāmā beautifully tallies with that of Manrique; and Partāb Bār was evidently no other than Pedro Tavares. Blochmann's and Beveridge's identifications of Partāb Bār should not therefore be taken as referring to two different persons.

Tavares must have exerted a great influence on Akbar. At his request Akbar exempted the Portuguese merchants from all the custom-duties of which they had defrauded the treasury until 1529.† To Tavares and two Jesuit Missionaries of Bengal must be given the credit of having convinced Akbar of the "truth of Law of Christ" or at least impressed him favourably towards the Christians. In consequence of a petition of Tavares, Akbar called for a priest named Fr. Juliano Pereira from Bengal so as to learn from him something more about the Christian Faith. Fr. Juliano Pereira having acquainted the Emperor with the tenets of the Christian religion asked him to send for more learned priests from Goa. From this resulted the famous Mission of Fr. Rodolfo Aquaviva.‡

When Hooghly was founded

When Tavares returned to Hooghly in 1579 or 1580 he was high in the estimation of the people and choosing a favourable site in Hooghly established the settlement, which grew into the greatest centre of trade in Bengal and supplanted the historic glory of Sātgāon. It is unfortunate that Manrique‡ does not specify the date of the foundation of Hooghly by Tavares. It can, however, be determined within close approximation from a consideration of contemporary writings. The

* *Ain-i-Akbari*, Vol. I. p. 440.

† Fr. F. de Souza, *Oriente Conq.* Pt. II, Conq. I, Div. ii, § 44.

‡ An excellent account of this Mission is given by Vincent Smith, *Akbar*, p. 170 *et seq.*

Akbarnāmā* records Tavares's visit to Akbar as occurring in 1579 (23rd year of Akbar's reign) but if Fr. du Jarric† is correct in dating Fr. Juliano Pereira's arrival at Fatehpur Sikrī in the year 1578 then Tavares must have gone to the Court of Akbar in 1577, or 1578 at the latest, since it was through his request that Fr. Pereira was called by Akbar. According to Fr. F. de Souza‡, Tavares must have been in Agra even upto 1579 because be obtained a decree from the Emperor exempting the Portuguese of Bengal from all their dues upto 1579. Now, it is certain that Tavares was in Bengal early in 1580 because Fr. A. Monseratte§ relates that when the first Jesuit Mission arrived at Akbar's Court on February 18, 1580, they found there some of Tavares's men while no mention is made of Tavares. The confirmation of the fact is found in the Akbarnāmā|| which relates that in 1580 Mirzā Najat Khān Akbar's *Faujdar* at Sātgāon being defeated by the king of Orissa, fled to Partāb Bār (Pedro Tavares) at Hooghly. Hence it may be asserted that the settlement of Hooghly was established either towards the close of 1579 or in the earlier months of 1580.

---

* Elliot, *Akbarnāmā* Vol. VI. p. 59.

† *Hist. Des. Choses plus Memorables.*

‡ *Oriente Conquistado* Pt. II, Conq. I, Div. ii, § 44.

§ *Mongol. Legat. Comment.* 20 *a*. 3. *Vide*, Fr. Hosten's annotations to Manrique, *Bengal Past and Present*, April—June, 1916, Ch. V.

|| Blochmann, *Akbarnāmā l.c. Ain-i-Akbari*, Vol. I. p. 440.

CHAPTER V

THE GROWTH OF THE SETTLEMENT OF HOOGHLY

The Portuguese settlement in Hooghly flourished with amazing rapidity. In 1580, about the same year that the settlement was made, the Portuguese influence was so well established that according to the Akbarnāmā* Mirza Najat Khān, Akbar's *Faujdar* at Sātgāon being defeated by the king of Orissa near Solimabad† fled to the Portuguese Governor at Hooghly for protection. Hooghly rose to be indeed "the richest, the most flourishing and the most populous" of all the Bandels that the Portuguese possessed in Bengal. As Fr. Cabral says, Hooghly became the common emporium of the vessels of India, China, Malacca and Manilla and a resort not only of a large number of the natives of the country but also of the Hindustanis (*sic*) the Mughals the Persians and the Armenians. Ralph Fitch who visited Hooghly in 1588 found the whole of the town in the hands of the Portuguese of whom he says it was the "chief keep." He adds the town was one league from Sātgāon, and was called *Porto Pequeno* in contradistinction to their *Porto Grande* which they had in Chittagong. Within the next ten years the Portuguese authority extended even to Sātgāon. The Ain-i-Akbari written in 1596-1597 says that in the *Sarkār* of Sātgāon there were two ports (Hooghly and Sātgāon) at a distance of half a *kos* from each other both of which were in possession of the Portuguese, Hooghly being the more important. Besides the Portuguese, had bought lands and possess-

Hooghly, 1580

* Cf. Blochmann *Ain-i-Akbari*, Vol. I. p. 440.

† A town south-east of Burdwan on the left bank of the Damodar.

ed villages on both sides of the river for a considerable distance from their town of Hooghly. Manrique, describing his voyage to Hooghly in 1628 says* "...we entered the mouth of the large and far-famed old Ganges at a distance of *Ganges* sixty leagues from the City of Vgolim (Hooghly). As we were navigating 'al uzane' which in the Bengala and Industana languages means going against the current we found it a very tough and tedious piece of work inspite of the many villages and towns, some of them the private property of the Portuguese of Vgolim which were covering both banks of the river all the way up to Vgolim." Fr. Cabral asserts the Portuguese did not confine themselves to the banks of the river but extended their settlement sixty leagues inland. The Portuguese population was fast increasing in Hooghly and so was the number of Christians who were converted by the Portuguese. The Augustinians built therefore in 1599, the year when the East India Company was formed, their great Convent at Bandel which still exists though not as originally built and not even on the original site.†

Towards the latter part of the sixteenth century, the greater part of the Bengal trade had passed into the hands of the Portuguese. Hooghly, Sātgāon and Chittagong were not their only ports and settlements, but they had also Hījīlī, Banja, Dacca and many other small ports. The extent of the Portuguese trade in Hooghly can be imagined from the fact that they paid over a 100,000 *tangas* or rupees as custom duties to the Mughals. For an account of the Portuguese trade in Bengal a separate chapter will be devoted.

The Portuguese were equally well thriving on the side of Chittagong and owned innumerable Bandels or *Bunders* on the

* Manrique, Fr. Cardon's Trans. *Bengal Past and Present* April—June 1916 p. 284.

† Fr. Hosten supposes the Convent stands on the same site as the old one. Cf. *A Week in Bandel Convent, Bengal Past and Present* Jan.—Mar. 1914. The question will be discussed below.

banks of the Ganges, of the Brahmaputra and of their various tributaries. In fact at this time more important events were occurring on the coast of Arakan and in the islands at the mouths of the Ganges than in Hooghly. In course of time the Portuguese of Hooghly became really independent of the Mughal Emperor in as much as they discontinued to pay the nominal tribute despite the remonstrations of the Mughal Governor. The Shāh Jahānnāmā* refers to the fact that the Portuguese had lands on both sides of the Hooghly and that they collected revenue from them. Even at the time when the *Ain-i-Akbarī* was written (1596-97), Hooghly had supplanted the historic Sātgāon, and both these ports were in the possession of the Portuguese.†

The Decline of Sātgāon

Two causes contributed to the decline of Sātgāon. The first was that the Portuguese, when they settled in Hooghly, diverted all the trade to their own port to the detriment of Sātgāon. The Mughal officers in Sātgāon actually complained to the Emperor that on account of the Portuguese, the revenue of Sātgāon was decreasing. The second cause was that the river Saraswatī on which Sātgāon was situated and through which flowed the main stream of the river Hooghly began silting up and was navigable only by smaller vessels. The Portuguese must have, indeed, chosen Hooghly for their settlement because they had noticed the main stream no longer flowing through the Saraswatī. This is one of the few examples in which the waters of the Ganges have played fast and loose with the ambitions of man. The holy Ganges does indeed work changes in its water system but it is not like other rivers such as the Indus, on which throughout its course no great city has ever flourished because it shifts its bed so very frequently. Well may it be called the Holy Ganga.

---

* Rev. Long, *Portuguese in North India*, Cal. Rev. Vol. V, June 1846.

† *Ain-i-Akbari*, Jarret. Vol. II. p. 125.

Question of a Fort in Hooghly

The Rev. Long remarks* that in 1599 the Portuguese erected a fort of a square form, flanked by four bastions, surrounded by a ditch on three sides and on the fourth by the Hooghly. This statement rests on no authority and it is one of the great many creations of his fancy. Each subsequent writer, probably relying upon him, has referred to the existence of the Portuguese fort in Hooghly, the remains of which are supposed to be the foundations of two walls that can be seen jutting out into the river at low tide.† The fact seems to be, however, that the Portuguese had not erected any fort in Hooghly.‡ No reference to it can be found in the Portuguese records. Ralph Fitch who was in Hooghly in 1686 makes no mention of a Portuguese fort and Van Linschoten (1593-97) distinctly says there was none.§ Most conclusive evidence is that of Manrique and Cabral who in their descriptions of the Siege of Hooghly regret that the Portuguese could not well defend themselves as they possessed no fort, having to content themselves with raising embankments and barricades, and converting their houses into citadels. It must be remarked Khāfi Khān|| in his description of the siege asserts that the Portuguese defended themselves from a fort ; but throughout his account he enlarges upon the *Bādshāhnāmā*,¶ which records that the Portuguese erected substantial buildings (not forts) which they fortified with cannon, muskets and other imple-

---

* Rev. Long, *Portuguese in North India, ut supra.*

† O'Malley, *Hooghly Gazetteer* p. 272.

‡ Fr. Hosten S. J. was the first to deny the existence of a Portuguese fort in Hooghly and to adduce evidence in support of it. *Vide Bengal Past and Present*, Jan.—Mar. 1915, p. 80 *et seq.*

§ Van Linschoten is however open to doubt as he says the Portuguese had no Government in Hooghly and lived like wild men, which could not be true.

|| Elliot, *Hist. of India*, Vol. VII. p. 211.

¶ *Ibidem*, pp. 31, 32.

RUINS OF THE SUPPOSED PORTUGUESE FORT IN HOOGHLY.

ments of war. It is not probable nor is there any evidence that the Portuguese built a fort after the Siege of Hooghly which took place in 1632.

The Rev. Long and Toynbee* refer to the fact that in 1603 Cervalius captured a Mughal fort with a garrison of 400 men all but one of whom were killed. This Cervalius was Domingo Carvalho who, as it will be seen, was the conqueror of the island of Sandwīp. Fr. du Jarric† gives some details about this interesting event. Carvalho came to Hooghly from Sripur (Bakargānj district) in order to take reinforcements for the capture of Sandwīp. He found there were about 5000 inhabitants in the Portuguese colony and that the Moors wanted to make them pay new tributes. Seeing the increasing prosperity of the Portuguese, the Moors had built a fortress near Hooghly so as to check their progress and had placed there a garrison of 400 Mughal soldiers. Whenever the Christians passed with their ships down the river, the Moors robbed them and even killed several of them inflicting indescribable cruelties. They tried to do the same with Carvalho when he was passing by their fortress with his thirty *Jaleas*‡ and began to discharge on him their arquebuzes. Carvalho jumped ashore with sixty Portuguese, and some seizing the gate of the fortress and others scaling its walls, they captured it and massacred the whole garrison excepting one Caffre who escaped through a channel. The further history of this fort, does not seem to exist in any records. Excepting this temporary hold on a Mughal fortress, the Portuguese cannot be said to have possessed a fort in Hooghly.

It is much to be deprecated that no adequate account is left

---

* *Sketch of the Administration of the Hooghly District*, p. 4.

† Cf. Fr du Jarric, *Histoire des Choses plus Memorables*, Part IV., Liv. VI p. 861-62.

‡ *Jalea* was a vessel used both for trading and fighting purposes; the word Jolly-boat is derived from it. *Cf. Hobson-Jobson* s. v. Gallevat.

Portuguese Government in Hooghly

of the Portuguese system of Government either in the official or individual writings. While so much is written about the Portuguese possessions in Western India, their doings in Bengal and the names of the chief actors have comparitively been consigned to oblivion. As to the names of the Portuguese Governors or Captains in Hooghly the only three names that can be given are Pedro Tavares (1580) Miguel Rodrigues (1623) and Manoel d' Azavedo (1632).*

The two of the earliest accounts of the Portuguese of Hooghly, throwing incidentaly some light on how they governed themselves, contain doubtful statements. Van Linschoten who travelled in India between 1583 and 1589, remarks in a brief description of the Portuguese of Chittagong and of Hooghly† "The Portingalles deale and traffique thether, and some places are inhabited by them, as the havens which they call Porto Grande (Chittagong) and Porto Pequeno (Hooghly) that is the great haven and the little haven but there they have no Fortes nor any government, nor policie, as in India [they have] but live in a manner like wild men, and untamed horses, for that every man doth there what

* In spite of repeated investigations I have not been able to find a list of the Portuguese Governors of Hooghly. Out of the three names given the first is mentioned on the authority of Manrique and others. As to Manoel d' Azavedo being Captain of the Portuguese of Hooghly we have the statement of Fr. Cabral, in his letter from Ceylon (1633) describing the Seige of Hooghly. Though Miguel Rodrigues is mentioned by Stewart, in his *History of Bengal*, and by others who have repeated his statement, as the Governor of Hooghly when Shāh Jahān fled to Bengal, yet there is considerable doubt about it. Stewart probably based his statement on Fr. Catrou's *History of the Mogol Empire*. But Manrique calls Miguel Rodrigues Captain of the Portuguese in Dacca. Fr. Catrou's is not a sure evidence because he makes Miguel Rodrigues a Captain of the Portuguese in Hooghly even in 1632, which cannot be true according to Fr. Cabral. Yet I have included Rodrigues's name among the Portuguese Captains of Hooghly for if he was a Captain of the Portuguese in Dacca he might have, at the same time, been Captain of those in Hooghly.

† Van Linschoten, Hakl. Ed. Vol I p. 95.

hee will, and every man is Lord [and maister], neyther esteeme they anything of justice, whether there be any or none, and in this manner doe certayne Portingalles dwell among them some here, some there, [scattered abroade] and are for the most part such as dare not stay in India for some wickednesse by them committed ; notwithstanding there is great trafficke used in those part es by diverse ships [and marchants] which all the year divers times both go to and from all the Orientall ports." As Van Linschoten was in Bengal not more than five years after the Portuguese had settled in Hooghly it is probable they had no perfect system of government and that there were many abuses but this writer seems to have been in some points either misinformed about Hooghly or else he applies to Hooghly what he saw in Chittagong, just as a later traveller Pyrard de Laval did. If in 1580 there was a. Portuguese governor in Hooghly to whom Mir Najat Khān fled for protection it is difficult to conceive how there could be no government at all only about five years after, especially since all evidence points to the fact that the Portuguese were flourishing rather than degenerating into "untamed horses". Ralph Fitch who was in Hooghly in 1588 saw a great town in the possession of the Portuguese and has nothing to say about their living like wild men. Pyrard de Laval who was in Chittagong in 1607 perpetrates the same blunder imagining that the condition of the Portuguese in Hooghly was the same as in Chittagong. It must be mentioned Pyrard de Laval did not visit Hooghly. "A large number of Portuguese", he says* "dwell in freedom at the ports on this coast of Bengal ; they are also very free in their lives being like exiles. They do only traffic, without any fort, order, or police, and live like natives of the country ; they durst not return to India, for certain misdeeds they have committed and they have no clergy among them." To say that the Portuguese had no

* **Pyrard de Laval, Hakl. Ed. Vol. I p. 334.**

clergy in Hooghly in 1607 is quite erroneous. As will be seen, the religious orders, Jesuits and the Augustinians, had erected in Hooghly many churches and undoubtedly there were priests in the great Augustinian convent built in 1599, which after being destroyed and re-built many times, still exists in Bandel.

Manrique who was in Hooghly in its palmiest days, devotes many pages to quite insignificant matters but as to the system of government or its officials he has scarcely to say anything beyond mentioning that "there was a government which did not think it fit to send an embassy to Shāh Jahān on his ascending the throne."* Fr. Cabral, however, gives some information, about how the Portuguese governed themselves in Hooghly.† He says the Portuguese enjoyed absolute independence, the Mughals being content with merely collecting custom duties and market dues. This is a fact which Shāh Jahānnāmā confirms. Not even the Emperor's Guazil could enter the Portuguese town except with the consent of the Portuguese and the Mughal ships had to submit themselves to many regulations which the Portuguese enforced in their port. The Portuguese government was under a *Captain Convidor* and four assistants annually elected by the citizens. This Captain was obeyed by common folk and even by the gentry of the place. It is worthy of remark that Fr. Cabral says that it was the King of Portugal who had these officials in Hooghly showing that the Portuguese of Hooghly were loyal to the crown. The reason why Manrique, Cabral and other Portuguese who were in Hooghly have not left any detailed description of the system of government was probably because

* Manrique's, *Itinerario*, Fr. Hosten's Trans. of the Siege of Hooghly, in Catholic Herald of India, Calcutta, Vol. XVI, April, 17th 1918 and succeeding Nos.

† Fr. João Cabral's Letter from Ceylon, dated 14th Nov. 1633. *Vide* Fr. Besse's Trans. Catholic Herald, *ut supra*. Jan. 30th 1918 and succeeding Nos.

it was the same as in the other Portuguese possessions, with only some modifications to suit the conditions of the country.

Mannuci who was in Hooghly about 1660, does not also refer in his *Storia do Mogor* to any Portuguese officials though he has a lot to say about opulent Portuguese merchants. It cannot be said that after the Siege of Hooghly in 1632 the Portuguese were mere traders without any officials or responsibilities. In the Diaries of Streynsham Master appears a deed, in the Portuguese language, enacted and signed by a Portuguese public notary named Antonio Gil de Brito in the year 1657.* In Bandel some tenants of the Augustinian Convent still possess deeds and documents in Portuguese, signed by public notaries at a comparatively recent date.†

The Portuguese in Hooghly were under the authority of the Ceylon government and not directly under the Portuguese Viceroy in Goa as communication with the latter place was only possible by sea and involved considerable delay. In a large measure the Portuguese managed their affairs independently, but they never shook off the authority of the Portuguese Viceroy who from time to time communicated to the King of Portugal the state of affairs in the Portuguese possession of Ugolim (Hooghly).

It is commonly supposed that the word Hooghly is derived from *hogla*, (*typha elephantina*) the name for the tall reeds growing in abundance on the banks of the river. This derivation

---

* *Diaries* Temple's Edition Vol. II p. 62. "I Antonio Gil (not Gonsalvez as Temple has) de Brito, notary public of deeds for his Majesty in this Bandel of Nossa Senhora de Guadelupe of Xahabad, certify that the signature above Gaspar de Breu is that of the said Gaspar de Breu, a Portuguese. I assured myself that the said Gaspar de Breu was his signature, in faith of which I have enacted this at present, signed by me with my public signature which is as follows.

To-day, 3rd Oct. 1657. He paid for this half a *tanga*."

† One deed, dated 22nd Sept. 1794 is signed by Thomas de Faria, *Escrivão Publico das notas d'esta Villa de Bandel*, and another, dated 21st Oct 1824 is signed by João Lobo, *Escrivão* e *Notario*.

first proposed by H. Blochmann,* does not seem to be true.

Derivation of 'Hooghly'

The *hogla* reeds which always grew on the river banks cannot alone account for a remarkable change of the name of the river from Bhāghīrathī or Ganges into Hooghly towards the end of the sixteenth century. The river acquired its name from the town of *Hooghly* which the Portuguese founded about 1580. Before this date Hooghly did not exist in name. The *Chandi* written in 1577 makes no mention of it though it refers to places close to it and opposite to it such as Harishar and Gouripur (Gorifa). O'Malley says † that Hooghly is mentioned in a Bengali poem dated 1495 but the reference which he gives, has no word about Hooghly and deals about quite different matters. The Portuguese obviously originated the name. The earliest mention of the word is in Ralph Fitch who in 1588 spells it *Hugeli.* Two years later we find in Fr. Monseratte's map the town marked *Goli.* The *Ain-i-Akbarī* (1596-97) has *Hugli.* As to the Portuguese historians, de Barros, Correa and Castanheda do not refer at all to Hooghly as their histories cover an earlier period than 1550, while Hooghly came into existence about 30 years later. Fr. Fernandes (1599) has Gullum or Gullo. Bocarro (1612-17) has *D'Ogolim, Golim, Dogolim* and Faria y Souza speaking about the Siege of Hooghly has *Golim.* Other forms are *Gollye* (Hughes and Parker 1620) ; *Ugolim* (Manrique, 1628) ; *Ugoli* (De Laet, 1630); *Oegli* or *hoegli* (Van den Broucke 1660); *Ogouli* (Bernier, 1665). Towards the end of the seventeenth century and after, *hughly, hooghly* began to be adopted.

It is very interesting to know whence arose the designation *Hooghly.* As already said it is not likely to be derived from the *hogla* alone, as it was not the river that was called

* Blochmann, J. A. S. B. 1873, p. 217 n.

† *Hooghly Gazetteer* p. 48.

Hooghly first but the town, where, as far as the Portuguese were concerned, the *hogla* reeds were not of any importance. Besides *hogla* reeds are to be found all over the banks of the river and not confined to the town of Hooghly. As Fr. Hosten suggests* the Portuguese might have named their settlement from the large amount of *golas* (store-houses) which they erected on the banks of the river. Fr. Hosten is not well inclined to adopt this derivation and raises many doubts. It has also been suggested that Hooghly is derived from *Gal* or *Goli* (Beng,) meaning a narrow passage, though there is nothing definite to justify such a conjecture. After all, the explanations suggested, resolve into attempting to suit facts to the theory. Whether Hooghly is derived from *hoglas* or *golas*, one thing certain at the present stage of historical research is that the name was originated by the Portuguese. Most probably both the words explain the origin of the name *Hooghly*, as the *golas* must have been covered with thatches of *hoglas*, as it is done even to this day.

---

* *Bengal Past and Present*, Jan.-Mar. 1915, *A week at the Bandel Convent*, pp. 89-91.

CHAPTER VI

PORTUGUESE SETTLEMENTS IN EASTERN BENGAL

From the earliest times Chittagong was the greatest harbour of Bengal, as already stated, and it continued to be so, as long as the far-famed Gaur remained the royal capital of Bengal, and one of the queens of Eastern cities.* All the early Portuguese captains João Silveira, Affonso de Mello and others, sailed up to Chittagong and stoutly braved the vicissitudes that the Bengal rulers subjected them to, until Mahmūd Shāh, in consideration of the help rendered him by the Portuguese, granted them in 1537 their settlement of Chittagong with a custom-house, and land and houses with powers to collect rent.† Unlike the one in Sātgāon, the settlement of Chittagong grew into a great centre of trade. Nuno Fernandes Freire who was appointed chief of the custom-house exercised vast powers in Chittagong and was asked to decide the quarrels between the Moorish Governors who did not fully acknowledge the authority of the King of Bengal.

Chittagong, 1537

---

* Camões thus speaks of Chittagong, *Lusiadas, Canto X, St. cxxi.*

Vê Cathigão, cidade das melhores
De Bengala, provincia que se preza
De abundante; mas olha que está posta
Para o Austro d'aqui virada a costa.

See Cathigam, amid the highest high
In Bengal province, proud of varied store
Abundant, but behold how placed the Post
Where sweeps the shore-line towards the southing Coast.
Burton's *Trans.*

† Vide Chapter IV; also Castanheda *Hist.* Liv. VIII. Chap. CXXVIII. p. 303.

Towards the last two decades of the sixteenth century, when the Portuguese settlement in Sātgāon was flourishing so well and the Portuguese were in high favour with Akbar and Jahāngīr, the Chittagong settlement was equally well progressing. The Mughal authority had not, however, yet extended to Chittagong side. The King of Arakan who held it, was favourably disposed towards the Portuguese. The Portuguese, it appears, had a skirmish with him and one Antonio de Souza Godinho about 1590 had captured by force of arms the fort of Chittagong and made the island of Sandwīp tributary to it.* But a reconciliation had taken place and the King was, in fact, permitting the Portuguese to build other forts in his kingdom, which the King of Portugal found were not quite necessary and difficult to maintain. The Portuguese and the King of Portugal spoke at this time in glowing terms of their settlement of Chittagong.

Capture of the Fort of Chittagong

Though Antonio de Souza Godinho had made the Sandwīp island tributary to the Portuguese Settlement of Chittagong it did not come completely in the possession of the Portuguese until 1602, when Domingo Carvalho and Manoel de Mattos captured it from the Mughals who had deprived Kedar Rai (Cedarai) from its possession. The details of this conquest have not been given by the Portuguese historians but fortunately much information about the feats of the Portuguese in Sandwip is found in Fr. Nicolau Pimenta, and Fr. Du Jarric. This island, where two hundred ships were annually laden with salt and which, indeed, according to Fr. Du Jarric supplied the whole of Bengal with salt, belonged to the famous Kedar Rai, one of the tradi-

Sandwīp, 1602

* *Archivo Portuguez Oriental*, Fasciculo III p. 257, King's letter, 12th January 1591. It is surprizing that the letters in Fr. Pimenta do not refer to this event which had occurred only eight years before they were written.

Sandwīp is a big island at the mouth of the Ganges in the district of Noakhali. According to Faria y Souza it is 70 leagues in length.

tional heroes of Bengal. The Mughals, however, after their conquest of Bengal deprived him of this possession. The Portuguese who for long had an eye on this rich island took advantage of this situation and under Domingo Carvalho, one of the most valliant Portuguese in Bengal or even in India, attacked and captured the fortress of Sandwīp in 1602.* But the inhabitants of Sandwīp (*naturels du pais*) having risen against the Portuguese, Carvalho appealed to the Portuguese of Chittagong for help. Manoel de Mattos who was captain of the Portuguese in Dianga came to succour Carvalho with 400 men and put the enemy to rout. This victory placed Sandwīp completely in the hands of Carvalho and Mattos who divided it between them. Fr. Du Jarric mentions that Carvalho was born in Montargil (Portugal) and was previously in the service of Kedar Rai.

Though Domingo Carvalho and Manoel de Mattos were jointly governing the island, the former wrote to the Portuguese King that they held authority under the crown of Portugal. In recognition of their brilliant services the King of Portugal created Carvalho and Mattos *Fidalgos da Casa Real* (i.e. nobles) and bestowed on them the Order of Christ.†

Battles with the King of Arakan.

The King of Arakan who had many Portuguese in his kingdom, was highly enraged at their conquest of Sandwīp, and apprehended that as they were becoming very powerful especially in Siriam (Pegu),‡

* This account is based on Fr. Du Jarric's *Histoire des Chose plus Memorables etc.* Part IV. Chap. XXXII & XXXIII. The passage referring to Kedar Rai has been mistranslated by Nikhil Nath Roy in his প্রতাপাদিত্য। It runs: "*Ceste Isle appartenoit de droiet á un des Roys de Bengala, qu'on appelle Cadaray: mais il y auoit plusieurs années qu'il n'en jouissoit pas á cause que les Mogores s'en estoient emparez par force. Or quād il sceut que les Portugais s'en estoient saisis, comme nous dirons bien tost, il la leur donna de fort bonne volunte renoncant en leur faveur a tous les droiets qu il y pouuoit pretendre.*" *Vide* op. cit. p. 848.

† *Doc. Rem.* Tom. I. p. 25.

‡ Phayre identifies Siriam with Thanhlyin. Cf. *History of Burma*, p. 124.

where they had built a fortress, they might prove a source of danger to his Kingdom. He prepared, therefore, a fleet consisting of hundred and fifty *jaleas*, *caturs*,* and other larger vessels well equipped and armed with guns and canon. Kedar Rai also joined the king of Arakan and sent hundred *cosses*† from Sripūr to help him in the attack. The Portuguese of Dianga and Caranja having got scent of the impending attack took to their ships and sailed off with all their goods since they could not face the enemy's enormous forces. Those of Chittagong also began to escape with their most precious things doubting the intentions of the King (*sic*) of Chittagong who was the uncle of the King of Arakan and who outwardly pretended to be a great friend of the Portuguese. On the 8th of November 1602, the Arakan fleet appeared in the port of Dianga where Manoel de Mattos was in a foist, with many other Portuguese in their *jaleas*, which being badly equipped, drew in the rear. The foist of Mattos bore the brunt of the attack in which many Arakanese were killed. Only one Portuguese was killed and seven were wounded of whom Mattos himself was one. The Arakanese captured four Portuguese vessels and in honour of their victory they drank and feasted in the wildest joy.

Two days after, things changed, as Domingo Carvalho came with relief from Sandwīp. He and Mattos got up fifty vessels among which were two *foists*, four *caturs*, three *barques*, the rest being *jaleas*. With this fleet they set out early in the morning and made a surprise attack on the enemy's ships with such fury and violence that they were completely routed. They became masters of all the Arakanese ships to the

---

* *Caturs* were light rowing vessels, 60 to 80 ft. long used in sea-fights. the word is probably the origin of the English marine term *cutter*. Cf. Hobson-Johnson S. V. Catur.

† *Cosses* were light boats suitable for fighting on the rivers and not at sea.

number of hundred and forty nine, with all the ammunition, arquebuzes, muskets and other implements of war. Many Arakanese lost their lives in this engagement, notably the uncle of the King of Arakan, named Sinabadi. Some escaped by jumping into the sea and swimming across to land.

When the news of the Portuguese victory reached Chittagong, all were panic-stricken. The people thinking that the Portuguese would march on the city began to run away carrying their valuable things on their shoulders and the Queen herself mounted on an elephant took to flight. The Portuguese, however, did not follow up their victory, though they could have easily taken possession of the fort of Chittagong as there was nobody to defend it.

The King of Arakan, though humbled in his pride at sea revenged himself on the Portuguese who were on land in his kingdom. He sacked their houses which they owned in many Bandels (*bunders*) on the river and imprisoned men, women and children in his fortress and subjected them to many cruelties. He, however, set to liberty the women on the day following their imprisonment. The Portuguese missionaries, Jesuits and Dominicans, who had come to Bengal in 1598 and 1599 and were carrying on very successful work also suffered immensely.* A treaty was, however, concluded by the Portuguese with the King of Arakan, and peace was restored for a time. According to the chronicles of the Dominicans the King of Arakan actually offered to rebuild at his own expense the church and the residence of the Dominicans which he had destroyed and requested them to stay in his kingdom.†

The Portuguese were now becoming very powerful in Eastern Bengal and Burma. Fillipe de Brito e Nicote had established a kingdom in Pegu and made treaties with the

* Vide Chapter IX.

† Frey Luis de Cacegas, *Historia de San Domingos*, 1767, Vol. III. Liv. V. Ch. XI.

kings of Tangu, Siam and Proem. After the conquest of Sandwīp the Portuguese conceived the grand project of holding the whole of the Eastern coast of the Bay of Bengal with Chittagong and Pegu as bases. Purchas remarks* the Portuguese feats were of great consequence for "here they (the Portuguese) might both build their Fleets, and be furnished of sustenance, might send at any time to all places in the South (which from Goa cannot be done but with the Monsons) and might cause that no ship of Moores should lade Pepper Cinamon or other commodities at Martavan, Reitav, Juncalao, Tanassarin and Queda, for Surat or Mecca, but with custome to them and passe from them."

The King of Arakan, dreading the Portuguese might oust him from his kingdom, decided to attack Sandwīp a second time and sent an enormous fleet of a thousand sail consisting of "the most Frigates, some greater, Catures and Cosses" against Carvalho. Again were the Portuguese victorious. The gallant Carvalho with only sixteen vessels destroyed the whole fleet of the Arakan King. Nearly two thousand Arakanese were killed and a hundred and thirty of their ships were destroyed, while the Portuguese lost only six men. This signal defeat enraged the King of Arakan beyond measure. He punished his captains by forcing them to put on women's clothes as they behaved so effeminately that they could not bring one Portuguese alive or dead.†

Second attack on Sandwīp

Though the Portuguese had won a brilliant victory their ships were badly damaged. Carvalho soon found out that he could not withstand another attack of the King of Arakan whose resources were unlimited. The Portuguese with the native converts of the place, therefore, evacuated Sandwīp and transported all their possessions to Sripūr, Bākla and

* Purchas, *His Pilgrimage*, Book V., Chap. vi., p. 582.

† Du Jarric, *Histoire*, Part IV., p. 860.

Chandecan, whereupon the King of Arakan at last became master of it. Carvalho curiously enough stayed with thirty frigates in Sripūr which was the seat of Kedar Rai. The Jesuit Father Blasio Nunes and three others who had begun building a church and a residence in Sandwīp abandoned their new ventures and repaired to their residence at Chandecan which was the only one left to them, all the others having been destroyed.

The Career of Carvalho

Even in Sripūr Carvalho was not destined to be left undisturbed. The Mughals who were extending their power all over Bengal and Arakan sent against Kedar Rai a fleet of hundred *cosses* under one Mandarai with a view to capture Sripūr. The Mughal captain find Carvalho in Sripūr directed his fleet against him. Carvalho had only thirty *jaleas* under him. But he who with sixteen vessels had defeated the King of Arakan's fleet of a thousand vessels could never hesitate to stand against only a hundred vessels of the Mughals. Not long after he engaged the Mughal fleet, he worked its destruction and even slew Mandarai who is described as "a very valiant man and very famous all over Bengal." Carvalho himself was wounded but he soon recovered and determined to embark on new ventures.

The re-capture of Sandwīp never ceased to haunt the dreams of Carvalho. As the Portuguese were very powerful in Hooghly, he personally went there in order to bring reinforcements for the execution of his plans. In Hooghly, still more stirring events were in store for him. He found that the Mughals gave the Portuguese a lot of trouble, demanding from them new tributes and imposts, and that in order to check their growing power they had built close to the Portuguese town of Hooghly a fortress garrisoned by four hundred soldiers. From this fortress the Mughals came down upon the Indian-born Christians when they passed by and inflicted on them untold cruelties. "Wishing therefore" adds Fr. Du Jarric,* "to do the same with Domingo Carvalho when he was passing by their fortress with his thirty Jaleas, those who were inside began to discharge on him many arquebuzes. Carvalho, unable to tolerate such an affront, promptly jumped ashore with eighty Portuguese soldiers, and at first seized the fortress, while others scaled the walls. Entering inside the fortress they made such a slaughter that of the four hundred soldiers who were there only one a Caffre escaped through a channel."

The victories of Carvalho won for him a legendary reputation in Bengal and Arakan. His name was so much dreaded that one of the Arakanese commanders who had fifty ships under him, having dreamt one night that he was assaulted by Carvalho he "terrified his fellowes and made them flie into the river; which when the king heard cost him his head." The grand career of Carvalho was brought to a tragic end by the cruel and treacherous king of Chandecan, who was, according to Beveridge,† no other than Raja Pratāpāditya, the great hero of Bengal. This unscrupulous chieftain desired to make friends with the King of Arakan who after taking possession of Sandwīp and conquering the kingdom of Bākla had become considerably powerful, and menaced the kingdom of Chandecan. As he knew that nothing would please the King of Arakan more than the death of Carvalho, he invited the latter to his court in Chandecan and had him treacherously murdered. The King of Arakan, indeed, prized the head of Carvalho more than Sandwīp. Not long after, Raja Pratāpāditya, a cruel monster as Beveridge calls him, expiated his crimes in an iron cage in which he died.

The identification of the exact sites of the Portuguese Settlements offers many difficulties. Old Chittagong or

---

* Du Jarric, *Histoire*, *Part IV.*, p. 862.

† *The District of Bākarganj Chap. V.*

The Sites of the Portuguese Settlements

Chatigam of the Portuguese writers was according to de Barros's map (1540), Bleav's map (1650), Broucke's map (1660) and other old maps, on the northern bank of the Karnaphuli river almost at its mouth. It is not the same, therefore, as the modern town of Chittagong which is situated ten and half miles to the east of the mouth of the Karnaphuli. Strangely enough in 1598 Van Linschoten* assigned to Chittagong a position fifty miles eastward from the mouth of the Karnaphuli. The first Portuguese settlement, founded by Affonso de Mello in 1537, was obviously in the real *Chatigam* as marked by de Barros in his map. There is no trace left of the Portuguese factory, their custom-house and their "circuit of houses". But the relics of their later establishments still survive.

O'Malley† refers to the remains of a Portuguese fort close to Pahartali which is two miles from the civil station of Chittagong and adds that according to tradition the Portuguese bucaneers buried their treasures in this fort. According to the Portuguese records ‡ the Portuguese possessed a fort in Chittagong before 1590 but it was rather in the port of Chittagong than close to Pahartali. If it is true that the Portuguese bucaneers buried their treasures in the Pahartali fort, it must have come into their possession after 1615, after which date they constituted themselves into a piratical power and settled in Dianga with the sanction of the King of Arakan. Yet Manrique does not refer to any Portuguese fort between 1621 and 1635 in Chittagong or Arakan. Fr. du Jarric§ mentions that in 1602 the Portuguese under Carvalho and Mattos could have easily taken possession of the fort of Chittagong,

* Linschoten, Hakl. Ed. Vol. I p. 94. "From this River Eastward 50 miles lyeth the towne of Chatigam which is the chief town of Bengala.'

† *Chittagong Gazetteer*, p. 176.

‡ *Arch. Port. Orient., Fasc. III*, p. 257.

§ *Histoire des Choses plus Memorables, Part IV.*, p. 851.

which seems to have been close to the mouth of the Karnaphuli. It is this fort on which the Portuguese must have had a temporary hold about 1590. The King of Chittagong was in fact willing to allow the Portuguese to build more fortresses but the King of Portugal in his letter to the Viceroy dated 12th January 1591 did not consider them necessary. "And thus I am told", the letter runs* "that Antonio de Souza Godinho has served me well in Bemgualla and has made the Island of Sundiva (Sandwīp) tributary to this State, and that he gained the fort of Chatiguão (Chittagong) by force of arms and that the King is making some offers (permitting the Portuguese) to build fortresses in his country. Because new fortresses when they are not quite necessary are useless and quite inconvenient to this State in which it behoves to have more garrisons to increase and preserve, than extra forts to guard and thus divert the forces of the same State, I do not consider it proper that the offers of this King should be accepted and it will be enough to maintain with him good friendship." Little did the King know that if the Portuguese had erected forts in Chittagong and Arakan they might have defied the King of Arakan on land as they defied his fleets at sea, in the constant struggles that arose in the next few years.

'Cidade de Bengala'

In the literature of the sixteenth and the seventeenth centuries and especially in the Portuguese writers, there are frequent references to a "City of Bengala," which is generally supposed to have been Chittagong. Varthema † as early as 1510 speaks of taking his route to this City of Bengala though according to Garcia de Orta,‡ he never came to Bengal. Duarte de Barbosa, who was one of the earliest Portuguese to write a geographical

* *Arch. Port. Orient, ut supra.*

† L. de Varthema, *Travels*, Hakl. Ed. p. 210.

‡ Garcia de Orta, *Colloquios* p. 30.

account of the African and Indian coasts says,* " .... this sea (Bay of Bengal) is a gulf which enters towards the north and at its inner extremity there is a very great city inhabited by Moors which is called Bengala, with a very a good harbour." Lord Stanley of Alderly understands this city of Bengala to have been Chittagong and in a note says that where Ortelius places Bengala, Hommanus places Chatigam, or Chittagong. Considering a chart of 1743 in Dalrymple Chittagong, as Yule remarks,† seems to have been the City of Bengala. Ovington‡ in giving the boundaries of the kingdom of Arakan remarks "*Teixeira* and generally the *Portuguese* writers reckon that (Chatigam) as a city of *Bengala* ; and not only so, but place the city of Bengala itself upon the same coast, more *south* than *Chatigam*." From this quotation, Fr. Hosten concludes§ that the City of Bengala was Dianga, which is opposite Chittagong on the southern bank of the river Karnaphuli ; and adds that Dianga was the first Portuguese Settlement in the Gulf of Bengal and that it was called Porto Grande. That the first Portuguese settlements in Bengal were Sātgāon and Chittagong has been already shown. In the Gulf of Bengal, however Piplī (Orissa) was the earliest settlement, being founded in 1514.|| To say that Dianga was called Porto Grande is to give it undue importance. The name Dianga does not occur except at the beginning of the seventeenth century¶ while *Chatigam* the real Porto Grande where the Portuguese settled, and the *City of Bengala* were referred

* *The Coasts of East Africa and Malabar*, Hakl. Ed. p. 178-9.

† *Hobson-Jobson* s. v. Bengal.

‡ *A Voyage to Suratt*, p. 554.

§ *Bengal Past and Present* 1916, Vol. XIII No. 25, p. 128.

|| See Chapter *VIII*.

¶ The earliest mention of Dianga I have found is in Fr. Fernandes's letter dated 22nd December 1599. *Vide*, Pimenta, or Du Jarric *Hist.* Part IV, p. 828.

to early in the sixteenth century. De Barros marks Chatigam in his map (1540) but neither Dianga nor the City of Bengala. Ovington, it must be remarked, reckons Chatigam or Chittagong as the City of Bengala and not Dianga though he says the Portuguese writers place the City of Bengala more south than Chittagong. Fr. Fernandes* in his letter written from Dianga on 22nd December 1599 calls Dianga a town (ville) in the Port of Chittagong. It was at about this time that it began to acquire some importance. Besides Dianga could not be the City of Bengala as it really formed a part of the Kingdom of Arakan.

In Blaev's map, which is not generally accurate, the City of Bengala is placed on the southern bank of the Karnaphuli more or less where Van den Broucke places Dianga. Vignola in a map of 1683 assigns the same position to the City of Bengala. But in an old Portuguese map in Thevenot† the City of Bengala is placed above *Xatigam* (Chittagong) or probably it is meant to be Chittagong itself. Without at all enquiring into the relative accuracy of these maps it may be safely asserted that all evidence points to the conclusion that Chittagong was the real City of Bengala, spoken of by the early writers. As Chittagong was the Great Port of Bengala it was more likely the Great City of Bengala. The Arabs and later on the Portuguese generally named a foreign important city or a seaport after the country in which it was situated.

The Settlement of Dianga

Dianga is now known as Bunder or Feringhi Bunder. The word Dianga still survives as *Diang Pahar* which is the name of a low ridge of red rock running along the last three miles of the southern bank of the Karnaphuli. The Portuguese who had established themselves in Chittagong extended their activities to Dianga towards the end of the sixteenth century.

---

* Du Jarric, *ut supra*.

† Thevenot, *Voyages Curieux*, Vol. 1, Map facing p. 128.

In the above mentioned letter, Fr. Fernandes referred to a great number of Portuguese of Dianga, who made their confessions. The captain of the Portuguese Dianga and of Chittagong was Manoel de Mattos. The King of Arakan owned both these ports at this time and in the letters-patent granted to the Portuguese Fathers he styled himself "the highest and the most powerful King of Arakan, of Tippera, of Chacomas, and of Bengala ; Lord of the Kingdoms of Pegu etc."* Fr. du Jarric though mentioning that Chittagong was subject to the King of Arakan says that the latter's uncle was King of Chittagong, probably meaning thereby that he was Governor of Chittagong. The King of Arakan was well disposed towards the Portuguese of Dianga and Chittagong until in 1602 he fell out with the Portuguese over their conquest of Sandwīp. A Portuguese map in Thevenot marks many houses and a Church in the locality of Dianga though this place is not mentioned. In 1607 there were six hundred Portuguese in Dianga who were put to the sword by the King of Arakan in a general massacre. The Portuguese settled in Dianga again after 1615 when the King of Arakan took the Portuguese adventurers in his service and with their conjoined efforts brought to a culmination an age of plunder and piracy. Till then the Portuguese of Dianga and Chittagong were loyal subjects of the crown of Portugal.

Filippe de Brito e Nicote

The circumstances that led to the massacre of Dianga belong more to the history of Pegu than of Bengal. Filippe de Brito e Nicote was a Portuguese settled in Pegu, who with his men helped the King of Arakan, Salim Shāh (*Xilimixa*)† in his battles with the King of Tangu and actually defeated the latter conquering the castle of *Mecao*. In recognition of his

---

* Du Jarric, *Histoire* Part IV., p. 830.

† Salim Shāh was the Muhammadan name of King Meng Râjâgyî, (1593-1612).

services, Salim Shāh conceded to Brito e Nicote* the title of *Changa* (the good man) and granted to the Portuguese the port of Siriam in Pegu. Encouraged by success, Brito e Nicote returned to Goa to consult with the Viceroy D. Ayres de Saldanha how to carry into effect his plan of conquering the whole of Pegu. He was received with great joy and eventually obtained the Order of Christ and was made *Fidalgo da Casa Real* (Noble). The Viceroy gave his niece in marriage to Brito e Nicote and conferred upon him the title of Commander of Siriam and General of the Conquests of Pegu. Meanwhile the King of Arakan finding that the Portuguese were fortifying themselves in Siriam, sent his captain Banadola with a large fleet and 6000 men against them, but he was routed by the brave Salvador Ribeiro de Souza, who was in command of the Portuguese. Three more attacks with enormous forces were withstood by Salvador Ribeiro de Souza, who with an epic gallantry would not surrender even after a siege of eight months. Help at last arrived from Goa, with which Salvador Ribeiro de Souza inflicted a crushing defeat on the whole of the fleet and army of Salim Shāh. Soon after, he gained another victory over the King of Massinga, drove him away from his kingdom, and was hailed by the people as the King of Massinga. Such was the high renown won by the Portuguese that they could easily command the services of twenty thousand natives of the place.

Brito e Nicote having returned from Goa, Salvador Ribeiro offered the crown of Massinga to him, who accepted it in the name of the King of Portugal. Salim Shāh astonished at the success of the Portuguese hastened to make friends with them, and the Kings of Tangu and Martaban entered into an alliance with Nicote. While Brito e Nicote was rising on the tide of fortune Salvador Ribeiro, the real hero of

* This brief account of Brito e Nicote is based on Bocarro, *Decada* XIII; Faria y Souza, *Asia*; and *Documentos Remettidos.*

the exploits returned to Portugal and died a poor man. In the letter of 12th September 1608, addressed to the Viceroy at Goa, the King of Portugal accepted the crown of Pegu.*

Brito e Nicote now formed the plan of taking possession of Dianga and as he exercised a great influence over the King of Arakan he sent his son with a fleet asking him to grant him that port. The King suspecting that Brito e Nicote wished to deprive him of the whole of his kingdom invited Brito e Nicote's son and his men to his court and put them all to the sword. A general massacre of the Portuguese in the kingdom was ordered and about six hundred Portuguese who were peacefully residing in Dianga were murdered in cold blood. From this massacre about ten Portuguese escaped with their ships and one of them was Sebastião Gonsalves Tibau who was destined not only to revenge the grim massacre but also to play an important part in the history of Bengal.

The Massacre of Dianga, 1607

* *Arch Port. Orient.* Fasc., VI. p. 975.

CHAPTER VII

THE RISE OF SEBASTIAO GONSALVES TIBAU

Sebastião Gonsalves Tibau, 1605-07

The history of the original Portuguese who settled in Chittagong and who were directly under the authority of the Portuguese Governor in Goa, is closely associated with the history of another section of the Portuguese who shook off the authority of the Governor and beginning life as adventurers eventually became so powerful as to establish an independent kingdom. The hero among these adventurers was Sebastião Gonsalves Tibau, a Portuguese of an obscure extraction born in Santo Antonio de Tojal.* He arrived in India in 1605 and having come to Bengal soon exchanged the profession of a soldier for that of a trader. He purchased a vessel of his own and filling it with salt went to Dianga at such an inopportune time that but for his cunning and bravery he would have perished in the general massacre of the Portuguese which the King of Arakan had ordered in 1607. He with nine or ten other Portuguese who had escaped with their ships, settled in the small islands at the mouth of the Ganges and sought the means of life in piracy. To revenge on the King of Arakan they ravaged his coast and carried off the booty to the King of Bākla's (Bacala)† ports, who was a friend of the Portuguese. With the massacre of Dianga, an era of piracy had dawned —piracy that led by the Arakanese, was to assume frightful proportions.

* The feats of Gonsalves are generally known through Stevens's Translation of Faria y Souza, Vol. III. p. 154, *et seq.* Bocarro, however, has a more detailed account in, *Decada* XIII, Chapters, 97—101.

† The Kingdom of Bākla included a large portion of the Bākarganj district and a part of Dacca; it was ruled by one of the *Bhuyās* of Bengal.

Sandwīp, Further History

It was mentioned that Manoel de Mattos was in sole possession of the island of Sandwīp since Domingo Carvalho had died in or about 1605. Wishing to absent himself for some time, Manoel de Mattos entrusted the government of the island to Fateh Khān, a Muhammadan in the Portuguese employ.* But this man learning that Manoel de Mattos had died proved treacherous and took possession of the Portuguese vessels. He murdered all the Portuguese and the native Christians with their wives and children and decided to drive away Gonsalves and other Portuguese, from the islands they had occupied. He prepared a fleet of forty vessels, embarked six hundred soldiers and went in pursuit of the few Portuguese who had escaped from the massacre of Dianga. At a time when these Portuguese adventurers were engaged in dividing their booty in the island of Dakhin Shāhbāzpur, Fateh Khān came to attack them. He was so confident of success that he inscribed these words upon his colours : "Fateh Khān, by the grace of God, Lord of Sandwīp, shedder of Christian blood and destroyer of the Portuguese nation."† The small band of the Portuguese who, driven by circumstances, were indeed now no better than corsairs determined to face Fateh Khān. They had only ten vessels and all the men numbered eighty. The fleets met at night and till the following morning there was a desperate struggle, in which one Sebastião Pinto distinguished himself very highly. Victory was on the Portuguese side. Not one vessel of the Moors escaped and those that were not killed were captured. Fateh Khān, who had styled himself the destroyer of the Portuguese nation, was among the dead. The victory did not

* According to the *Dec. Rem. Tom. I. pp. 175-76* Manoel de Mattos died leaving a minor son and appointing Pero Gomes, Governor of the island. Fateh Khān probably siezed the island from Pero Gomes.

† Faria y Souza Vol. III. p. 155 ; Bocarro, *Decada* XIII, p. 433.

cost the Portuguese anything, save the death of Sebastião Pinto, who was loved by all on account of his noble character.

The Portuguese who though victorious were merely roaming vagabonds felt the necessity of a captain who could train and discipline them, and chose Estevão Palmeyro "a man of years, experience and discretion" to command them. But he refused to be at the head of men who, though brave, had proved themselves to be wicked by their ravages, and appointed Sebastião Gonsalves Tibau as the commander whom all agreed to obey.

The Second Conquest of Sandwīp, 1610

Under the new commander, the Portuguese determined to gain Sandwīp that was lost to them through the thoughtlessness of Mattos. They gathered the Portuguese from the various neighbouring ports and by March 1609 they managed to collect a force of forty sail and four hundred men. Gonsalves arranged with the King of Bākla for assistance on the promise of giving him half the revenue of the island. The King, indeed, sent some ships and two hundred horse. Fateh Khān's brother who conducted the defence of the island met the Portuguese at the landing place but was forced to retire into the fort. The Portuguese then besieged the island for two months, but ran short of provisions and amunition, which could not be brought up on account of the enemy's opposition. At a time when all seemed to be lost a Spaniard named Gaspar de Pina at the head of fifty men came to the rescue from Hījilī, with only a ship but much courage and ingenuity. He approached by night with shouts, blare of trumpets, noises of drums and a blaze of lights, creating an impression that a powerful succour had come. In this confusion Gaspar de Pina and the whole of the Portuguese force effected a landing and took possession of the island. The Hindu inhabitants of the island, who were already accustomed to the Portuguese rule during the time of Manoel de Mattos welcomed the entry of

Gonsalves. He received them well on condition they brought to him every Moor in the island. They gladly brought to him about a thousand Moors who were all murdered in cold blood. The massacre of Dianga and Fateh Khān's murder of the Portuguese in Sandwīp were thus revenged.

Gonsalves, an Independent Ruler, 1607—1610.

Gonsalves became now the sole master of the island, independent of the Portuguese of Hooghly or of the Goa Government. Besides, he owned lands on the coast of Arakan. He had under him one thousand Portuguese, two thousand soldiers, all well armed, two hundred horse and eighty ships with canon. Many merchants of Bengal and of the coasts of Tenasserim and Choromandel resorted to Sandwīp and paid duty at the custom-house which Gonsalves had erected. He dictated the laws of the place. The neighbouring princes sought his friendship and his alliance. He was at this time at the height of his power and glory ; but power dazzled him. He grew insolent and ungrateful. He took back the lands from the very Portuguese who had raised him to power. Instead of paying half the revenue of Sandwīp to the King of Bākla as he had promised he made an attack on him and seized the islands of Dakhin Shāhbāzpur and Patelbanga.

In the year 1609 disputes arose between the Prince (Heir-apparent) of Arakan and his brother Anaporan* over trifling matter such as the possession of an elephant. The Prince actually fought a battle against his brother who being defeated fled to Gonsalves. Gonsalves promised to succour him and kept his daughter† as a hostage. He and Anaporan, combining their armies, marched against the Prince of Arakan but as

* Faria y Souza calls Anaporan brother of the King of Arakan and in *Documentos Remettidos* he is said to be nephew of the King of Arakan. I have followed Bocarro.

† Sister, according to Faria y Souza.

the latter came with an army of eighty thousand men and seven hundred fighting elephants, they returned to Sandwīp In the sea fight, however, Gonsalves's brother Antonio captured a hundred sail of the enemy with only five vessels on his side. Anaporan brought over to Sandwīp his wife, children and all his treasures. It is an interesting fact that on her becoming Christian, Gonsalves married Anaporan's daughter whom he had kept as a hostage. Shortly after, Anaporan died and as Gonsalves seized his treasures it was suspected he caused his death. To suppress this suspicion Gonsalves wanted to marry his brother Antonio Carvalho Tibau to Anaporan's widow but she refused to embrace Christianity and hence his project was not realized.

Marriage Relations between the Portuguese and the Royal Family of Arakan

Many were the marriage relations contracted between the Portuguese and the Royal Family of Arakan. Not only did Sebastião Gonsalves marry the daughter of Anaporan (Meng Phaloung?) who was, as Bocarro says, the second son of the King reigning in 1610 (Xalamixa I or Meng Radzagyi), but also according to Manrique a son of Gonsalves married a daughter of Alamanja whom he calls the younger son of Xalamixa I (and of Xalamixa II in another place). It would seem that the Alamanja of Manrique is the same as Anaporan of Bocarro. But Manrique seems to speak of them as two different persons. According to Faria y Souza, Anaporan was the brother, and according to *Documentos Remettidos*, the nephew of the King of Arakan who ruled in 1607, that is Xalamixa I or Meng Radzagyi. It is curious that all the Portuguese writings should differ on this point. The daughter of Alamanja who married the son of Sebastião Gonsalves was baptized under the name of Maxima. After the death of Alamanja his two other children, a boy and a girl, were baptized under the names of Martinho and Petronilla respectively. Martinho was brought up by the Augustinians at

Goa, and at the age of eighteen he joined the Portuguese navy in the hope of gaining the crown of Arakan which he claimed on the ground that he was "the legitimate son of Alamanja, and grandson of Xalamixa II (sic)". He served in the Armada of Dom Ruy Freire de Andrade and then in the fleet of Nuno Alvares Botelho. He fought on the Portuguese fleet against the King of Achin in Malacca (1627-28) being wounded in the attack. He went to Portugal when D. João IV was proclaimed King of Portugal (1640) and died when returning to India. His sister Petronilla died at Hooghly*. It may be added, Brito e Nicote's son married the daughter of the King of Martaban, and another of his son was about to marry the daughter of Anaporan.†

Gonsalves, a Treacherous Ally 1610

The Mughals since the fall of Daud Khan in 1577 were in possession of Bengal and Orissa and according to Bocarro had overthrown the *Bhuyās* by 1610. They had not, however, yet penetrated into Arakan and were now planning the conquest of the kingdom of Bhulua.‡ As this kingdom was close to Sandwīp as well as to Arakan, Gonsalves and the King of Arakan thinking the Mughals would be a danger to their kingdoms forgot their enmity and entered into a mutual agreement to combat them. Stewart however says§ that the reason of this alliance was that they planned between themselves to invade Bengal, the agreement being that the King of Arakan was to proceed with an army by land and the Portuguese in a fleet by sea. The King of Arakan entrusted the whole of his fleet to Gonsalves keeping his nephew as a hostage. During

* Cf. Fr. Hosten's *Annotations to Manrique, Bengal Past and Present*, 1916, Vol. XIII, No. 25, p. 130.

† *Documentos Remettidos* Tom. I, p. 356.

‡ Bhulua is the largest pargana in the Noakhali district of Bengal. The village of Bhulua is a few miles west of Noakhali on the Lakhipur Road.

§ *History of Bengal* p. 236.

these negotiations Gonsalves gave back the widow of Anaporan who afterwards married the governor of Chittagong. The King of Arakan and the Portuguese attacked the Mughals and drove them out of the kingdom of Bhulua and took Lakhipur, while Gonsalves barred their advance from the sea.

Gonsalves, however, soon changed his mind and whether he was influenced by a bribe or actuated by a desire for revenge on the former crimes of the King of Arakan, he allowed the Mughals to pass to Bhulua up the river. They then easily attacked the King of Arakan and routed his army. The unfortunate King with his nobles fled towards the forests of Tippera for safety. The King of Tippera who was the vassal of the King of Arakan rebelled at this time and put to the sword the nobles of Arakan. The King of Arakan with great difficulty escaped, mounted on a swift elephant and at last arrived in Chittagong.

Seeing the King of Arakan defeated and driven to his own limits, Gonsalves took possession of the Arakan fleet with which he was entrusted and murdered all the Arakan captains. What is more, with a bold effrontery he set out with his fleet and plundered all the forts on the Arakan coast especially those of Chittagong, Maju and Ramu and destroyed many ships some of which belonged to other nations. Amongst these ships was one the loss of which the King felt most. "It was," says Farya y Souza,* "of a vast Bigness and wonderful Workmanship with several Apartments like a palace all covered with Gold and Ivory and yet the curiosity of the Work surpassed all the rest." All that the King could do in revenge was to order a stake to run through Gonsalves's nephew who was kept as a hostage. He impaled him on a high place near the Port of Arakan in order that his uncle might see him as he departed from the coast of Arakan. But he, to whom treachery and insolence were ordinary affairs, had no feelings for a nephew.

* Faria y Souza, Stevens Trans. Vol. III, p. 161; Cf. also Bocarro *Decada XIII* p. 433.

CHAPTER VIII

MINOR SETTLEMENTS OF THE PORTUGUESE

Dacca

Situated on the banks of the Bouriganga, or as Manrique says, on the banks of the famous (and at that place fertilizing) Ganges, Dacca commanded an extensive trade and was the resort of many foreign merchants especially since Islam Khān made it the capital of Bengal in 1608. At the time of the Portuguese settlement in about 1580, Dacca did not hold this proud position though it was noted for its rich industries. After the Portuguese had settled in Hooghly, they were not slow to avail themselves of the benevolence of Akbar and establish themselves in Dacca to secure the trade of this important centre. Her richest muslins and her various kinds of cloth found their way to Portugal, Italy, Malacca, Sumatra and Goa in the Portuguese ships. Ralph Fitch describes Dacca in 1586, as abounding in rice, cotton and silk goods. From the account of Ralph Fitch it can be gathered that only six years after the Portuguese had settled in the Dacca district they had grown into traders of much importance especially in Sripūr. Manrique says that Akbar as well as Jahāngīr offered the Portuguese Fathers lands for their maintenance or as an assignment of revenue, which they refused because the Asiatic princes were wont to take advantage of the favours they conferred to turn the foreigners out. When the natives of Dacca were terrifying the people against the Portuguese because they ate pork, and drank wine, Akbar sent a positive order that no harm should be done to them. Caesar de Federici found the Nawab of Dacca in very friendly terms with the Portuguese and the Christians ; and Tavernier records that in 1670 he saw in Dacca a Church of the Augustinians, built of brick, and of a very fine workmanship.*

These Portuguese settlers did not belong to the other section of the Portuguese who were powerful in Sandwīp and in Arakan and who during Shaista Khān's viceroyalty settled in Dacca at a place called Feringhi Bazar. In fact, when Shaista Khān was bent upon the conquest of Chittagong he sent Shaikh Ziāuddin Yusuf to the original Portuguese settlers trading in salt in Loricul near Dacca asking their countrymen in Chittagong to abandon the King of Arakan and enter the Mughal service.† They having agreed to do so, were given by Shaista Khān the land known as Feringhi Bazar. About twelve miles from the city, springing from the banks of the Ishamutti, lies this Feringhi Bazar calling to mind the days of the Portuguese domination in Bengal. Dacca possesses another relic of the Portuguese. Though every trace of the factories of the Dutch, of the French and even of the English is gone,‡ a part of the Portuguese factory, beautiful in its ruins, still exists in Dacca close to the Church of O. L. Rosary. Bradley-Birt remarks§ "All that remains to-day of the various factories (in Dacca) is a portion of the house which the Portuguese once made their headquarters. It must have been in those days a fine commodious building, but like every thing else in this city of the long sleep it is sadly fallen and decayed retaining but a memory of its better days." Many, many of the early European archæological remains are so ignominously disappearing and crumbling into dust that a

---

* Tavernier, Ball's, Ed. Vol. I, p. 128.

† Shiabuddin Talish, *The Conquest of Chatgaon*, J. A. S. B. 1907 p. 407.

‡ The Dacca College stands on the site of the English Factory; the palace of the Nawab of Dacca covers the French factory; and the Milford Hospital tends to suffering humanity where the Dutch factory once stood.

§ F. Bradley-Birt, *Romance of an Eastern Capital*, p. 286.

Lucretius might have well exclaimed "*et etiam perierunt ruinae.*"

In the Dacca, Bāckarganj, and Noakhali Districts the Portuguese had numerous minor settlements where they did not erect factories or forts, though they carried on a considerable trade. Many of them were entirely Christian centres, where the Portuguese Missionaries built their churches and effected the conversions of the inhabitants. Most of the names of these places, once the scene of considerable activities are no longer current. But Dr. Wise and Beveridge, and latterly Fr. Hosten have thrown much light on the identification of the places that belonged to the twelve *Bhuyās* of Bengal.

Sripūr.

Sripūr, situated according to Ralph Fitch six leagues below Sonargaon, has played an important part in the history of Bengal, being the seat of the kingdom of Chand Rai and Kedar Rai. De Barros, Blaev and Van den Broucke differ in the exact locality which they assign to it in their maps but all of them place it south of Sonārgāon. De Barros and Blaev, whose map as far as relates to Bengal is almost a re-print of that of de Barrros, mark Sripūr as *Bunder.* Van den Brouke calls it Sherpur Feringhi, which shows it was an important Portuguese settlement. Ralph Fitch says in 1586 that the Portuguese had sole authority in Sripūr. He speaks of having gone to Pegu from Sripūr in a Portuguese ship belonging to one Alberto Carvalho.*

Chandecan.

Chandecan was another small settlement of the Portuguese, where the Jesuits built their first Church. Beveridge considers Chandecan to be identical with Dhumghat or Jessore after an elaborate discussion.† He has not however considered Van Linschoten's references in his *Le Grand Routier de Mer* to the river of Chandecan which

* Purchas, *His Pilgrimes,* Ralph Fitch p. 185.

† *The District of Bákarganj* p. 176 *et seq.*

appears to have been a part of the river Hooghly or one of its channels near Saugor Island. Though, he says, he could not find Chandecan in any maps, it is marked in Sir Thomas Roe's map of 1632 and in Fr. Monseratte's map of 1580-1600. Much information about Chandecan can be derived from the letters of Fr. Fernandes and his companions who carried on missionary work in Chandecan at the express invitation of the King*. The Portuguese built a Church in Chandecan which was formally opened on January 1st, 1600. As it has been shown, the Portuguese activities in Chandecan were checked when the King of Chandecan, whom Beveridge supposes to be Raja Pratāpāditya soon changed his attitude towards the Portuguese, and in order to please the King of Arakan treacherously murdered Domingo Carvalho, the gallant captain of the Portuguese.

Bākla

The Portuguese had a small settlement in Bākla which according to Beveridge included a great part of the Bākarganj district and was really identical with the Chandradwip *pargūna*. Fr. Melchior Fonseca who came to Bengal in 1599 has left a very good account of Bākla, which materialy helped later investigators in tracing on the history of its rulers. Bākla, was under the rule of a Hindu prince who was one of the twelve *Bhuyās* of of Bengal.† He was well disposed towards the Portuguese and granted Fr. Fonseca a decree allowing the Jesuits free liberty to preach their religion and erect their churches. Fr. Fonseca found a colony of the Portuguese under a captain Il (Capitano) in Bākla, which for many years had not been visited by priests.

Catrabo called by Manrique one of the Kingdoms of

* Du Jarric, *Histoire*, Part IV, Chap. XXIX.

† According to Fr. du Jarric out of the twelve *Bhuyās* of Bengal only three were Hindus, those of Sripūr, of Bākla and of Chandecan.

Bengal was under the rule of one of the twelve *Bhuyās*

Catrabo

of Bengal. Van den Broucke places it below Sonārgāon and Beveridge identifies it with Katrabuh or Katibari in the Mānikganj sub-division.* Dr. Wise however suggests† "Catrabo is Katrabo, now a 'tappa' on the Lakhya opposite Khizrpúr which for long was the property of the descendants of 'Isā Khān Masnad-i-'Alī". Fr. Fernandes was in 1599 in Catrabo and relates that the population was mainly Muhammadan. The people were convinced through his efforts that the Christian law was true and good but they were not willing to be converted.‡ It was a place where the Portuguese founded a small colony which at one time was very influential.

Loricul, twenty eight miles south of Dacca, was another Christian settlement of the Portuguese. It appears in Van den

Loricul

Broucke's map (1660) as Noricoel and is marked by a cross like all the other christian settlements. La Touche very curiously suggests§ the place was so named after the Portuguese Viceroy, Marquis of Louriçal, who ruled from 1741 to 1742, but as Fr. Hosten points out, the place was much older. Blochmann identifies it with Morculij of Blaev's map (1650). Merculij also is marked in de Barros's map, which was the origin of Blaev's information about Bengal. Manrique mentions that the Augustinians built a Church in Loricul though he does not give the date. It must have been built towards the end of the sixteenth century when the Augustinians had spread all over Dacca. According to Sicardo, the Augustinian historian, the Church existed in

---

* Proc. A. S. B. 1903, pp. 133-134.

† J. A. S. B. 1875, XLIV p. 182.

‡ Du Jarric, *Histoire*, Part IV, p. 829.

§ La Touche, *The Journals of Major James Rennel* etc, Mem. A. S. B. Vol. III No. 3, 1910 No, 39.

1682 but Rennel wrote on February 14, 1765 "Here are ye ruins of a Portuguese Church and of many brick houses."*

The famous Portuguese merchant Nicolo de Paiva who left twenty thousand xerafins for the upkeep of the Jesuits at Hooghly and farmed the customs of the Nawab of Dacca lived in Loricol in 1675.† One Nicola Pareres, a "Portugall Merchant," probably the same as Nicolo de Paiva, as Fr. Hosten supposes, assured William Hedges in 1684 that "their (Portuguese) whole community had wrott ye Vice King of Goa and besought him earnestly to send them two or three frigates with aid and assistance of soldiers to possess themselves of ye Islands of Kegeria and Ingelee (Khijri and Hījīlī) for which purpose they had sent him draughts and large descriptions of ye said Islands." ‡

In Bhulua, which was an independent principality in the seventeenth century there was a colony of the Portuguese.

Bhulua

There were also numerous Portuguese converts in Bhulua who were very influential. Glanius who has left a graphic description of the wreek of *Ter Schelling* remarks§, "The Prince's Guard (in Bhulua) consists wholly of Christians which are there in great esteem and although perhaps they are only Christians in name being *Negroes* born; subjects to the King of Portugal ; yet they are counted such brave fellows, that they have a particular respect shew'd them and therefore the grandees of the court so highly prize their familiarity, that they relate to them whatsoever passes in Council." The Portuguese influence was so completely established in Bhulua that many of the people spoke Portuguese.||

* *The Journals of Rennel*, *ut supra.*

† J. A. S. B. 1911 pp. 27, 29.

‡ Yule, *Diary of Hedges* Vol. I p. 172.

§ Glanius, *A Voyage to Kingdom of Bengal*, pp. 138-9.

|| Glanius, *ut supra*, p. 136, "we bought Milk and Rice which we drest in a Pot that was lent us by Moors that spoke Portugaise."

Hījīlī (Angelim)

Hījīlī is a littoral tract extending from the mouth of the Rupnarayan along the western side of the Hooghly estuary and forming part of the Midnapore district. It was formerly an island now united to the mainland and was a district of Orissa under native rulers. At the time of the Portuguese occupation it had its own chiefs but in 1505 according to the local traditions the Muhammadans under Taj Khān and his brother, took possession of it.* After a period of eight years however a Hindu chieftain recovered it. The Portuguese settlement in Hījīlī can be said to be the earliest European settlement in Bengal. The Portuguese not long after establishing themselves in Pipli (Orissa) in 1514 migrated northwards towards Hījīlī. Before the town of Hījīlī existed as such, the author of the *Chandi* was referred in 1577 to a Portuguese territory in or near Hījīlī as the "*Feringhee Desh* where they (the poet and his companion) ply their boats night and day for fear of the *Harams* (a term of abuse applied to the Feringhis) and pass it in twenty days."† If the boats plying night and day, took twenty days to pass the country under the Feringhi influence the Portuguese occupation of the Hījīlī coast must have been an extensive one. On the return journey of the poet he refers to another *Feringhi desh* on the Orissa coast where *they* visited Jagannath Puri.

The Augustinians built in Hījīlī two Churches both dedicated to Our Lady of Rosary. In 1582 both Churches contained three hundred parishioners grown to an age of confession.‡ Sicardo refers to another Church built by the Augustinians in the Bandel or village of Banja (which Manrique places in the kingdom of Hījīlī), dedicated to Our Lady of

* Blochmann, *Contributions to the Geog. and Hist. of Bengal*, p. 17.

† *Calcutta Review*, Oct. 1891, No. 186, p. 373.

‡ Fray J. Sicardo O. S. A. *Christiandad del Japon* Ch. III. (Quoted by Fr. Hosten).

Salvation, "the Christian community there counting five hundred souls exclusive of those whom the commerce of that Port brought to the place albeit the climate is little salubrious." Manrique throws some light on the commerce of Hījīlī. Referring to the Church of Banja he says* it was built "to be able to cope with the great number of merchants who gather there to buy sugar, wax and Ginghams (*guingones*) which I have said is a kind of cloth made of grass (*yerua*) and silk, a very nice and cooling texture to wear during the hot summer." An earlier account of Ralph Fitch (1586) says† "To this hauen of Angeli (Hijili) come euery yere many ships out of India Negapatam, Sumatra, Malacca & divers other places & lode from thence much store of Rice & much cloth of cotton wool, much sugar, & long pepper, great store of butter & other victuals for India."

W. Hedges mentions‡ in his Diary that the Portuguese were ousted from Hījīlī in 1636 by the Mughals and in 1724 Valentyn referred to Hījīlī as a *former* Portuguese settlement. The Arakanese and Portuguese pirates now began to commit depredations on the Orissa coast and in Hījīlī. Tracts of lands became depopulated and the ryots left their fields. Shāh Jahān thereupon annexed Hījīlī to Bengal so as to enable the imperial fleets stationed at Dacca to guard against these piratical raids.

The ruins of the Portuguese settlements in Hījīlī can still be seen. A couple of miles south of Geonkhali lies Merepore, known still as *Feringhi Para*, where the S. P. C. Mission found in 1838 some Christians who declared that they were descendants of the Portuguese from Goa who were given the village of Merepore rent free as a reward for some services

* *Bengal Past and Present*, Cardon's Trans. 1915, Vol. XII p. 48.

† Horton Ryley's, *Ralph Fitch*, p. 114.

‡ Yule, *Diary of Hedges*, Vol. II. p. 240.

rendered by them to the Raja of Mysadal, which is now in the Hooghly District.*

In Midnapore the Portuguese also had another important settlement in Tamlūk. Tamlūk is situated on the southern bank of the Rupnarayan and was an important seaport in ancient times deserving a mention as *Tamalites* in Ptolemy's geography.† But it lost its importance towards the tenth century as the channel that afforded an easy communication with the sea gradually silted up. Hījīlī then rose into prominence. It is noteworthy, however, that the Portuguese settlement in Tamlūk remained long after they were driven away from Hījīlī. In 1635 a church was built there through Manrique's influence. Gemelli Careri refers ‡ to it in 1695 as having been subdued by the Portuguese and in 1724 Valentyn remarks§ "Tamboli and Banzia (Banja) are two villages where the Portuguese have their Church and their southern trade. There is much dealing in wax here".

Tamlūk

Tamlūk, like Piplī and Balasore in Orissa, had a great slave market where the Arakan and Portuguese pirates brought their captives for sale. In a description of the exploits of these pirates Shiab-ud-din Talish (about 1665) says,|| "sometimes they brought the captives for sale at a high price to Tamlūk and the port of Baleswar (Balasore), which is a part of the imperial dominions and a dependency of the province of Orissa. The manner of the sales was this. The wretches used to bring the prisoners in their ships, anchor at a short distance from the shores of Tamlūk or

* *Indo-European Correspondence*, Calcutta 1869 pp. 80-81. (Quoted by Fr. Hosten).

† M. Chakravarti, J. A. S. B. May 1908, p. 289.

‡ *A Voyage Round the World*, Churchill's Collection, Vol. IV p. 109.

§ Valentyn, *Oud en Nieuw Oost-Indien* V de Deel p. 159.

|| *The Feringhi Pirates of Chatgaon*, J. A. S. B. 1917, p. 422.

Baleswar, and send a man ashore with the news. The local officers, fearing lest the pirates should commit any depredation or kidnapping there, stood on the shore with a number of followers and sent a man with a sum of money to the pirates. If the terms were satisfactory, the pirates took the money and sent the prisoners with the man." As the Portuguese pirates did not actually land ashore, it is obvious that the Tamlūk settlement was not founded by these renegades but by the loyal Portuguese, like those of Hooghly, who according to Valentyn carried on a southern trade and possessed Churches even in the eighteenth century.

Piplī

The earliest European settlements in the Gulf of Bengal were established in Orissa. It was the same with the Portuguese as with the English and the Dutch.* Ascending along the western shore of the Bay of Bengal the coast of Orissa was the first to offer a landing place. In the beginning of the sixteenth century, that is, a short time after the discovery of the sea-route to India (1498) the Portuguese established themselves on the coast of Madras. Alarmed at the growth of a foreign power, the natives rose against the Portuguese who escaped northward and in 1514 founded a town in Piplī† about four miles from the mouth of the Subarnareka River, establishing their earliest settlement on the coast of the Bay of Bengal. Piplī was then an important harbour on the Orissa coast and a great centre of Portuguese trade when their fleets commanded the whole sea-board from Chittagong to Orissa. It was also a great slave market where the Arakanese and the Portuguese pirates sold their prisoners.

Joannes De Laet refers in 1631 to this port as being in the possession of the Portuguese. Early in the seventeenth century

* Before the English had any footing in Bengal, they settled in Piplī in 1625 and in Balasore in 1625.

† W. Hunter, *Orissa* 1872, p. 37. O'Malley in his *Balasore Gazetteer* asserts that the Portuguese settled in Piplī in 1599, Cf. p. 36 and 204.

the Augustinians had built a Church and a residence in Piplī, the Church being dedicated to Our Lady of Rosary.

The Portuguese settlement in Piplī continued to be a trading centre for a long period of time. Bruton describes Piplī in 1683 as a "Port town of the Portuguese where the Portugals are resident" and Fr. Barbier in his description of the Episcopal visitation of Bishop Laines in 1723 refers to a large Portuguese or *Topaz* congregation.

When the East India Company sought for trade in Orissa there arose bitter hostilities between them and the Portuguese settlers. W. Hunter, in his *History of British India*, gives a graphic description of a fight between an English and a Portuguese vessel.* A Portuguese frigate from Piplī, launched an attack in Harishar, a port in Orissa, against the first English junk that came to Bengal in 1633 and assisted by some "ribble-rabble rascals of the town," nearly finished with the English. Ralph Cartwright, a merchant of E. I. Co., claimed before the Mughal Governor the Portuguese frigate as a redress for the Portuguese attack in a Mughal harbour. The Portuguese also entered their protests. The Mughals who were ill disposed towards the Portuguese and only a year before had sacked their settlement of Hooghly confiscated the Portuguese vessel for themselves to the great chagrin of Cartwright.

The famous English ship Swan which came to Bengal in the same year received a quite different treatment from the Portuguese. According to the Diary of Hedges† the Portuguese redeemed the Swan when seized by the Arakanese. "Last year (1633)," it says, "when the Swann was in Bengalla her boat beinge sent on shoare for water was suddenly surprized by some of the Kinge of Arackans *Gelliaes*

---

* Cf. also C. R. Wilson, *Early Annals of the English*, Vol. I. p. 1 *et seq.*

† Yule, *Diary of Hedges*, Vol. III p. 180.

of Warr : 3 : of her men killed, and the rest taken and carryed to a place in Bengalla called Piplee where a Portugal Captain that came thither on a small vessel from Macassar redeemed them for 400 : Ruppes which mony was presently sent him from Ballasarra.........for which affront we doe away all opportunitye to force a satisfaction." This account is in marked contrast with that of the first junk in which the English came to Bengal.

Balasore

The Portuguese also had a small settlement in Balasore of which no vestige now remains. Stirling however says* that in his time the only relic of this settlement was a small Roman Catholic Chapel with a wooden cross over the principal doorway. Even this has now disappeared. This Chapel or really a Church was dedicated to Our Lady of Rosary.

* *Account of Orissa.*

CHAPTER IX

PORTUGUESE MISSIONARIES

The ecclesiastical history of the Portuguese in Bengal would fill up volumes. No nation came to India with a religious zeal more fervent than that of the Portuguese. Their conversions went *pari-passu* with their conquests. The sword always allied itself with the Cross and while the one extended the domain of the Empire the other propagated the Christian faith. The first words of a sailor of Vasco da Gama in reply to the question of a Tunisian Moor, were "we have come to seek Christians and spices." In the propagation of faith, the methods as well as the agents would in many cases be open to reproach if judged according to the modern canons of liberty and justice. One may, indeed, blame the aggressive proselytism of the Portuguese missionaries, as the Portuguese themselves have condemned it, but it cannot be denied it was through their zeal and efforts that the best fruits of Christian civilization were spread even in the most recondite parts of India.

The first members of the illustrious Order of the Jesuits, came to India in 1542, among whom was St. Francis Xavier. Before them the Franciscans and the Dominicans had begun

The Jesuits

the work of evangelization in India. The Jesuits and the secular priests were, however, the earliest on record to have come to Bengal. The Jesuit Fathers Antonio Vaz and Pedro Dias arrived in Bengal in 1576,* and a secular priest named Juliano Pereira, *Gangarides Archimystes*, as Monserratte calls him is mentioned as a vicar in Sätgäon in 1578. Akbar invited him to his court in Fatehpur

---

* Fr. Delaunoit gives the date as 1579, *Cf. Catholic Encyclopedia*, s. v. Calcutta.

Sikri to explain to him the tenets of the Christian religion and he having done so as best as he could, requested Akbar to summon more learned priests from Goa.

The work of the Jesuits who came to Bengal between 1598 and 1600 is aptly described in their letters to Fr. Nicolau de Pimenta who was in Goa.* Pimenta sent in 1598 two Jesuits named Francisco Fernandes and Domingo de Souza from Cochin and two more in the following year, Melchior da Fonseca and André Boves. They arrived in Hooghly in May of the same year and preached in the bigger Church (*summo temple*) which was built before their arrival. They erected a school and a hospital, evidently the first one in Bengal. In Hooghly they received an invitation from the King of Chandecan to pay him a visit but they first went to Chittagong in the course of their missionary tour, leaving their school and their hospital in the hands of the Vicar of Hooghly probably a secular priest. They erected in Chittagong two Churches and a residence. Though Chittagong belonged at this time to the King of Arakan they found it almost entirely in the hands of the Portuguese. Fr. Fernandes gives the text of the letters-patent† which the King of Arakan granted to the Portuguese, allowing them to preach the Christian religion and build Churches in his kingdom. As the King of Chandecan was angry with the Jesuits for their not having responded to his invitation, Fr. Fernandes sent Fr. de Souza to Chandecan and he was received favourably. In October 1599, Fr. Fernandes himself went to Chandecan and obtaining from the King letters-patent with full authority to carry on his mission and to erect a Church and a residence. The Church was formally consecrated on the 1st January 1600. This was the first Jesuit Church in Bengal and was therefore dedicated to Jesus Christ. Fr. Fonseca was very successful in the kingdom of Bākla where

* Pimenta's *Carta.* Cf. Du Jarric, *Histoire*, Part IV., Chapters XXIX and XXX.

he found many Portuguese. He obtained free permission from the King of Bākla to preach the Christian religion in his kingdom and the Jesuits actually built a residence and appear to have begun a Church.*

The successes of Fr. Fernandes and his companions unfortunately came to a melancholy end. In connection with the disputes between the Portuguese and the King of Arakan, already described, a tumult arose in Chittagong in which the Portuguese suffered heavily. Fr. Fernandes having attempted to save some children who were being forced into slavery by the Arakanese was mercilessly thrashed and deprived of one eye. On the 14th November 1602 he expired in prison. Fr. Andre Boves was also cast into prison with chains round his neck and legs. To crown all this ill-treatment, the Arakanese used the sacred *chalice* as a spittoon. Following the fortunes of Carvalho, they took refuge in Sandwīp and then in Sripūr, Bākla, and Chandecan. Carvalho was soon after murdered by the King of Chandecan. Under these melancholy circumstances the surviving fathers eventually left Bengal, some going to Pegu and some to Cochin.

Bengali Children, educated in Goa

From the letters of Fr. Fernandes and his three companions, it appears that long before them, the Portuguese Fathers had begun missionary work in Bengal. The Jesuits, then as now, not only converted the people of Bengal but also sent Bengali children to be educated in the great Jesuit College of Santa Fé in Goa, which was afterwards known as the College of São Paulo. Fr. H. Josson S. J. mentions* the names of five Bengali children who were pupils of the College of Santa Fé in 1558—Filippe, Gaspar de Deus, Antonio do Ermo, and two Pedros. In the catalogue of the pupils of that College, dated 1559, and still preserved in

* *Mission Belges.* 1913, Sept. p. 331. Cf. H. Hosten, *Bengal Past and Present*, 1915, Vol. XII, No. 24 p. 45.

the Royal Library of Ajuda, Portugal, several names of Bengali children are mentioned.*

From 1599 to 1617 there is no record of any Jesuits in Hooghly. The Augustinians meanwhile had established themselves in Hooghly and when the Jesuits came back in 1617 they found that the former claimed the sole right of evangelisation. The Jesuits however, took possession of their College of St. Paul and their hospital and in the same year they erected in Hooghly their first Church and residence. Three years after, both these buildings had to be re-constructed, because they were too close to the river.

Jesuits, 1617

The Augustinians accomplished the most important work in Bengal. They were the fourth religious Order to come to India, their first batch of twelve missionaries having arrived in Goa in 1572. When they came to Bengal, is a disputable point. Sicardo and other Augustinian historians say that they came to Bengal in 1599. Manrique however asserts that they came after the Portuguese had settled in Hooghly in 1580. When Tavares came to Bengal with a *farman* from Akbar granting the Portuguese full religious liberty and permission to preach openly the Christian faith, to erect Churches and to baptize the natives, who would consent to be Christians, he applied to the Viceroy at Goa and the Bishop of Cochin for missionaries. The Augustinians having been chosen to minister in Bengal they came to Bengal as soon as the season permitted, with Frei Bernardo de Jesus as superior and in his absence Frei João de Cruz. Probably Sicardo has lost sight of the first batch of missionaries that came to Bengal. Tavares and his Portuguese certainly required religious missionaries to carry on their religious work and as the two Jesuits who were in

Augustinians

* Fr. Cros S. J. *Lettres de St. François Xavier*, Vol. I, p. 484.

Hooghly had gone away, only secular priests or Augustinians could have ministered in Hooghly at this time. Whatever be the truth, all agree that five Augustinians came to Hooghly in 1599 and the same year they built their Convent dedicated to Sam Nicolau de Tolentino, to which was attached the Church of Our Lady of Rosary. They took possession of all the Churches existing there. They also built a *Casa de Misericordia* (Alms House) with an attached Chapel. The parishioners of the Churches numbered five thousand including the Portuguese, their descendants and Indian converts. The next batch of seven Augustinians came in the following year, that is, in 1600.

The Diocese of Cochin formed in 1557 was at the head of all the Catholic missions in Bengal but Dom Frei André, a Franciscan Bishop of Cochin, transferred the sole possession of the Churches and right of evangelization to the Augustinians of Goa. These Augustinians extended their labours all over Bengal. They established themselves in Hījīlī (Angelim) where they built two Churches dedicated to Our Lady of Rosary; in Piplī where they also erected a Church dedicated to Our Lady of Rosary, and in Tamlūk (Tumbolim) where they built a Church in honour of Our Lady of Hope. In 1606 the Diocese of Mylapore was created and the jurisdiction of Bengal passed from the diocese of Cochin to that of Mylapore. But the Augustinians continued to enjoy their privileges. In 1612 they established themselves in Dacca where they built a Church dedicated to Our Lady of Assumption. They also erected Churches in Nuricol, Sripūr and Catrabo.

Augustinians in Chittagong, 1621

The Augustinians extended their activities to Chittagong in 1621 and, in fact, took the place of the Jesuits who had up to that time ministered there and had undergone many troubles. In 1598 there were 2500 Portuguese and their descendants in Chittagong and Arakan; besides these there were Indian

Christians. In the massacre of Dianga which followed Brito e Nicote demand of this port, all the Churches of the Jesuits were pulled down and some of the missionaries were killed. Those who escaped to Sandwīp and established the Catholic religion there, were afterwards massacred by Fateh Khān. When the Augustinians established themselves there in 1621, a revival of Christianity took place. They built a Church and residence in Angaracale, and also a chapel in Arakan dedicated to Our Lady of Success. This was the time, it must be remembered, when the Portuguese were in the service of the King of Arakan and along with the Maghs were committing frightful depredations all along the banks of the rivers in the Sunderbunds carrying off Musalmans and Hindus as captives. Between 1621 and 1624 the Portuguese brought to Chittagong 42,000 slaves of whom 28,000 were baptised by the Augustinians. Besides these, they converted 5000 Arakanese or Maghs.* In 1640 the Augustinians spread to Balasore where they built a Church dedicated to our Lady of the Rosary. They also built a Church in Ossampur and two Churches in Rangamati dedicated to Our Lady of the Rosary and Our Lady of Guadeloupe.

Missionary Disasters, 1632

Though the Christian religion was flourishing in Eastern Bengal, it received in 1622 a great check in Western Bengal owing to the siege of Hooghly. During the sack the lofty Convent of the Augustinians was burnt down and all the Churches and buildings belonging to the missionaries were destroyed. Only the Jesuit College and a few other houses escaped destruction as the Mughal officers took up their abode in them. According to Fr. Cabral four Augustinians, six or seven secular priests and three Jesuits lost their lives in the siege. But the number of Jesuits killed must have been more

* Fr. Delaunoit, *Catholic Encyclopedia* s. v. Calcutta.

because he records that Fr. Fialho S. J. died during the night and that Br. John Rodrigues S. J. died in the vessel which Pedro de Couto blew up and that the corpses of three Jesuits more, Fathers Pedro Gomes Benedicto Rodrigues and Gaspar Ferreira were dug up from the graves by the Moors, who surprized at their not being decomposed very respectfully deposited them again in the Jesuit Church which was broken down. Four Jesuits, including Father Cabral escaped with those who took refuge in the Saugor island, numbering in all three thousand Christians of whom two hundred were Portuguese. Among the four thousand Christian prisoners who were taken to Agra there were two Augustinians, Frei Antonio de Christo and Frei Francisco De Incarnação and two secular priests Manoel Garcia and Manoel da Anhaya. Considering the brilliant arguments of Father Hosten, it is doubtful whether Frei João da Cruz, the hero of a miracle in Agra was among these captives.* According to Manrique he was severely wounded across the shoulders while escaping during the siege of Hooghly with some Portuguese descendants (*Topasses*) and was left for dead. These *Topasses* carried him to a neighbouring Hindu village from where a Hindu merchant took him to his own house. His wounds were so bad that worms set in. A *Topass* removed the festering flesh and cured him with applications of coçoanut oil and tamarind. Frei Bernardo de Jesus who was superior of the mission, was thrashed to death in Dacca at the time of the siege.

The siege of Hooghly, however, checked the progress of the Catholic religion only for a short time. The following year the Christian Fathers and other Portuguese returned with a grant of 777 *bighas* of land (about 260 acres) from Shāh Jahān and with privileges the like of which they had never enjoyed

The Return of the Augustinians, 1633

* *Bengal Past and Present* Jan.—Mar. 1915, p. 49 *et seq.*

before in Hooghly. They did not establish themselves at their former site in Hooghly proper but a little outside the town in Balagarh, the present Bandel. Fr. Hosten supposes that they must have erected new Churches on the ruins of the former buildings. The Augustinians took possession of the 777 *bighas* of land, about 280 *bighas* of which still belong to the Bandel Convent. They spread themselves all over Bengal, and it is chiefly through their efforts that numerous people in Bengal were converted to Christianity. In 1666 Bernier wrote that Hooghly (Ogouli) alone, contained eight to nine thousand Christians and that the Jesuits and the Augustinians possessed there large Churches.

Although the Augustinians had raised in Goa a monastery to St. Augustine which as Mandelso said,* looked from a distance like one of the noblest palaces in the world and in which there was a Library the sight of which made Dr. Buchanan suddenly transport himself to one of the libraries of Cambridge, yet their Mission in Bengal was the wealthiest. Cottineau says † regarding the Augustinians in Bengal, "The Mission of Bengal is the chief source of their opulent situation; the two churches in Calcutta, one of which is the richest now in all India (probably Murgihatta Cathedral) and all the other Churches in Bengal under the British Dominions are exclusively entrusted to the care of the members of this Order sent directly from Goa though they take the faculties or licences of exercising the ministry from the Bishop or Administrator of St. Thomé of Mylapore near Madras who is commonly since near a century a member of the same Order." Their chief seat was the Bandel Convent and Church, on which depended all the Churches and parishes in Dacca, Solicur, Chandpur, Banja, Piplī, Balasore, Tamlūk, Jessore, Hījīlī, Tesgāon Chittagong Dīanga, Rangamati, Catroba, Sripūr and Arakan.

* *Voyages and Travels*, p. 81.

† *Historical Sketch of Goa* p. 123.

When the French started a factory in Chandernagore in 1688, the Augustinians erected their Churches there and claimed sole jurisdiction to the chagrin of the French Jesuits. But the French Government intervened and the Bishop of Mylapore created in 1696 a parish for the French Jesuits. The Capuchins built a Church there in 1796. In 1753 the Catholic population in Chandernagore was four thousand.

The Return of the Jesuits, 1640

The Jesuits got back their property in 1640 through the good offices of Fr. Joseph de Castro S. J. but they did not get permission to build a Church until 1663, when the historian Manucci interviewed the Mughal Governor Mirzagol on their behalf.* Manucci remarks that he was told in Hooghly by the Jesuit Fathers that before 1663 they had built a tiny Church made of straw. When a new Governor succeeded Mirzagol in 1664 he forced the Portuguese to pay Rs. 1,000 because they had built without permission a Church, which, as Fr. Hosten supposes, must have really been the Jesuit Church. Abbate Ripa called it a fine Church in 1709. They had a residence and a garden which is still known as *Sam Paulo Bagan*† and which marks the site of the Jesuit residence and College. Various writers refer to a College of Jesuits in Hooghly and their superior was indeed called the Rector. According to Fr. Barbier S. J. who wrote an account ‡ of the Episcopal Visitation of Bishop Laines of Mylapore in 1712-15 this Bishop died at the College of Hooghly. Fr. J. Tieffentaller S. J. who wrote a sort of a statistical account of Hooghly§ in 1765 speaks of the Jesuit College as already in ruins. But

* *Storia do Mogor*, Irvine's Ed., Vol. II, p. 90.

† The Jesuits were known as Paulists in India from their great institution in Goa, Collegio de Sam Paulo de Sante Fé.

‡ *Bengal Past and Present*, 1910, Vol. VI, p. 223 *et seq*.

§ *Vide* Tieffentaller in Bernoulli, *Description historique et geographique de L'Inde.*

FR. TIEFFENTHALLER'S PLAN OF HOOGHLY, (1765).

The ground plan of the Bandel Convent and Church (A and B) is not quite accurate. The site of the Jesuit Church (C) corresponds with Muktodasi's Garden, (*vide* map facing p. 149) in which its ruins can still be seen.

Fr. Hosten holds that this College was nothing but the Jesuit residence in which only two or three Jesuit Fathers lived with occasionally a lay brother. * The Jesuit Mission ministered in Hooghly till 1740 when Fr. George Deistermann the last Jesuit Rector died. But Fr. Delaunoit says † there was one Jesuit managing the Church and the college even up to 1746 when they were given up. At present there is no trace of the Jesuit Church and college but Fr. Hosten unearthed in 1915 in the *Sam Paulo Bagan* a wall 47 ft. long and 2 ft. 11 in. broad, which he believes formed part of the Jesuit Church. Most visitors to Bandel have probably seen this Jesuit garden, about four acres in area, now occupied by Bengali tenants and planted with various kinds of trees including cocoanut trees, mango trees and plaintain trees. Excepting the southern wall the other walls are decaying.

When Job Charnock founded Calcutta in 1690, the Portuguese and other Christians followed him and obtained a plot of ground where the Augustinians built a Chapel. In 1797 this Chapel was replaced by a Church dedicated to Our Lady of Rosary now known as the Cathedral Church. Its history will be dealt with later. As Calcutta was growing in importance and in population a need for another place of worship was felt; consequently a new Church was erected by Mrs. Grace Elizabeth at Boitakhana in 1808. The Church of the Sacred Heart of Jesus in Dharamtolla Street was built in 1834 by a Portuguese lady, Mrs. Sabina Barretto de Souza in fulfilment of a vow. The Barretto family is noted for the erection of many chapels and for munificent donations for the Churches in Calcutta and in its neighbourhood.

The year 1834 marked a new era in the history of the Catholicism in India. Hitherto the work of evangelization

---

* *Bengal Past and Present*, Jan.—Mar., 1915 p. 66.

† *Catholic Encyclopedia*, S. V. Calcutta.

was carried on only by the Portuguese Missions under the sanction and protection of the Portuguese Government. The Pope with a view to supply the growing needs of the Church created an Apostolic Vicariate and entrusted it to English Jesuits. But Portugal claimed the sole right of religious (Catholic) jurisdiction, known as *Padroado*, which she had received from the Pope for her zeal in the propagation of the faith in the East. The Marquis of Pombal, the Portuguese premier aggravated matters in 1835 by suppressing all Portuguese Religious Orders. Thus interminable disputes and controversies went on between the Courts of Rome and Portugal for over fifty years. This period may be passed over in silence while mention may be made of only a few points of interest to the Church in Bengal. An Irish Jesuit, Robert St. Leger, was appointed the first Vicar Apostolic of Bengal and he took possession of the Portuguese Murgihatta Church. By the suppression of the Religious Orders in 1835 very few friars were able to come to Bengal to carry on the work of the Mission among the Christians that were converted by the early Portuguese missionaries. The vast field of the Vicar Apostolic in Bengal was divided in 1850 and a new Vicar Apostolic was appointed for Eastern Bengal and Assam.

The Rivalry between the Portuguese and other Missions, 1834

In 1857 the Concordat between the Holy See and the King of Portugal curtailed furthermore the rights of the Portuguese Mission. The Augustinians having now left Bengal the Goanese who had stood up for the rights of the Portuguese began to supply missionaries for Bengal while the English Jesuits being unable to cope with the work, the Pope entrusted the Mission to the Belgian Jesuits while the Fathers of the Order of the Cross took the place of the Benedictines. The rivalry did not subside until 1887, when the Delegate Apostolic Mon. Agliardi came to carry out the clauses of the Concordat entered into between the Holy See and the King of Portugal Dom Luis I. By that Concordat it was decided that the following parishes and Churches should belong to the Portuguese Mission in Bengal under the jurisdiction of the Bishop of Mylapore :— Boitakhana in the town of Calcutta ; Chinsurah and Bandel in the district of Hooghly ; in Eastern Bengal Dacca, Tesgong, Nagory, Hashnabad, Sripūr, Tangrakali and Tuital ; while all other places passed on to the Jurisdictions of the Archbishop of Calcutta and of the Bishop of Dacca.

CHAPTER X

PORTUGUESE TRADE IN BENGAL

The high hopes which the Portuguese had entertained regarding the possibilities of trade in Bengal were realized beyond their expectation. Towards the middle of the sixteenth century a great part of the Bengal trade and shipping passed into the hands of the Portuguese. As early as 1535 Diogo Rebello had forbidden any alien ship to touch at Sātgāon without the permission of the Portuguese. The Portuguese applied to Bengal the law they had enforced in the Indian seas in order to destroy the Moorish trade. Any ship that travelled without a Portuguese pass was treated as an enemy ship and was either not allowed to sail or captured. The superiority of Portuguese vessels over native craft rendered the enforcement of this principle practicable, though sometimes the Portuguese met with their rivals elsewhere in the Turkish and the Egyptian ships. The ordinary merchant vessels of the Portuguese consisted of a captain, a master and a pilot, while among the crew there would be Moors or any class of Asiatic people. Until the Portuguese established their great settlement of Hooghly in 1580 their ships did not permanently stay in Bengal. However, the Portuguese ships commanded the whole sea-board from Orissa to Chittagong from about 1537, when they had founded their settlements on both the arms of the Bay of Bengal. Kabi Kankan mentions in the *Chandi*, written in 1577, that the coast near Hījīlī was dangerous on account of the Feringhi ships. The Portuguese came with their goods before the monsoons set in and spent the rainy months in Bengal buying and selling goods and transacting their business. When the monsoons were over the ships would repair to Goa and other Portuguese ports laden with the merchandise of Bengal.

The earliest commercial relations of the Portuguese in Bengal were with Chittagong (Porto Grande). De Barros wrote

Porto Grande

in 1532 "Chittagong is the most famous and wealthy city of the kingdom of Bengal, on account of its port, at which meets the traffic of all that eastern region." From 1517 expedition after expedition had come to Chittagong with no great success until the Portuguese founded their settlements in 1537 and owned independent custom-houses both in Chittagong (Porto Grande) and Sātgāon (Porto Pequeno). Ever since the fall of Gaur and especially after the foundation of the Portuguese settlement in Hooghly, Chittagong had begun to lose its commercial importance. Even then Eastern Bengal and the kingdom of Arakan continued to be the seat of many industries and Portuguese ships used to go to Chitagong with their goods, though Hooghly was a more frequented port. In 1567 Cæsar de Federici found more than eighteen ships anchored in Chittagong, and he writes that from this port the traders carried to the Indies "great store of rice, very great quantities of bombast cloth of every sort, sugar, corn, and money with other merchandise."*

In Western Bengal, Sātgāon was the emporium of Portuguese trade since 1537. It was then the chief mart where all

Porto Pequeno

the merchants of Northern India flocked with their merchandise. After the Portuguese had settled in Hooghly in 1580 this port became the centre of their trade while Sātgāon gradually dwindled into in significance. Hooghly was then termed Porto Pequeno.

The Portuguese ships of the larger type, came up to Garden Reach or rather Betor (Howrah) where they anchored because the river Hooghly was not navigable higher up than

* Purchas, *His Pilgrimes*, C. Frederick, Vol. X. p. 138.

Adhiganga (now Tolly's Nollah) except by smaller vessels. Cæsar de Federici who was in Hooghly in 1567 says* that in the Hooghly river the large ships of the Portuguese came up to Betor (near Sibpur, the modern Howrah), whence the smaller ships sailed up to Sātgāon and laded "Rice, Cloth of Bombast of divers sorts, Lacca, great abundance of Sugar, Myrobolans dried and preserved, long Pepper, Oyle of Zerseline and many other sorts of merchandise." In Betor the goods were stored in thatched houses of straw or bamboo and were either sold or exchanged in big local markets or taken to other places. Gradually these goods swelled the markets of Calcutta and Chitpore, which were then very insignificant villages. It is to these thatched houses and villages which as Federici and Manrique say, were made and unmade by the Portuguese when they went back, that can be traced the origin of the great city Job Charnock founded. It is in those marts of Betor, Chitpore and Sutanuti which were supplied by Portuguese goods that can be seen the first glimmerings of the great commercial importance that Calcutta attained many years later. C. R. Wilson well remarks,† "It is under their (Portuguese) commercial supremacy that the place which we know by the name of Calcutta first began to have any importance; it is to them that we are chiefly indebted for our first reliable information about Hughli and its markets."

Manrique's Account of Portuguese Trade

The best account of the Portuguese trade in Bengal is found in Manrique's *Itinerario.*‡ Manrique, it must be stated, was in Bengal during the palmiest days of the Portuguese and actually saw what he described. The Portuguese imported into Bengal various kinds of goods from other places which

* Purchas, *His Pilgrimes*, C. Frederick, Vol. X. p. 114.

† *Early Annals of the English in Bengal.*

‡ *Vide* Fr. Cardon's Trans. of the chapters relating to Bengal in *Bengal Past and Present* 1915; Vol. XII, No. 24.

were visited by the Portuguese vessels. The principal things they brought to Bengal were from Malacca, Sumatra and Borneo, such as "Brocades, Brocateles, Cloth, Velvets, Damasks, Satins, Taffetas, Tafiosinas, Tafissirias Escomillas or Muslins" of all colours but black, which colour was considered ill-omened in Bengal. From Malacca they also brought cloves nutmegs, and mace; and from Borneo the highly prized camphor. They brought cinammon from Ceylon and pepper from Malabar. From China they brought silks, gilt furniture such as bedsteads, tables, coffers, chests, writing-desks, boxes and very valuable pearls and jewels, for labour being cheap in China "these were made in European style but with greater skill and cheaper." From the islands of Maldives they brought sea-shells (*kaurim*) which were, during the period of Hindu kings, current in Bengal as coins and were known as *cowries*. The bigger kind of shells called *chanquos* were brought from their fisheries on the Choromandel Coast. They imported from Solor and Timor both the white and the red varieties of sandalwood which was in Bengal a rich commodity. These commodities fetched such high prices that according to Tavernier, if the Dutch had not come to India there would be no piece of iron in the Portuguese factories but all would be gold and silver, for the Portuguese with two or three voyages to China, Japan, Philipines and Mollucas would earn as much as a thousand per cent on their goods. In spite of the Dutch having come, however, gold and silver abounded in Portuguese houses in Goa and other parts of India.

East India Co., Records

From the records of the East India Company we learn a good deal about the trade and power of the Portuguese in Hooghly and in the rivers of Bengal. In a letter dated the 26th February 1616, the English factors at Surat communicated to the East India Company, "that hitherto they had not found it practicable to open a trade in the countries bordering on the Ganges, the Portuguese being in exclusive possession of the commerce in this part of the Peninsula." Another communication in 1618 says that "for small shipping there were no ports but such as the Portuguese possessed." The Portuguese extended their commerce to Patna in Bihar, in which connection Hughes and Parker, who had gone there from Surat to found a factory, write in 1620,* "The Portingalls of late yeares, have had a trade here in Puttana, cominge up with theire friggitts from the bottom of Bengalla where theye have two porttes, th, one called Gollye, th, other Pieppullye and therein are licenced by this kinge to inhabitt. Gollye is theire cheefest porte where theye are in greate multitudes, and have yearlye shipping both from Mallacka and Cochine. The commodites theye usiallye bringe up hether is for the most part tyne, spices, and China wares, in live whereof theye transporte ambertye callicoes, carpets and and all sortes of thine cloth, which theye die into redds purposlye for saile to the sothwards. This cittye stands upon the river Ganges, whose suifte currant transportes theire friggits with such dexteritye that in five or six dayes theye usiallye go hence to theire portes, but in repairinge up againe spend thrice the tyme."

In their other communications, Hughes and Parker throw some light on the Portuguese trade. "There are" they wrote on July 12th 1620,† "some Portingalls at present in towne and more are latlye gon for theire portes in Bengala ; into whose trafique I have made enquirye and gather that theye usialye bringe vendable here all sorts of spices and silke stufes of Chyna, tyne and some jewelleres ware ; in lewe whereof theye transporte course Carpets of Junapore (Jaunpore), ambertyes cassaes (a kind of cloth) and some alike." On the 6th of

---

* Foster, *The English Factories in India (1618-1621)*, p. 213-4.

† *Ibidem*, p. 115.

August 1620 Hughes and Parker spoke of many Portuguese frigates having come to Patna from Sātgāon and remarked that the Portuguese merchants were wont to buy all they could lay hands on.*

Portuguese Exports

The Portuguese shipped various things from Bengal, seat as it was of a great many industries and manufactures. Pyrard de Laval who travelled in Bengal in the beginning of the 17th century says,† "The inhabitants (of Bengal), both men and women, are wonderously adroit in all such manufactures such as of cotton, cloth and silks and in needlework, such as embroideries which are worked so skilfully, down to the smallest stitches that nothing prettier is to be seen anywhere." The natural products of Bengal were also abundant, and various are the travellers who have dwelt on the fertility of the soil of Bengal watered as it is by the holy Ganges. When Manrique came to Bengal in 1628 he found there plenty of foodstuffs, fowls, pigeons, castrated goats whose meat the people preferred to mutton, veal, vegetables, rice, butter, sweetmeats and milk, sweets. To export such commodities as rice butter, oil and wax 100 ships were annually laden in the ports of Bengal. Rice was very cheap, a *candi* (about 500 lbs. but in Bengal 1200lbs.) costing only three or four rupees; one *contaro* of butter (75lbs) cost only two rupees. Twenty or twenty-five fowls cost also about two rupees (one *peso*). A cow cost a rupee (three or four *reals*); 200 lbs of sugar seven or eight annas. These prices which Manrique gives may seem extraordinarily cheap but many others confirm him. In Bowrey's time (1669-1679) prices had gone a little high excepting of fowls. He says ‡ "A very good cowe is sold for foure shillings six pence *viz.*, two rupees, a good hogg for ¾ of a rupee, 45 or 50 fowls for one

* *The English Factories, ut supra*, p. 197.

† Pyrard de Laval, Hak. Ed. Vol. I. 329.

‡ *Countries Round the Bay of Bengal.* pp. 193, 194.

rupee." Bowrey adds that the Portuguese themselves used to prepare in Hooghly all sorts of sweatmeats from mangoes, oranges, lemons, ginger, mirabolans, ringroots etc. and also make pickles from mangoes, bamboo, lemon etc., which were all good and cheap.

Local Commerce and Industries

Fruits seem to have been abundant in Bengal, the daintiest of all being mangoes on which unstincted praise has always been lavished by European writers. There were no wines in Bengal but spirit distilled from rice and jogree was plentiful. The trade in opium and its extracts was very great as it was used as an aphrodisiac. Dacca was then the Gangetic emporium of trade. It was there that those priceless muslins were made even as early as the Roman days. Its thread was so delicate that it could hardly be discerned by the eye. Tavernier mentions,* "Muhammad Ali Beg when returning to Persia from his embassy to India presented Cha Safi III with a cocoanut of the size of an ostrich egg, enriched with precious stones, and when it was opened a turban was drawn from it 60 cubits in length, and of a muslin so fine that you would scarcely know what it was you had in your hand." These muslins were made fifty and sixty yards in length and two yards in breadth and the extremities were embroidered in gold, silver and coloured silk. The Emperor appointed a supervisor in Dacca to see that the richest muslins and other varieties of cloth did not find their way anywhere else except to the Court of Delhi. Strain on the weavers' eyes was so great that only sixteen to thirty years old people were engaged to weave. These are the men who with their simple instruments produced those far-famed muslins that no scientific appliances of civilized times could have turned out.

The betel-leaf alone brought four thousand rupees of revenue to the Governor of Dacca. In Midnapore scents were manufac-

* Tavernier, Ball's Ed., Vol. II, pp. 7–8.

tured from flowers and scented oils from a kind of grain and they were highly valued because they were used by the people to rub themselves with, after bath. In Hījīlī there was a great trade in salt, sugar, wax, silk and cloth made from grass (*Ginghams*). There was a vast trade in salt in Sandwīp and annualy as many as two hundred ships laden with it sailed from there. Ship-building material was very cheap in Sandwīp and Cæsar de Federici says that the Sultan of Constantinople had found it cheaper to have his ships built there rather than at Alexandria. He calls Sandwīp "the fertilest Iland in all the world." Speaking about the cheapness of goods he remarks,* "And when the people of the Iland (of Sandwīp) saw the ship, and that we were coming a land : presently they made a place of Bazar or Market, with Shops right over against the ship with all manner of provision of victuals to eate, which they brought downe in great abundance, and sold it so good cheape, that wee were amazed at the cheapnesse there of. I bought many salted Kine there, for the provision of the ship, for halfe a Larine a piece, which Larine may be twelve shillings sixe pence, being very good and fatte, and foure wilde Hogges ready dressed for a Larine ; great fat Hennes for a Bizze a piece which is at the most a Penie ; and the people told us that we were deceived the half of our money, because we bought things so deare. Also a sacke of fine rice for a thing of nothing and consequently all other things for humaine sustenance were there in such abundance that it is a thing incredible but to them that have seene it." In the beginning of the eighteenth century Captain A. Hamilton says† that he was informed by one who wintered there "that he bought 580 pound weight of rice for a rupee or half a crown, eight geese for the same money and sixty good tame poultry for the same, and cloth is also incredibly cheap, it is but thinly inhabited."

* Purchas, *His Pilgrimes*, Frederick, Vol. X, p. 137.

† *A New Account of the East Indies* Vol. II, pp. 23-24.

The Portuguese took full advantage of the cheapness of goods in Bengal and sold them at an enormous profit in their numerous ports in the East. The wealth that such commerce brought to the Portuguese is unimaginable. It also brought luxury in its train. Pyrard de Laval says* that the Portuguese men of quality travelled on horseback, and that the harness of horses coming from Bengal, China, and Persia was all of silk embroidery enriched with gold and silver and fine pearls. The stirrups were of silver gilt, the bridle was adorned with precious stones and silver bells. The grooms carried fine horsecloths of red velvet fringed with gold and embroidery for covering the horses when their masters dismounted. It would be out of place here to relate the luxuries and wealth, which the trade of Bengal as of the whole East brought to the Portuguese. One of the reasons why Akbar asked two Portuguese from Hooghly to come to him was that he was charmed to see the precious goods they brought there. The Portuguese had found the trade of Bengal so profitable that even in the latter half of the eighteenth century there was an attempt in Lisbon at the proposal of Viceroy Conde de Ega tó form a Company exclusively to trade with Bengal.† The Company was however soon wound up and the plan, like most of the plans at this time, was never realized.

* Pyrard de Laval, Hakl. Edition, pt. II. pp. 75-80.

† *Conselho Ultramarino No. 32. Vide* Danvers, *Report on the Portuguese Records etc.* p. 15.

PART II

THE DECLINE AND FALL

OF THE

PORTUGUESE IN BENGAL

CHAPTER XI

THE PERIOD OF DECADENCE

...Ah ! Que desmaio
Apaga o marcio ardor da Lusa gente ?*
Barbosa du Bocage

General Decline

With the dawn of the seventeenth century the Portuguese power in the East had begun to decline. After spreading her influence over two worlds, Portugal had exhausted herself. The task undertaken was too great for a small nation. The energy soon spent itself out. Sailors could not be found to man her fleets even when outlaws and convicts were set at liberty. Even the expedition of the Governor Estevão da Gama who came to India in 1540 was chiefly composed of convicts. The later Portuguese were not of the type of Albuquerque, Cunha or Castro. In judging of the Portuguese of the seventeenth century, one should remember that the ships which sailed from the Tagus brought chiefly the refuse of Portugal to India The last flash of Portuguese genius shone in D. João de Castro, Viceroy of Goa, 1545-1548. The subsequent half a century marks the period of transition from glory to actual decadence.

Pampered by wealth, the Portuguese in India had grown indolent. Luxury bred vice and profligacy. The civic virtues of the earlier rulers had given place to venality and corruption. Concealed beneath the pomp and splendour of the Portuguese grandees in India lay the seeds of decay and dissolution. Vice and corruption as in the days of the

---

* Ah ! Lusians, what dull gloom o'erspreads, what dire dismay
Quells the conquering fire, where heroes held their sway ?
Trans J. C.

Roman Empire were but the symptoms of the impending collapse.. The earlier Portuguese were schooled in hard facts, while those who followed were easy-going and reaped the harvest which had been sown after years of hard struggles. Growing immensely rich without any difficulty they lost themselves in a whirl of orgies.

The ecclesiastical supremacy in the political atmosphere had also its own results. In 1560, during King Sebastião's reign, the Inquisition was introduced in India. Its excesses in Europe alienated other European nations from the Portuguese who in a religious zeal cultivated this institution. Diogo de Couto has painted in vivid colours how the interference and preponderance of priests in politics contributed to the downfall of Portugal.* Ennes calls Dom Henrique, the Cardinal King, the grave-digger of Portugal, for tolerating ecclesiastical abuses and allowing a free hand to the Inquisition.†

The monastic orders in India had really grown to be an *imperium in imperio.* The Viceroys of India though beset with numerous enemies, considered the friars and secular priests the most dangerous of all. The Jesuits not only arrogated to themselves magisterial power but even collected custom duties from the vessels, sailing past their convents, threatening to open fire from the cannon planted on the towers.‡ The government could hardly enforce submission and even when the Portuguese galleys threatened to bombard the Franciscan monastery in Goa they had to retreat when the Sacred Host was exposed to their view. As it has been said, one does not know how far, the abuses of power and the defiance of law, were the causes or symptoms of the collapse of Portuguese power in India.

---

* *Dialogos do Soldado Pratico*, Lisbon, 1790.
† *Historia de Portugal.*
‡ *O Chronista de Tissuari*, Vol. II, pp. 70-71.

The Follies of the Spanish King

When King Dom Sebastião, "a beardless youth enamoured of glory" was killed whilst fighting on the sands of Kassr-el-kebir and his successor the Cardinal King Dom Henrique died before a year was over, the crowns of Spain and Portugal were united in 1580 under Philip II of Spain, (Philip I of Portugal). The event sealed the fate of Portugal. The Spanish King had no sympathies with Portugal, and treated her as a conquered country. A nation fettered with the bonds of captivity and slavery could no longer rule the world. Another little nation was now destined to break her bonds of servitude. Spain dominated at this time the Low Countries which possessed the two great ports of Antwerp and Amsterdam. It was to these ports that the Portuguese commerce of the East was shipped and thence transported all over Europe. But the Flemish and the Dutch having broken with Spain, the "fatal Philip" closed all the Portuguese ports against the Dutch in 1594. Being thus deprived of their trade in eastern commodities, the Dutch determined to sail to the East with a view to secure it for themselves. Portugal paid dearly for Philip's crime by the loss of an Empire.

The Dutch not only wrested a great part of the trade from the Portuguese but in the constant struggles that followed for the next sixty-nine years, at length emerged victorious. Portugal whom "Neptune and Mars feared" was unable to stand before a small nation but recently under the Spanish yoke. It was not that the Dutch were bolder than the Portuguese. A nation that had won the supremacy of the seas from the Arabs and the Turks when the Crescent was supreme even in Europe, cannot be said to have been excelled in maritime power and enterprise. The fact was that the Dutch, free from a foreign yoke, found the Portuguese demoralized and groaning under the oppression of the Spanish monarch. The Dutch first captured from the Portuguese the fort of Amboina and then the forts of Ternate and of Tidore in the Moluccas. In 1641 fell Malacca, the rich gateway of commerce and the scene of the heroic feats of Albuquerque. Galle, Trincomali, Baticola, Negumbo, Calacature and Colombo in Ceylon were then captured. The fort of Jafnapatam, the Island of Manar noted for its pearl fisheries, Tuticorin, Negapatam, the forts of Quilon, Cranganore, Cannanore and the city of Cochin successively passed into the hands of the Dutch.

The English followed in the wake of the Dutch and bitter hostilities arose between them and the Portuguese. The English and the Dutch, indeed, combined to overthrow the Portuguese supremacy in the Indian Seas Three English vessels* and four Dutch ones blockaded Goa in January 1623 but were forced to retire by the middle of March. The English, did not wrest so many places from the Portuguese as the Dutch. They, however, lent assistance to the Persians in conquering Ormuz and were indirectly responsible for many Portuguese losses which followed.

The Dutch in Bengal

The rivalry of the European nations was no less keen in Bengal. The Dutch ships arrived in Bengal for the first time in 1615, though Dutchmen like Van Linschoten† visited Bengal towards the latter half of the sixteenth century. The Dutch fleet joined the King of Arakan and signalized its first appearance in Bengal by fighting with the Portuguese, near the coast of Arakan‡. The battle lasted one day but the victory was indecisive. Thereafter the Dutch continued to trade with Bengàl but did not settle permanently in Bengal until towards the middle of the seventeenth century§ when they

---

* The names of the vessels were *Exchange*, *Ann*, and *Diamond.*

† It may be mentioned that Van Linschoten served in the Portuguese Indian fleet.

‡ *Vide* Chapter XIV.

§ Orme loosely says that the Dutch settled in Bengal in 1625. Cf.

established their factory in Hooghly. The Dutch rapidly extended their sphere of activities while the Portuguese settlement in Hooghly sustained a severe disaster in at the hands of the Mughals in 1632. Though the Portuguese continued to trade in Hooghly long after, the Dutch easily outrivalled them. The Dutch erected their Fort Gustavus in Chinsura, founded a silk factory in Cassimbazar, another factory for salting pork in Baranagar, north of Calcutta, owned a beautiful garden near Chandernagore and later on established a station at Fulta for their merchant vessels.

The English in Bengal

The first attempt of the English to open a trade with Bengal in 1617 through the influence of Sir Thomas Roe was unsuccessful. The attempts of Hughes and Parker in 1620 and of Peter Mundy in 1632 to establish factories in Patna also proved failures. The first English vessel that came to Bengal or rather Orissa, fared badly in a fight with a Portuguese frigate. In the letters of the early English factors who strove to secure trading concessions in Bengal there are various references to the supremacy of the Portuguese and to their possession of most of the ports in Bengal. Through the good offices of Dr. Gabriel Boughton who cured the Emperor Shāh Jahān of an illness, the English obtained a *farman* from the Emperor permitting them free trade in Bengal. In 1651 the English founded their first factory in Bengal and six years later they established subordinate agencies at Balasore, Cossimbazar and Patna. How the English spread all over Bengal and triumphed in the end is ably dealt with by other writers.

History of Hindustan Vol. II, p. 8. Bowrey remarks that both the English and the Dutch owned factories in Hooghly about the time of the massacre of the English in Amboina (1623) Yule however has shown that the the English had no factory in Hooghly before 1651. In the English Factories records there are references to the Dutch trade but not to their factory till after 1650. Toynbee's reference to the Dutch *farman* of 1638 is not confirmed by Stavorinus in his List of Dutch *farmans*.

The first French settlement in Bengal was the result of an accident. The first French ship, the Fleming, which made its appearance in Bengal in 1674 did not come of its own accord but was brought a captive by the Dutch from Balasore to Hooghly. The vessel was however set at liberty and the Frenchmen established near the Dutch garden, a small factory, which is mentioned by Streynsham Master.* The foundation of the great French settlement of Chandernagore is believed to have originated in the *farman* of Aurangzeb granted in 1688. The French, however, did not put any difficulties in the way of the Portuguese trade in Bengal. Until Joseph François Dupleix was appointed Intendant of Chandernagore in 1731, this little French territory was an insignificant place containing a few families and, as Alexander Hamilton said, "a pretty little church to hear mass in which is the chief business of the French in Bengal."

The French in Bengal

The first factory of the Danes was established at Balasore about 1636, and in Hooghly they settled sometime after 1676. The factory was built in Gondalpara to the south-east of Chandernagore. A part of Gondalpara is still called *Dinemardanga,* that is, the land of the Danes. They obtained the settlement of Serampore in 1755 from Ali Vardi Khān. As the rise of the Danes, the Prussians, and the Flemish who successively established themselves in Bengal, did not contribute to the downfall of the Portuguese in any way, their account need not be given here.

The Danes in Bengal

It was the Mughals who struck the fatal blow at the Portuguese power in Bengal. Once their best friends, the Mughals proved to be their worst enemies. The siege of Hooghly in 1632 was the beginning of the downfall of the Portuguese in

* Yule, *Hedge's Diary, Vol. II*, p. 233.

Western Bengal. In Eastern Bengal the Portuguese were, indeed, flourishing at this time, but only as adventurers and pirates. When Shaista Khān conquered Chittagong in 1668 the era of piracy was over. From this date onward the Portuguese cannot be said to have wielded paramount influence in Bengal. The day of the Portuguese was gone while that of the other European nations had dawned.

CHAPTER XII

THE FALL OF HOOGHLY

The privileges which Akbar had granted to the Portuguese were well maintained by his son Jahāngīr ; for the latter like his father was glad at the promise made by the Portuguese to keep the Bay clear of pirates. He was, however, a weak-minded man and was entirely ruled by his wife, Nur Jahān. This fact had its influence on the history of Bengal. Nur Jahān favoured the fourth son of the emperor, Shāhryar, who had married the daughter of her first husband and tried to secure the throne for him. Prince Khurrum (Shāh Jahān) raised the standard of revolt in 1621, but being defeated he fled to Bengal and resided in Burdwan. During the time of the Mughals, every Mughal prince who was driven away from Delhi or had fallen into trouble in some way or other, looked to Bengal as a place of refuge, as it was far from the influence of Delhi and not peopled by warlike races. Humāyūn had done the same, then the Afghan Sher Shāh, and then again Prince Khurrum. From Burdwan Prince Khurrum asked Miguel Rodrigues, the Portuguese Governor of Dacca (or Hooghly), to help him with men and artillery and promised in return immense riches and vast tracts of land. Rodrigues declined to help him because he was a rebel son.* This insult cut the future Emperor to the quick and he swore revenge. Whatever the intention of the Portuguese Governor might have been, whether he thought it was unjust to help a rebel or that by helping the son he would incur the displeasure of the father,

The Siege of Hooghly (1632), Causes

Manrique, Fr. Hosten's Trans, *Catholic Herald of India*, May 8, 1918, p 354.

his rebuke was destined to cost the Portuguese a good deal. According to Fr. Cabral S. J., a Portuguese actually went to help him with a few ships and then deserted him.* Prince Khurrum fought the Mughal Governor on the banks of the Ganges, defeated him and he became the sole master of Bengal in 1622.. But under the conditions he was placed in, he could not muster a force strong enough to give any trouble to the Portuguese. Two years later the imperial army engaged Prince Khurrum again and defeated him, but on his asking pardon his kindly father forgave him. On the death of Jahāngīr, Prince Khurrum ascended the throne in 1627 as Shāh Jahān and appointed his best friend, Kasim Khān, Governor of Bengal ordering him to keep a watchful eye on the Portuguese, so that the earliest opportunity might be taken to drive them from Hooghly. Another cause which heightened Shāh Jahān's wrath against the Portuguese was that the year before the siege of Hooghly he had sustained serious defeats losing more than 50,000 horse in his quarrel with Adil Khān of Bijapore and he attributed the latter's success to the help which the Adil Khān had received from the Portuguese.†

Fr. Cabral S. J. and Manrique who have left the best accounts of the siege of Hooghly enumerate many other causes which led to that tragic event. Fr. Cabral was an eye-witness of the siege and was one of those who escaped. Manrique was in Bengal at the time and was in fact mixed up with the causes of the siege. Shāh Jahān, relates Fr. Cabral, felt the affront of one Manoel Tavares, a country-born Portuguese who having gone to his help with a few galleys when he rose in revolt against his father, had abandoned him at a critical moment. To add to the insult, the Portuguese of Hooghly had not sent him an embassy to congratulate him on

* Fr. Cabral, Fr. Besse's Trans. *Catholic Herald of India*, Feb. 6, 1918, p. 111.

† Faria y Souza, *Asia*, Steven's Trans., Vol. III, p. 402.

his ascending the throne. They were, it was alleged, in league with the King of Arakan who committed depredations on the Mughal territories and were supplying him with men, munitions and galleys. Above all the Mughals seem to have been exasperated at the conduct of a Portuguese captain of Chittagong who seized a fair and pretty Mughal lady during one of his piratical raids. Manrique dwells at length on this episode in which he intervened the lady to console her daughter and mother-in-law in their misfortune. It was this incident which according to him precipitated the siege. Fr. Cabral S. J. supposes that the Mughals were indeed afraid that the Portuguese might possess themselves of the 'kingdoms of Bengal,' considering their increasing power in Bandel (Hooghly) and the high regard in which they were held by the native Hindus.

Muhammadan version of the 'Casus Belli'

According to the Muhammadan historians the causes of the siege of Hooghly were quite different. Kasim Khān the Governor of Bengal is said to have sent a report to Shāh Jahān complaining "that instead of confining their attention to the business of merchants, the Portuguese had fortified themselves in that place (Hooghly), and were become so insolent that they committed many acts of violence upon the subjects of the empire, and presumed to exact duties from all the boats and vessels which passed their factory, and had completely drawn away all the commerce from the ancient port of Satgong, that the Portuguese were in the habit of kidnapping or purchasing poor children and sending them as slaves to other parts of India and that their pirates in consort with the Mughs committed innumerable aggressions on the inhabitants of the districts on the eastern branch of the Ganges." * Though it is true that the Portuguese in Hooghly had grown insolent and took many liberties, they were not in league with the Chittagong pirates. They

* Stewart, *History of Bengal*, p. 240.

however, bought the slaves sold by the pirates as they would buy of any body else. Kidnapping people and committing aggressions were not the practices of the Portuguese of Hooghly but of the Portuguese of Chittagong and lower Bengal, who had disowned their King and country and were mercenaries in the pay of the King of Arakan. As to the alleged aggressions in Hooghly the Mughals themselves indulged in them freely as can be seen from Fr. Du Jarric's description of the visit of Domingo Carvalho to the Portuguese of Hooghly *

There might have been some private Portuguese individuals against whom the accusations made by the Mughals might have been rightly made. But considering as a whole, it is necessary to differentiate between the adventurers of Chittagong and the Portuguese of Hooghly. It was thus that the Portuguese replied to the Mughals during the peace negotiations, "To the complaints of the two Moors, the captain and his assistants answered in writing stating that the greater part of the charges against the city were mere falsehoods, the inventions of Martin Afonso and his crew. If necessary they would prove it by the authoritative evidence of the merhants, Moors and Pagans who had been for many years trading at Hugli. The other accusations concerned private persons, they contended, and they were in possession of a document confirmed by king Jehangir and Sultan Paraves, his son, to the effect that the Bandel would never be held responsible as a body for the misdemeanours of particular individuals."†

It may be added that Asiaticus mentions as the cause of the siege of Hooghly, that "In 1632 the Portguese committed excesses on the Imperial Mahal at Hooghly: the emperor demanded satisfaction which was denied him." It is difficult

---

* *Vide* Chapter IV, p. 72-73.

† Fr. Cabral, *Catholic Herald of India*, Feb. 13, 1918, p. 130.

to say what was the source of Asiaticus's information but the fact, is that as Fr. Hosten S. J. says, the Emperor never had any Imperial Mahal in Hooghly. There is also a Mughal story to the effect that the Empress who had a dislike for the Portuguese prevailed on Shāh Jahān to crush their power in Bengal. When she was in Bengal she is said to have been offended at the sight of the holy pictures and images which were in the Portuguese Churches. Manucci * says that she was enraged with the Portuguese because when she was residing near Hooghly (Burdwan) with his husband, the Portuguese seized two of her beloved slaves, which they refused to return in spite of her urging them to do so.

The Siege

Of the plan and the conduct of the siege there are excellent accounts in Fr. Cabral's Letter, Abdul Hamid Lāhorī's *Bādshāhnāma* and Khafi Khān's *Muntakhābul-lubār*. The latter repeats more or less the *Bādshāhnāmā* and Stewart's description is chiefly based on them. The most graphic and certainly faithful description is that of Fr. Cabral S. J. who took part in the siege and was one of those who escaped. Other accounts can be found in Faria y Souza's *Asia Portuguesa*, Manucci's *Storia do Mogor*, Bernier's *Travels* and Fr. Catrou's "*General History of the Mogol Empire.*" The Muhammadan historians are at great variance with the Portuguese historians, who themselves do not exactly agree in certain points.

When Kasim Khān got orders to march against Hooghly he knew it was no easy task. He postponed the attack as long as he could, till it happened that a Portuguese half-caste named Martim Affonso de Mello, whose evil doings had alienated him from the sympathy of the Portuguese, went especially to Dacca and prevailed upon him to march on Hooghly. De Mello disclosed to Kasim Khān the treasures of the Portuguese

* Manucci, *Storia de Mogor*, Irvine's Ed., Vol. I, p. 175.

and informed him that the defences were not as strong as he supposed. Being thus assured, Kasim Khān delayed no more in making preparations for the attack and ordered all his ships and his land forces to be in readiness.

The Forces engaged in the Attack and in the Defence

Kasim Khān's son 'Ināyath-ulla was given charge of the army though Allāh Yār Khān was the real commander. Bahadur Kambu with five hundred horse and a large force of infantry was sent with another army making it ostensibly appear that he was going to capture some lands in Macksusaba. The object of all these forces was rumoured to be an attack against Hījīlī. According to Manrique the armies were commanded by fourteen Nawabs (Muraos); according to Frei Nicolau by eighteen Nawabs and according to Asiaticus by twenty-two *Omrahs* or Nawabs. A fleet consisting of five hundred ships (Manrique says 600) was sent under Khwaja Shere to operate from the river and cut off the retreat of the Portuguese. This fleet appeared on the 24th June 1632* in the river about ten leagues south of Hooghly and only two days later the army consisting of hundred and fifty thousand men† ninety castled elephants and fourteen thousand horse (Manrique) began the operations by advancing from the north within a league from the town. Captain Manoel de Azavedo‡ conducted the defence. The Portuguese

* I have followed the dates of Fr. Cabral. Various incorrect dates have been assigned to the siege. Elphinstone (*Hist. of India*) Beale (*Orient. Biog. Dict.*), Ma,āsir-ul-Umara give the date as 1631 and Faria y Souza as 1633. The *Bādshāhnāmā* relates that the first attack was made on 2nd Zil-hijja 1241. The Portuguese official account says that the siege lasted from June, 21 to Sept. 29, 1633, *Vide* Danvers *Records* p. 29.

† This is according to Fr. Cabral. Faria y Souza's number is 200,000.

‡ Fr Catrou an then Asiaticus say that Michael (Miguel) Rodrigues who had refused help and insulted Shāh Jahān in 1621 was captain of the Portuguese in Hooghly at the time of the siege. This is wrong. Fr. Cabral and Manrique have a greater right to be believed.

forces consisted of only three hundred Portuguese including their descendants and about six hundred Native Christians.* According to Cabral and Manrique the Portuguese had neither a fort nor even artillery. Khafi Khān distinctly says† that the Portuguese had a strong fort with towers and embattlements furnished with artillery, but his description is only an enlargement upon the *Bādshāhnāmā*‡ which does not make any distinct mention of a fort though it says that the Portuguese had erected large substantial buildings fortified with canon and muskets and other implements of war and that the town was defended by the river on one side and on the other three sides by a ditch filled from the river. Manrique says,§ "The town was situated in an open plain along the banks of the Ganges and was exposed on all sides. It had neither wall nor rampart but only an earthen parapet which they had thrown up, a thing of little value and still lesser strength." Fr. Cabral also asserts that the Portuguese had only erected barricades and built palisades from house to house, during the siege.

The plan of the Mughals was to attack both by land and by sea. The siege began on the 24th June, 1632 when Khwaja Shere's fleet appeared before Hooghly advancing from the south, while on the 26th the army began to operate from the north. First of all, the Mughals captured the lands which the Portuguese possessed on both sides of the river outside the town. By July 2nd all the northern suburbs and the *Casa de Misericordia* with its

First Attack

* The numbers given by Fr. Cabral are three hundred whites besides natives. Manrique gives 180 Portuguese and 600 slaves. The official version puts down the Portuguese forces to 200 Portuguese and 600 Christian slaves. Cf. *Doc. Remet. Liv. 30 fols. 281 and 288*, or see Danvers *Records etc.* p. 29.

† Elliot, *Hist of India*, Vol. VII, p. 211.

‡ *Ibidem*, Vol. VII, pp. 31-32.

§ *Catholic Herald of India*, May 29th, 1918, p. 414.

Church was in the hands of the enemy. But the attack cost them a good deal. An Augustinian friar converted the tower of his Church into a citadel and delivered such blows from there with seven or eight Portuguese and ten or twelve natives that after the attack was over, it was found that the compound was strewn over with many corpses of the enemy. The *Bādshāh-nāmā* says that the Mughals captured or killed all the Portuguese they could get hold of before attacking the town itself and forced four thousand Bengali boatmen, who were serving the Portuguese, to join them. After playing the havoc, both sides desired for peace, and entered into negotiations. The Portuguese delivered to the Moors four vessels and ninety Christian slaves on promise that the siege would be raised. But Kasim Khān again demanded 700,000 *patacas** from the *Santa Casa de Misericordia* and the moiety of all the goods of the inhabitants. After much fruitless dallying, the fight was resumed.

The fight continues

The Mughal forces pressed on and the handful of Portuguese gave up the defence of Bali where all the Churches and the buildings of the Augustinians were situated and retired southwards to their main town of Hooghly. While retiring, the Portuguese set fire to their buildings and to the great Augustinian convent. The Moors who occupied Bali completed the destruction of the Portuguese buildings but spared the Jesuit College where their officers stayed. From the 31st July the Moors began to attack the main town of Hooghly and that little band of Portuguese under the command of Captain Manoel de Azavedo offered a stubborn resistance although without any defences.

The Moors hurled repeated attacks, the fleet co-operating now and then, but each time they were repulsed. Hardly a

* *Pataca* was a silver coin worth about two rupees eight annas.

day passed without fighting. The Portuguese were so few in number that they kept themselves mainly on the defensive, content to work as much havoc as possible in the enemy ranks. Meanwhile the Moors received reinforcements, artillery and ships from Rajmahal, Dacca and Burdwan. They dug up new trenches and mined the whole of the Bandel. They launched a naval and a land attack, but the Portuguese ships stood the attack bravely. Fighting continued in this way for a month and half. The Moors entered again into negotiations and the Portuguese eager to rid themselves of the scourge paid 100,000 *tangas* (rupees) to them. They however never meant to make peace but only under false promises to extort money from the Portuguese in order to pay the soldiers that were clamouring for salaries. Meanwhile Martim Affonso was preparing to bar the flight of the Portuguese down the river. He bridged the river with a pontoon of boats and also threw across the river many thick cables and iron-chains. Fire-ships were kept in readiness and trenches were dug along the banks of the river for more than five leagues.

The Flight, Sept. 24th 1632

Hostilities were again resumed and the Portuguese unable to hold the town any longer took to their vessels under cover of darkness and began their disastrous flight on the night of September 24th. About fifty or sixty Portuguese remained in Hooghly and kept on the fire to give an idea that the town was not evacuated, but on the next day the Moors launched a violent attack capturing the town*. The description of the flight down the river by Fr. Cabral, is one of the grandest pages in the history

* The town was therefore captured according to Fr. Cabral on the 25th September, 1632. The Portuguese official account fixes the date of the capture on the 29th September and the *Bādshāhnāmā* on the 14th Rabi-al-Awul 1241 (Elliot). Stewart, however, gives the date 14th Rabi-al-Awul 1042 (*Hist. of Bengal*). According to Fr. Cabral the siege lasted exactly for three months and according to the *Bādshāhnāmā* for three months and half.

of the Portuguese in the East. The bravery the Portuguese ships displayed has been seldom surpassed. In fact the defence of Hooghly can only be compared to D. João de Castro's defence of Diu, and well may Fr. Cabral say, "Ours did wonders never heard of before". Each of the Portuguese *pataches*, and there were many, contained about twenty-five or thirty Portuguese and some natives and few falconets and guns. With these they had to pass through the narrow width of the Hooghly river opposing five hundred ships, a land force of a hundred thousand strong and a hundred and twenty pieces of artillery protected by trenches extending on either side of the river for a distance of five leagues. The *pataches* commanded by Pantaleão de Seixas, Luis de Maya, Pedro de Couto and Gomes Bareiros did wonders. But the tactics of Khwaja Shere and Martim Affonso cut off all means of escape. Most of the Portuguese ships were sunk. On September 27th Pedro de Couto's boat was blown up and it went down with 60,000 *tangas* belonging to private individuals. The widow of Pedro de Couto and many Portuguese and natives jumped into the river and kept on swimming and diving until they were rescued by six boats that had managed to escape. Even these six boats met with opposition at Betor (Howrah) in the iron chains that were put across the river. The *patache* of Domingos (Ds[os]) De Seixas cut asunder an iron chain and passed proudly on leading two other boats but capsized further down. At the pass of Betor the *pataches* of Luis de Maya and of Pantaleão de Seixas were lost, after desperate and heroic fighting against both land and sea forces. Some Portuguese ships however escaped safely carrying three thousand people, a hundred and odd Portuguese, sixty or seventy Portuguese ladies (whites) the rest being country-born people and slaves. The King of Arakan sent to the Portuguese an expedition consisting of some galleys, and manned by Portuguese soldiers but the help arrived when the tragedy was over and the town of Hooghly had passed into the hands of the Mughals.

The Losses on Either Side

About a hundred Portuguese were either killed or capcured; besides them four Augustinians, three Jesuits, six or seven secular priests and twenty-five married soldiers with their boys and girls lost their lives.* Fr. Cabral does not give the number of the "slaves and the coloured people" lost, but the *Bādshāhnāmā* says that ten thousand Feringhis and *rayots* died. This number is probably correct if it includes all the Portuguese, their descendants and the natives who died during the siege and in course of their flight. They could not be, however, all fighting men whose number did not exceed a thousand (300 Portuguese and 600 natives) and a vast majority must have been of the civil population. In the *Batavia Dagh Register 1631-1634*, it is mentioned that the Dutch heard that 1,560 Portuguese had been killed and 1,500 taken prisoners. The Mughals captured four thousand Christian prisoners and sent them to Agra. Regarding the Portuguese fleet, the *Bādshāhnāmā* says that out of 64 *Dinghas* (large vessels) 57 *grabs* and 200 *Jalies*, only one *Ghrab* and two *Jalies* escaped.†

On the Mughal side the losses were enormous. The *Bādshāhnāmā* admits that only 1,000 of the Imperial army died in the conflict. Fr. Cabral holds as probable the estimate which a Mughal gave him in Arakan, namely 4,300 dead or missing.‡ This number does not agree with the number of Faria y Souza who says§ 50,000 Mughals were killed. It may, however, be taken as the probable one. As to the vessels of the Mughals, Fr. Cabral says "they lost 32 boats in the fire

* Fr. Cabral, *Catholic Herald of India*, March 27, 1918, p. 243.

† Elliot, *Hist. of India*, Vol. VII, p. 34.

‡ *Catholic Herald of India*, March 27, 1918 p. 243.

§ *Asia Portugueza*, Stevens's Trans., Vol. III, p. 403.

raft engagement more than 60 in the pontoon affair, and more than a hundred of their ships remained stranded on the shore, disabled for ever".*

The Survivors

The three thousand survivors, among whom was Fr. Cabral, fled to the Saugor Island where they took refuge, but sometime after a plague broke out, and those who escaped its ravages migrated to Hījilī and Banja. Meanwhile they obtained permission from the King of Arakan to build a fortress in Saugor and Manoel de Azavedo proceeded with the work. The King of Arakan who was in league with the Portuguese of Dianga granted many other concessions to them and to the survivors of Hooghly. He ordered the captains of his fleet to be always in readiness to help the Portuguese in Saugor if the Mughals attempted to do them any harm.

The Prisoners

On the other hand the fate of the four thousand Christian prisoners taken to Agra, where they reached in July 1633, was indeed lamentable. Manrique dwells at length on the martyrdom of these men and fortunately for the historian, completes the description of Fr. Cabral. Bernier in a few words summarises the cruelties to which the prisoners were subjected in Agra.† He says, they were all made slaves; the handsome women were shut up in the seraglio, the old women and others were distributed among different *Omrahs*. The young lads were circumcised and made pages; and men of age renounced for the most part their faith, either terrified by the threatenings they heard daily, that they should be trampled upon by elephants or drawn away by fair promises. Some Friars persisted in their faith and the Missionaries of Agra, who notwithstanding all this unhappiness remained in their houses, found means after-

---

* *Catholic Herald of India, ut supra.*

† Bernier's *Travels* etc. Constable Ed. p. 177.

wards, partly by friends, partly by money, to get many of them away, and to have them conveyed to Goa, and to other places belonging to the Portuguese. According to the Portuguese records the Viceroy of Goa really sent an expedition to Bengal in 1643 to rescue the Portuguese survivors. *

* Danvers, *Report on the Portuguese Records* etc. p. 29.

CHAPTER XIII

THE RETURN OF THE PORTUGUESE TO HOOGHLY

It is really surprizing how the Portuguese established themselves again in Hooghly scarcely a year after the siege of Hooghly. This is all the more surprising because Shāh Jahān was at the time badly disposed towards the Christians and had not ceased persecuting them, even up to 1635. Yet it is true the Portuguese returned to Bengal with full liberty and a grant of 777 *bighas* of rent-free land by July 1633. The account of their return is found in a letter (July 17, 1633) written from Harishpur (Orissa) to Mr. Cartwright of Balasore regarding the possibilities of English trade in Bengal.* The writer says "Those Portinggalls whilome exspelled [from] Hugly hath found greate favour with Shawgahan (Shah Jahan) and re-entered that place to the number of 20 persones ; hows cavidall (whose capital) for theirs commensing a new investment is the third part of there goods formerly cessed on, which with large priveliges and tashareefes (presents) with honer the King hath beestowed on them. So that our exspectation [of] Hugly is frusstrayt and I feare likwise Pippoly will n [ot by] us be obtainened beeing a nancient (convenient) Randyvoes of the [irs] how som 10 parsones have latly complained to this Nabob of our seeking to put them from that porte ; have answered we intended on such matter but only for Bollasary [Balasore] or Harssapoore

The Return to Hooghly, 1633

---

* Forster, *The English Factories in India*, 1630-1633, p. 308-309. This letter is not signed. Sainsbury in his *Calendar* supposed that the letter was written by John Powell (Poule) and Yule accepting the conjecture printed part of the letter in his *Hedge's Diary*, Vol. III p. 177. The fact is however that John Powell does not seem to have been in Harishpur until Sept. 19. C. R. Wilson therefore changed the date of the letter to Oct. 17 (*Early Annals*, *Vol. I*, *p. 17*). Forster discussing this question in a note (p. 307) concludes that it was Thomas Colley who wrote the letter.

(Harishpur) so with great delassa (encouragement) they were dismissed." It will be seen from this letter that the English agent distinctly says that the Portuguese who had been expelled had now returned with such powers that all hopes of the English to establish trade in Hooghly and even in Piplī were frustrated. This is well confirmed by Frei João de S. Nicolau in his memorial * of 1785 and also by Frei Luiz de Santa Rita, the prior and administrator of the Convent of Bandel in another memorial † prepared by him in 1820 for the Provincial of the Augustinians who had been requested by the Portuguese Viceroy of Goa to furnish information about the grant of seven hundred and seventy-seven *bighas* of land which he wanted to transfer for the Crown of Portugal. Frei Luiz de Santa Rita reported that in the archives of Bandel he found a MSS. memorial from which it was clear that Shāh Jahān's *farman* was given in 1633 to the Augustinian Missionaries and the Christians of Bandel. He added that this *farman* was lost in 1756 when Sirāj-ud-daulā besieged the English in Hooghly and sacked Bandel. He however found in the archives of the Convent a copy of the *farman* written in Persian with a Portuguese version attached to it.

The Privileges of the Portuguese

Besides the grant of 777 *bighas* of rent-free land it conceded to the Portuguese the following seventeen religious and commercial privileges‡ :—

---

* J. F. J. Biker's *Coleccão de Tratados e Concertos de Pazes, Tom. XII*, Lisboa, 1886 pp. 17-25. J. H. Cunha Rivara first published it as an addition to Teixeira Pinto's *Memorias Sobre as Possessões Portuguezas na India*, Nova-Goa, 1859.

† Biker's *Collecção etc. ut supra*, Tom. XII, pp. 12-17. It was first published by Cunha Rivara in *O Chronista de Tissuari* Vol. I, pp. 60-62.

‡ The English translations of the Memorials of Frei Nicolau and of Frei Luiz de Santa Rita were first published by Fr. H. Hosten S. J. in *Bengal Past and Present*, Jan.-Mar., 1915 pp. 106-118. Regarding these privileges I have not, however, availed myself of Fr. Hosten's translation wherever I found that it did not strictly conform to the original.

1. That at the time of the Mass, no Moor, or *pião*, (footman, soldier) shall have the power to enter the Church to cause a disturbance.

2. That the Padre of Bandel shall administer justice to its inhabitants in all matters except in crimes punishable with death, not excepting theft.

3. That the Padre shall give the property of the deceased to their heirs or creditors, and the surplus to the poor, and the *Sercar* (government) shall not interfere in this matter.

4. That, if the owners of the ships of both the Portuguese and the Dutch which land there, happen to die, the *Dorbar** shall not interfere with any of the ship's goods, but only the custom-dues for the said goods shall belong to him (the *Dorbar*).

5. That the Dutch ships shall not have the power to seize the Portuguese ships coming to Bengal.

6. That the Portuguese ships coming to Bengal shall sell their goods in any harbour of Bengal, and that no change shall be made in the custom-dues.

7. That, should the slaves of the Christians run away and be caught again in any place whatever, no Moor shall have the power to hinder them (being caught) and still less to make them Moors.

8. That no Dorbar shall be allowed to retain the servants or employees (*officiaes*) of whatever class of Christians if they run away to another territory.

9. That, in time of scarcity, no ships shall be allowed to take in rice for exportation.

10. If the Christians are found to live in concubinage, the Dorbar shall have nothing to do with this matter.

---

* *Dorbar* or *Durbar* means a court, levee or government. Here, however, it seems to stand for a government official as, a little below, *Dorbar* is qualified by *nenhum* (no).

11. Should fires break out in the houses of Bandel, and bambus, stakes and straw be necessary for rebuilding them, the Sercar of the Moor shall not have the power to levy tolls, (*tomar direitos*) or to prevent their being bought or obtained from any other place.

12. That, if some married families come from Europe, and wish to take a house to live in this Houguli, it shall be given them free and no customs (*fretes*) shall be taken from them.

13. That all eatables coming to this Bandel, shall not be liable to custom-duties.

14. That in criminal cases the father shall not pay for his son, nor the son for his father, but each one for himself.

15. That families coming from Europe shall have the power to remain here for what time they like, and no one shall have the power to stop them, when they wish to return to Europe.

16. That the Fordar (*Faujdar*) shall not have the power to call all the Christians for military service in case of war, but only four or five of the oldest and the best counsellors.

17. That the two *xequis* (Shaikhs) who were down the river (*para baixo* : lower down) should not take from the Franguis more than was at first customary.

In 1641 Shāh Shuja granted a new *farman* confirming all the privileges of the first *farman* and promising the Portuguese his protection. Toynbee also refers to this new *farman*.* Dr. Wise who says he based his Statistical Account of Hooghly on MSS records and must have, probably, seen the document of Frei Rita or perhaps the *farman* of 1646 which seems to have escaped the ravages of 1746, says of the re-settlement of the Portuguese,† "A firman was promulgated by beat of tom-tom through all the country ordering the immediate return of the

* *Sketch of the Administration of Hughly.*

† *Bengal Catholic Herald*, 21st May, 1842.

captives (Portuguese) who were loaded with presents and sent back to their former residence. The Portuguese thus received into favour obtained a charter (sunud) signed by the Emperor by which he allowed them to return to Hooghly and to build a town to the north of the former Fort, still known by the Europeans as Bandel and by the natives by that of Balaghur (strong house). The land thus assigned to the Christians consisting of 777 beeghas was given free of rent and the Friars were declared exempted from the authority of the Subadars, Fouzdars and other officers of state. They were even allowed to exercise magisterial power with regard to Christians but were denied that of life and death—at the same time the Emperor ordered all his officers and subjects in Bengal to assist the brave Portuguese. The Christians returned to Bengal in 1633..."

The Explanation of the Return

It is difficult to make out how the Portuguese could have been allowed to come to Hooghly, and given such great power by the Emperor only ten months after the siege of Hooghly and at a time when he persisted in persecuting the Portuguese and the Christians in other parts of his Empire. Almost all the writers on Hooghly, Rev. Long. Dr. Wise, Crawford, Asiaticus and others attributed the return of the Portuguese to a miracle worked by God in the case of Frei João de Cruz who was they say among the captives taken to Delhi. The first account of this story about Frei João de Cruz's miracle was given in 1785 by Frei João de S. Nicolau who was prior of Bandel 1782-84, in a memorial drawn up by him after his retirement to Goa. The later writers especially Asiaticus and Dr. Wise added much to what Frei Nicolau related and the recollection of which, he said, was fresh in the memory of the people living there. Between the occurrence of the miracle, it may be added, and its account by Frei Nicolau a full century and a half had passed.

Divested of its embellishments, the story of the miracle is that after all the Christian prisoners from Hooghly were dealt with, Frei João de Cruz, being well known for his piety, was reserved for a special punishment. The Emperor and his court having assembled on a gala day Frei de Cruz was placed in a large hall before them and a wild and infuriated elephant was let loose. To the surprise of all, the elephant did no harm to the kneeling friar but on the contrary lay prostrate before him in reverence and caressed him with his trunk. This created such a profound impression on the Emperor's mind that he pardoned Frei de Cruz, whereupon, the elephant as an expression of joy made three profound bows before the Emperor. The Emperor then granted Frei de Cruz and the Christians of Hooghly a charter allowing them to return to Hooghly and build a new town.

The Miracle

Fr. Hosten has very forcibly questioned the truth of this story and asserted that Frei João de Cruz never went to Agra at all and that Shāh Jahān did not grant liberty to the Christians brought from Hooghly.* He adduces the authority of Manrique who saw Frei João de Cruz in Hooghly in 1628, who was in Arakan from 1630 to 1635 and again visited Bengal in 1640, and who surely would have known everything about the miracle if it were true. Manrique far from referring to any such story, says that Frei João de Cruz was severely wounded when trying to escape from the siege of Hooghly that he was saved from death only by a miracle and that he lived in great sanctity in Goa where he died. "If Frei João da Cruz" asks Fr. Hosten, "had been the chief hero in the wonderful events which legend has grouped around his name, how is it that the Jesuit letters from Agra say nothing about him, and that Manrique says hardly more about him for the period

---

* *Bengal Past and Present*, Jan.-Mar. 1915, pp. 49-50 and *J. A. S. B* 1911, Vol. VII, No. 3 pp. 53-56.

1633-38 than what we have related ; how is it that in the large collection of letters of the English and the Dutch factors or in the accounts of travellers we do not find the slightest allusion to the scene of the rescue alleged to have occurred at Agra ; chiefly how it is that the writer of his menology who intended the private edification of his brethren in religion should not have picked up the most marvellous facts of his history ? The reason must be that he did not find them in the Augustinian histories or that he found them contradicted or self-contradicting". These arguments and Manrique's evidence conclusively prove that Frei João de Cruz could not have worked the miracle which tradition and modern writers have ascribed to him. It cannot be denied, however, that by itself, the grant of land by Shāh Jahān only ten months after the siege of Hooghly and at a time when he was persecuting the Portuguese elsewhere is nothing short of a miracle. On the other hand Manrique says that Frei João de Cruz, indeed, escaped death from his festering wounds only by a miracle. Seeing that Frei João de Cruz's recovery was indeed associated with a miracle it is quite possible that his name has been mixed up with another miraculous event, or a wonderful physical occurrence which had actually taken place. Fr. Hosten suggests that Shāh Jahān never made this grant, though the copy of the original *farman* which was destroyed in 1756, says that in 1633 'Emperor Sajan Mahameo Sujakam' made the grant of land and the privileges to the Fathers and Christians of Bandel. If the Christian captives taken from Hooghly did not get the concession of *777 bighas* of land and other privileges from Shāh Jahān, what other Portuguese could have got them and who gave them ? The constructive part of Father Hosten's arguments and the explanation of this concession is not as striking as the destructive one. He surmises that perhaps through a bribe Mīr Muhammad Azīm Khān, Governor of Bengal, 1632-39, made the grant on the sly to a few Portuguese families (from where ?) and that this grant was probably a confirmation of a part or whole of the grant made by Akbar to Tavares before 1580. It is not probable that Azim Khān could have taken such a step when Shāh Jahān's wrath had not yet abated and when it was quite certain that the Emperor would come to know of such an important concession through some of the numerous Mughals who were in Bengal and who could not have been well disposed towards the Portuguese only a few months after the siege. As a matter fàct, Azim Khān continued to be Governor of Bengal for six years after this suggested treachery with full confidence of the Emperor. Hence all that can be said at the present state of our historian researches is that the return of the Portuguese to Hooghly, under the sanction of Shāh Jahān only a few months after the seige, remains unexplained.

The Property of the Crown or the Church

The Augustinians took possession of the 777 *bighas* of rent-free land and out of them about 280 *bighas* still belong to the Bandel Convent, the rest being lost through many litigations and bad management of the Priors. It is questionable, however, whether the grant of land was made to the Church, or to the Portuguese government. In 1782 the Portuguese ambassador in London learnt from an English merchant who had returned home from Madras that the Portuguese possessed an important commercial port near Calcutta managed by some runaway Portuguese who lived without any order or government but who raised a Portuguese flag, maintained a priest and abided by his authority. The Portuguese ambassador having informed the Home Government about this Portuguese possession, the Viceroy at Goa was asked to furnish detailed information regarding it. The Viceroy however knew no more about the affairs in Bengal than the Government at Lisbon and asked the Provincial of

HOOGHLY SURVEY MAP OF 1886, SHEET NO. 1, SECT. 1, SCALE 16″=1 MILE

The Portuguese Settlement of 1633 included all the foreshore from the present jail, which is to the south of the area covered by the map, to the northern limit of the Circuit House Compound.

the Bengal Missions to furnish the desired infomation. As a result of those dealings, Fr. João de S. Nicolau, who had been many years Prior of the Bandel Convent, drew up in 1785 after having retired to Goa a memorial, referred to above. In this memorial he stated that the flag, raised in Bandel, was that of Our Lady of Rosary and not of the Portuguese Government and that the lands or the settlement belonged to the Augustinians, since the *farman* was granted to Fr. João de Cruz by the Mughal Emperor "signed with his own hand and sealed with his royal seal, bestowing on him 760 bighas of land in a place left to the Father's choice." When the Portuguese Government raised the question of the property again in 1820 and asked the Augustinian Provincial for a copy of the *farman*, Frei Luis de Santa Rita, vicar of Bandel drew up another memorial in which he gave a detailed account of the settlement. He stated the *farman* was granted by the Mughal Emperor to the Fathers and the Christians, that it was destroyed during Sirāj-ud-daulā's sack of Hooghly, and that its copy existed in the Bandel Convent, from which he had copied the seventeen privileges they enjoyed.

From what the Augustinian Fathers asserted in the memorials, it would appear that the Bandel lands belonged to the Church and not to the Portuguese Government, or to private persons. According to Manrique, an Augustinian friar, the Augustinian Fathers always refused to accept the grant of lands. "The Padchá or Emperor Acabar," he says,* "as well as his son Zia-hianguir or Ianguir as he is more commonly called, tried more than once to give the Fathers lands for their maintenance, or assign to them mainás, that is a monthly allowance to be paid from their nacassares or Royal treasuries, but the religious of St. Augustin always refused to accept such income, not only in this Empire (Bengal) but also in Persia

* Manrique, Fr. Cardon's Trans. *Bengal Past and Present*, 1915 Vol. XII, p. 50.

and other infidel kingdoms where they live." In view of this, it would seem that the Augustinians could not have accepted the lands even if they were given to them. The grant was made in 1633 and Manrique's experience is of the same time, since he was in Bengal and Arakan from 1628-1636 and again in 1640. Thomas Colley or John Poule said that twenty Portuguese occupied the Bandel lands, without mentioning, however, whether they represented the Church or the Government.* There is a petition which a Portuguese named George Germain made, on the 31st December 1784, to the Queen of Portugal requesting her government to take possession of the lands that he declared belonged to the government and not to the Church.† This petition is earlier in date than the memorial of Frei João de S. Nicolau by two months and did not seem to have reached Portugal before the Portuguese minister in London communicated to his government the information he had received through an English source. George Germain maintains in the petition that the settlement of Bandel belonged to the Portuguese ; that when the number of European Portuguese was diminishing in Bandel the Augustinians took charge of the lands and that these Fathers thinking themselves masters of the property lost the *farman* under conditions which he describes. He states that Fr. da Cruz influenced Shah Jahān to confirm the earlier grant of 777 *bighas* of land to the Portuguese, though he does not refer to any miracle. It is difficult to say how much credence the different statements deserve. It may be, taken for granted on the authority of John Poule or Thomas Colley, at least until the copies of the original *farmans* are discovered, that the grant of the lands was made to twenty private Portuguese persons who subsequently made

* *Vide* p. 141.

† This important document has been published in *O Oriente Português*, 1906, Vol. III, pp. 129-134. For its translation *Vide* Addenda II.

over the lands to the Church. Frey de Santa Rita said in 1820 that the Prior of Bandel delivered Shāh Shuja's *farman* of 1646 to the English government in 1786. It is possible, therefore, to find it in the Imperial Records Department. German in his Appeal of 1784, gives detailed directions regarding the finding of the copies of the *farmans* in the Mughal Records (*vide* Addenda II).

After the Return

In whatever way the Portuguese might have settled again in Hooghly in 1633, they never regained their former power and political importance. As it has been already said, the Portuguese power in the East had long begun to decline and the Portuguese that came to India at this time were no longer the Portuguese of the days of Albuquerque. Besides, it was the time when European rival nations had come to Bengal and were striving to establish their supremacy by supplanting the power of the Portuguese. The Dutch obtained a *farman* from Shāh Jahān in 1625 to erect a factory in Hooghly and to trade in Bengal, and the Portuguese who had wrested the trade from the Moors, when their power was at its zenith even in Europe, could not compete with this brave little nation. The English who were for long powerless in Bengal on account of the Portuguese supremacy, obtained permission from Shāh Jahān to trade in Bengal in 1638 and gradually other nations stepped in where the Portuguese had an undisputed sway. Still the Portuguese trade continued to flourish to a considerable extent.

It is thus that the Venetian Manucci speaks of the Portuguese whom he saw in Hooghly about 1660 : "Here I found the chief inhabitants of Hooghly, all of them rich Portuguese for in those days they alone were allowed to deal in salt throughout the province of Bengal."* He also adds "there were many Portuguese of good sense, of good family, well establish-

* *Storia do Mogor*, Irvine's Ed., Vol. II, p. 89.

ed merchants at Hugli." Six years later Bernier says* that there were eight or nine thousand Portuguese and *mesticos* at Hooghly and that the Portuguese, driven from other quarters by the Dutch, resorted there. In 1669-1679 the number of the Portuguese and their descendants all over Bengal was no less than 20,000, according to Bowrey,† half of whom were in Hooghly. As in the palmiest days of the Portuguese in Hooghly, the number of the pure Portuguese did not exceed three hundred, Bowrey's numbers evidently include most of their descendants. Regarding the Portuguese trade in Hooghly Bowrey adds that many Portuguese ships sailed there transporting sundry commodities.‡

Commercial Rivalry

Though the English and the Dutch had obtained important commercial concessions, they met with a keen rivalry on the part of the earlier traders, though the latter had lost many of their own privileges. In the *Diaries* of Streynsham Master, who was Governor of Fort St. George and agent deputed by the Court of Directors to Bengal, several pages are devoted to the description of the business of a Portuguese merchant named João Gomes de Soito.§ This rich merchant rebuilt the Bandel Church (Hooghly) in 1661, and was buried in the Bandel Churchyard but unfortunately the tablet with the inscription on his tomb, which Asiaticus copied in 1803 is no longer to be found.|| On the ground that the E. I. Company refused to pay him a sum of about Rs. 6,000 due to him in 1652 on a consignment of cinnamon, sent by him to Persia in a Company's ship, he managed to have the English factors seized and imprisoned. A few years after, his son Pascal and his widow referred the

* Bernier's *Travels*, Constable's Ed., p. 439.
† *Countries Round the Bay of Bengal*, Temple's Ed., p. 195.
‡ *Ibidem* p. 133.
§ *Diaries of Streynsham Master*, Temple's Ed., *Vide Index s. v.* De Soito.
|| *Vide* p. 230

matter to the Nawab of Dacca and obtained a decree that the Company should pay him a thousand rupees. Such disputes frequently arose among the European traders in Bengal. In the struggle the Portuguese eventually fell. But up to the end of the seventeenth century they may be said to have maintained against powerful odds their sway over the commercial activities of Bengal. In the eighteenth century the Portuguese played a subordinate part in Bengal and their history merges into that of their descendants.

CHAPTER XIV

EASTERN BENGAL

The Fall of Gonsalves and the Rise of Piracy

The Fall of Gonsalves, 1615-1616

The power which Sebastião Gonsalves had acquired in Sandwīp was not destined to last long. In 1615 Gonsalves conceived the plan of conquering Arakan. Though he had always ruled as an absolute and independent prince he proposed to the Portuguese Viceroy in Goa offering to acknowledge the suzerainty of the King of Portugal and deliver every year a galleot of rice either at Malacca or Goa as a yearly tribute if he would help him in the conquest of Arakan. He further assured the vast treasures of the King of Arakan would be at their disposal. The Viceroy Jeronymo de Azavedo, who was quite pleased with this offer, fitted out an expedition of fourteen galleots, a flyboat, and a pink under the command of Dom Francisco de Menezes Roxo, the former Governor of Ceylon*. This expedition arrived on the 3rd of October 1615 and after a consultation with Gonsalves it was decided that Menezes should attack Arakan, the head quarters of the King and that Gonsalves should follow him. A new power had however come to help the Arakanese, a power that eventually contributed a good deal towards the downfall of the Portuguese in the East. On the 15th October the Portuguese saw a Dutch fleet coming down the river composed of such a large number of ships that, as Faria y Souza says†, the Portuguese could not see the end of it.

---

* This expedition is described by Bocarro, *Decada XIII*, and by Faria y Souza, *Asia*, Stevens, Vol. III, p. 226.

† *Asia Portugueza*, Stevens, Vol. III. p. 224 *et seq.*

Against this force Menezes had to defend only with sixteen vessels, nay, only with fourteen, because one had fled and another had gone in pursuit of it. Yet they engaged the combined fleet of the Dutch and the Arakanese. The fight lasted the whole day. Though the Portuguese lost four galleots they wrought terrific havoc among the Dutch. In the evening the Dutch retreated thinking fresh succour had come to the Portuguese, while it was only the pink that had gone in search of the running vessel. Gonsalves now joined Menezes with fifty ships and they arranged themselves in two squadrons. The fight commenced again and all throughout, the advantage was on the side of Portuguese, but at about sunset D. Francisco de Menezes fell struck with two musket balls. Ebbtide then set in and the fleets parted. The Victory was more on the side of the Portuguese than of the Dutch.* About two hundred Portuguese died and were buried in the sea. The Portuguese sailed back to Sandwīp and D. Luiz de Azavedo who had succeeded Menezes in command, returned with his squadron to Goa inspite of Gonsalves's repeated requests not to do so. Many of Gonsalves's men took this opportunity to abandon him and returned with D. Luis de Azavedo to Goa. In the following year (1616) Gonsalves being quite abandoned by many of his followers, the King of Arakan invaded Sandwīp, defeated Gonsalves and took possession of the island besides some-other islands in the Sundarbans. Gonsalves was, as Faria y Souza says, reduced to his former miserable condition.

Character of Gonsalves

In estimating the character of Sebastião Gonsalves one cannot ignore from what beginnings he rose to be a potentate, whose alliance was sought for by the ruling princes of Bengal, though more from

* L. S. S. O'Malley says in the *Chittagong Gazeteer p. 28*, that the Portuguese were defeated by the Dutch. This is inaccurate according to the Portuguese historians. The most that can be said is that the victory was indecisive.

fear of his power than from a friendly feeling for him as a ruler. He was an adventurer, unscrupulous and remorseless. But he was not, as he is supposed to be, a pirate, in the strict sense of the word. He committed at the outset of his career some piratical raids on the coast of Arakan, but it was in revenge for the massacre of Dianga. There is no evidence that during the eight or nine years of his rule (1607-1616) in Sandwip, he fostered piracy. However, many of his treacherous acts stain his character with the darkest blots. As in Rob Roy of old, wickedness and worth are often curiously blended together. It is wonderful, indeed, how Gonsalves was able maintain his sovereignty, beset as he was with such powerful enemies as the Mughals and the King of Arakan, not to speak of the chiefs of the other principalities that lay near his kingdom. Referring himself to Faria y Souza's remarks that the kingdom of Gonsalves passed like a shadow, that his pride was humbled and his vileness punished, H. Beveridge justly makes the following observations,* "such are the unsympathising remarks of the Portuguese historian about a man who at least possessed vigour and ability, and who owed his fall in great measure to the impetuosity of the Portuguese officer who was sent from Goa to assist him, but who was too proud or too rash to co-operate fully with him. The Viceroy was also to blame, for he directed his officer not to wait for Gonzales. We cannot but think that if Gonzales had been an Englishman and his historian of the same nationality, we would have heard a great deal about Anglo-Saxon energy, the Barseker-spirit and the Vikings." If D. Luis de Azavedo had, indeed, co-operated with Gonsalves and had not sailed back to Goa, the the fate of the Portuguese possession of Sandwīp might have been different. Incidentally, the dispersal of the Portuguese in Eastern Bengal and Arakan would not have taken place if

* *District of Bákarganj*, p.38.

they had not lost their possession of Sandwīp, and thus no occasion would have arisen for them to live mainly by piracy, which has sullied their name.

The Rise of Piracy

From the time of the fall of Gonsalves upto 1665, the history of the Portuguese in Eastern Bengal is a history of the Portuguese in their worst form. The fall of Gonsalves did not mean the end of his men. The vast rivers of Bengal and their banks became their homes. Schooled as they were not to recognise any law or authority, they sought the means of subsistence in plundering and piracy. Arising as a necessity, piracy eventually became an art, a trade. It was a time, morever, when plundering was generally accepted as the best method of avenging wrongs, real or supposed and of punishing the enemy. The Afghan Kings of Bengal, the Kings of Arakan and of Tippera ravaged one another's territories without the least scruple. But this game was generally carried on from land. The Portuguese introduced a new element with their fast sloops and newer methods of ship-building, so that depredations began to be carried more from the sea and the rivers of the delta. The Portuguese were neither the originators of these nefarious practices nor the only culprits. The Mughals themselves indulged in them and the Arakanese or the Maghs were the greatest of all plunderers. Wonderful legends connected with the famous pirate and bandit Dilal Khān are still current in Sandwīp. He is said, however, to have protected the poor, though he plundered the rich.* It was Husain Bey, the general of Shaista Khān who eventually captured Dilal Khān and confined him in a prison at Dacca, where he ended his days. Still more striking is the story of the English free-booter J. Shepherd, who made the Sunderbans the scene of his piratical exploits until he was arrested and banished for life only a few years ago.

* J. E. Webster, *Noakhali Gazetteer*, pp. 19-20.

The Offer of Chittagong to the Mughals

An event occurred in 1638 which gave an additional impetus to the game of piracy in its most frightful form. Ever since the Mughals had made themselves masters of Bengal, they were bent upon conquering Chittagong from the King of Arakan and, if possible, the whole of his kingdom. A favourable opportunity arose in 1638. Matak Rai, the Governor of Chittagong rebelled against the King of Arakan, named Islam Khān Mushaddi, and acknowledging himself the vassal of the Mughal Emperor handed over Chittagong, though nominally to the Mughal Governor of Bengal. This action of the Governor of Chittagong did not materialize into anything, but it served to light up the fire of a long-standing enmity. To revenge on the Mughal kingdom of Bengal, the King of Arakan made friends with the Portuguese adventurers, took them into his service, paid them high salaries and settled them in Dianga. With their help he built vessels large enough to carry cannon. Thus equipped he began ravaging and laying waste the Mughal territory, and extended his depredations even up to Dacca. These cruel practices of the Arakanese and the Portuguese, to which the people of Bengal were subjected, continued till 1665 when Shaista Khan conquered Chittagong and broke their power for ever.

Portuguese Relations with Piracy

Various statements have been made to the effect that all the Portuguese in Bengal were generally pirates or adventurers, and even to-day in the folk tales of Bengal the name of the Portuguese is always associated with piracy. Nothing could be farther from the truth, than a generalized statement of this kind. It was only the Eastern and not Western Bengal that was a haunt of the Portuguese adventurers. These men were taken into the employ of the Arakanese who in conjunction with them devastated the southern part of Bengal, especially the Sunderbans. The Portuguese of Western Bengal were quite a different section. In the Hooghly river there were, however, a few Portuguese pirates about twelve miles above the Saugor Island whence the river or one of its branches at that part of its course was known as the *Rogue's River.** Their field of operations was the coast of Hījīlī (Midnapore) and Orissa. These men who had leagued themselves with the Arakanese were not of the type of the Portuguese from Hooghly, but were outlaws and fugitives from Goa and other Portuguese places. They were disowned by their own Government in Goa and were not recognized by their own brethren in Hooghly. It is true the Portuguese Viceroy sent help to Gonsalves, but then he was not a pirate but an independent prince who agreed to pay a yearly tribute of a ship of rice to the King of Portugal, in return for the help received. Even before Gonsalves and his troops had taken to buccaneering, Stephen Palmeyro who was an aged and a genuine type of Portuguese, refused to command them because they had committed a few justifiable depredations on the coast of Arakan out of revenge on the massacre of the Portuguese in Dianga. Ruy Vaz Pereira who saw in Chittagong a Moorish ship, built after the Portuguese fashion, being used in privateering, seized it because such practices would unjustly sully the name of the Portuguese.†

The Pirate Damião Bernaldes

An excellent example of how different the real Portuguese in Bengal were from the adventurers in the Sunderbans, was afforded on the very coast of Bengal. Nuno da Cunha, the Portuguese Governor, gave in 1531, to Damião Bernaldes a license for a voyage to Bengal.‡ After rounding the Cape Comorin he turned a corsair and in Nicobar captured a Moorish

---

* A Hamilton, *A New Account of the East Indies*, Vol. II, p. 3. Also *vide*, *Yule*, *Hobson-Jobson* s. v. Rogue's River.

† *Vide* pp. 30-31.

‡ Castanheda, *Historia*, Vol. VIII, p. 46. Also Correa, *Lendas* Vol. III, p 446.

ship worth £9000. Nuno da Cunha, on hearing of this, asked Khājeh Shiāb-ud-dīn, who as already said,* was a friend of the Portuguese, to seize Bernaldes when he landed in Chittagong or else to kill him and his crew on the spot. There were then seventeen Portuguese vessels in Chittagong which in concert with Khājeh Shiāb-ud-dīn awaited the arrival of Bernaldes. When this pirate actually arrived they did him no harm immediately, believing that he would ask for pardon and give up his mode of life. Far from doing so he seized a influential Moor and though his men who had landed were captured, he refused to exchange this Moor with his men except for a ransom of £2000. The Portuguese spared no efforts to capture him and he was at last caught in their settlement of Negapatam, sent to the Governor in Goa in chains and banished for ten years, during which he died. Such was the punishment accorded by the Portuguese to the pirates. When the Portuguese became the masters of the whole Bay and rivers of Bengal they indeed, enforced their principle of not allowing any ships to sail without their passes but they granted these passes freely and these ships were absolutely safe except when they fell into the hands of the adventurers lurking at the mouths of the Ganges. Even the Muhammadan historian Khafi Khān gives the credit to the Portuguese while he has much to complain against the English. Speaking generally of the Portuguese he says† "On the sea they (Portuguese) are not like the English; and do not attack other ships, except those ships which have not received their pass according to rule, or the ships of Arabia or Maskat with which two countries they have a long-standing enmity, and they attack each other whenever opportunity occurs. If a ship from a distant port is wrecked and falls into their hands they look upon it as their prize." The author of the *Bādshāh-*

---

* *Vide* p. 33.

† Elliot, *Hist. of India*, Vol. VII, p. 344.

nāmā has another story about the Portuguese. He says* "The village and districts of Húglí were on both sides of the river and these the Europeans got possession of at a low rent. Some of the inhabitants by force, and more by hopes of gain, they infected with their Nazarene teaching and sent them off in ships to Europe. In the hope of an everlasting reward, but in reality of an exquisite torture, they consoled themselves with the profits of their trade for the loss of rent which arose from the removal of the cultivators. These hateful practices were not confined to the lands they occupied, but they seized and carried off every one they could lay their hands upon along the sides of the river." This contrasts very strongly with what Khafi Khān says about the Portuguese. The passage in the *Bādshāhnāmā* is really based upon the report of Kasim Khān whom Shāh Jahān had sent with preconceived ideas against the Portuguese and who in spite of his constant and minute watching could not find any *casus belli* for four years to overthrow their power. In this report the charge of piracy and aggressions was, however, levelled only against the Portuguese of Eastern Bengal, while it accused the Portuguese of Hooghly of fortifying themselves, of drawing away all the trade from Sātgāon and of having committed many acts of violence, presuming to exact duties from all the boats and vessels which passed their factory.† It is true, the Portuguese of Hooghly had grown insolent and haughty but they cannot be said to have been pirates. Writers who have never cared to differentiate the real Portuguese from the outlaws of Sunderbans have made sweeping generalizations against them all. Far from being pirates, the Portuguese of Hooghly promised Akbar and also Jahanghír to stamp out piracy and agreed to keep the Bay clear of the pirates that nestled

* Elliot, *Hist. of India* Vol. VII. p. 32.

† Stewart, *History of Bengal*, pp. 266-267.

there. They did not however keep their word. Yet it must be said they did not in general indulge in the very thing they had promised to extirpate.

The Practices of the Pirates

As to the Portuguese in Eastern Bengal in the seventeenth century no amount of vituperation and invectives would be too strong for them. As Manucci says* they had reached the very acme of evil doing and at one time even a priest named Frei Vicente acted as their leader. The horror of their practices can better be imagined than described. Yet they held a secondary place to the Maghs. François Bernier gives a very graphic account of them. He says† "For many years there have always been Portuguese in the kingdom of *Rukan* (Arakan) or *Mog*, and with them a great number of their *Mestices* or Christian slaves and other *Franguis* gathered together from all parts. This was the retreat of fugitives from Goa, Ceylon, Cochin, Malacca and all the other places once occupied by the Portuguese in the Indies. Those who had fled from their convent, who had married twice or three times, assassins—in a word, outlaws and ruffians, were here welcomed and held in repute, and led a detestable life, utterly unworthy of Christians, going so far as to massacre and poison each other with impunity, and to assassinate their own priests, who were often no better than themselves. The king of Rakan, in perpetual terror of the Mughal, kept these people for the defence of his frontier at a port called *Chatigon* (Chittagong) assigning them lands and letting them live and follow their own devices. Their ordinary pursuit and occupation was theft and piracy. With small and light half-galleys called *galleasses* they did nothing but sweep the sea on this side; and entering all rivers, canals, and arms of the Ganges, and passing between the islands of

* *Storia do Mogor*, Vol. II, p. 117.

† Bernier, *Travels*, Constable Ed. p. 174-175. The translation adopted is from *Calcutta Review* 1871, Vol. LIII, pp. 65-66.

Lower Bengal—often even penetrating as far as forty or fifty leagues into the interior—they surprised and carried off whole villages and harried the poor gentiles, and other inhabitants of this quarter at their assemblies, their markets, their festivals and weddings, seizing as slaves both men and women, small and great, perpetrating strange, cruelties and burning all that they could not carry away. It is owing to this that at the present day are seen so many lovely but deserted isles at the mouth of the Ganges, once thickly populated, but now infested only by savage beasts, principally tigers". It must be said to the credit of Bernier that however bitterly he may vent his wrath on the Portuguese he acknowledged that the Portuguese who carried on these frightful depredations were outlaws, fugitives and ruffians, that fled to this convenient buccaneering haunt in the River Delta of Bengal from other Portuguese settlements. The practices referred to here by Bernier are correct but he ascribes them all to Feringhis while the fact is that the main offenders were the Maghs. In Rennel's map of Bengal published in 1794, the note "this part of the country has been deserted on account of the ravages of the Maghs", is written across the portion of the Sundarbans, south of Băckarganj. Bolts refers to the Maghs alone and not to the Portuguese as plunderers of the Sunderbans.* The Sunderbans, at least the greater part of them, were never in a flourishing condition, and as it has been shown, the portion, south of Băckarganj, was plundered more by the Maghs than by the Portuguese. Bernier continuing says that the Feringhis sold a part of their slaves in Goa, Ceylon, St. Thomé and to the Portuguese of Hooghly, and that a part of them were converted to Christianity and were trained in theft, murder and rapine. He concludes that in spite of the strong militia and numerous bodies and guards and also a small

---

* Bolts, *Indian Affairs.*

naval armament of *galleasses* which the Mughals maintained, the Portuguese did not "cease to make frequent and strange ravages and to penetrate into the country, laughing at all this army of Mughals, having become so bold and so expert in the use of arms and in navigating these galliasses that four or five of their vessels would not hesitate to attack fourteen or fifteen of those of the Mughal—destroying, taking or sinking them, and coming off with flying colours."* The Muhammadan historian Shiāb-ud-dīn Talish gives a much more detailed account of the practices of the pirates in the Bay of Bengal and apportions the blame both to the Maghs as well as to the Feringhis, though the translation of Mr. Jadunath Sarkar is headed "The Feringi Pirates of Chatgaon".†

Shaista Khān's Conquest of Chittagong (1665-66)

No sooner was Shaista Khān appointed Viceroy of Bengal than he determined to invade Arakan and conquer Chittagong in order to put an end to the piratical raids of the Arakanese and the Portuguese and also to avenge the murder of his nephew Shāh Shuja whom the King of Arakan had put to death when he had gone to take refuge there, after his defeat by his brother Mir Jumla.‡ Shaista Khān assembled a large fleet of 300 ships and an army of 13000 men. Abul Hassan was ordered with 200 ships in Sangrangar to oppose the Arakanese and the Feringhis. Muhammad Beg Abakash with 100 ships was to stay at Dhapa and re-inforce Abul Hassan when necessary. His own son Buzurg Umed Khān was appointed to command the army, consisting of 4000

* *Calcutta Review* 1871, Vol. LIII, p. 68.

† *J. A. S. B.* 1907, June, Vol. III, pp. 419-425.

‡ In this short account of the conquest of Chittagong, I have mainly followed Shiāb-ud-dīn Talish's *Fahiyyah-i-ibriyyah* (J. A. S. B. June, 1907) and the *Alamgirnama*, (*Vide*, an extract in M. A. Salam's Trans. of *Rizazu-s-Salatin* p. 229 *et seq.*). Cf. also Manucci's version of the Conquest of Chittagong, *Storia*, Vol. II pp. 117-118 and Bernier's version, *Travels* pp. 179-182.

men, which was to march by land and co-operate with the fleet. Seeing that the conquest of Chittagong would be no easy task so long as the Portuguese defended it, Shaista Khān sent his officer Shaikh Zia-ud-dīn Yusūf to the Portuguese captain of the port of Hooghly, requesting him to write to the Portuguese of Chittagong to desert the King of Arakan and enter his service and offering them a large grant of land where their families could form a colony. He promised imperial favours and offered much better terms than those granted by the Raja of Arakan. The Portuguese gladly accepted the terms, but according to the *Alamgīrnāma*, all the Feringhis did not desert the Raja. Some of them informed the Raja of Arakan about the desertion and he planned to murder them all. The *Alamgīrnāma* says that some letters fell into hands of a Magh who communicated them to the King of Arakan. What followed is described in the *Alamgīrnāma** : "The Feringis learning of [the intended Arracanese treachery] resisted and fought the Arracanese, burnt some of the ships of the latter and started for service in Bengal with all their goods and ships. On the 19th December 1665, fifty *jalbas* (Shiāb-ud-dīn says 42 *Jalbas* or *Jaleas*) of the Feringis full of guns, muskets and munitions and all the Feringi families reached Noakhali". As soon as the Feringhis left Arakan, Shaista Khān decided to attack Chittagong and, as Shiāb-ud-dīn Talish says, considered the coming over of the Feringhis as the commencement of the victory. They were taken, says Shiāb-ud-dīn Talish, in the imperial army and liberally rewarded, but Bernier very unjustly remarks that Shaista Khān ill-treated them and put an end to those wretches.† The ablest of the Portuguese were chosen to take part in the campaign against the King of Arakan and the rest were sent to the Governor,

* *J. A. S. B.* June, 1907, p. 408, n.

† Bernier's *Travels*, pp. 181-182.

who allotted to them a large area, twelve miles south of Dacca, known as Feringhi Bazar, where still the Portuguese descendants reside.*

Shiāb-ud-dīn Talish gives a spirited account of what passed after the Feringhis left Chittagong† : "In December, 1665, the Feringis of Chātgāon, partly in fear of Arracanese treachery and partly won over by Shaista Khan's tempting overtures came with all their families in 42 *jalbas* and took refuge with Farhād Khan the Mughal *thanadar* of Noakhali. The Khan sent their chief, Captain Moor ‡ with a few of their great men to Shaista Khan at Dacca, while he kept all the others with their ships a Noakhali, with great attention and kindness. The captain and other leaders of Feringis had audience of the Nawwāb at night and received splendid robes of honour and other unexpected favours. The Nawwāb asked them, 'What did the zeminder of Maghs fix as your salary ?' The Feringis replied, 'Our salary was the Imperial dominion ! We considered the whole of Bengal as our *jāgīr*.

---

* Manucci has a different version, *Storia*, Vol. II p. 118. He says Shaista Khān sent for a Portuguese, named Antonio de Rego, who was in Hooghly and had a brother named Sebastião Gonsalves in Chittagong. The Nawab paid Rego Rs. 25,000 and Rs. 50,000 more for his brother Gonsalves in order to deliver Chittagong to him. Gonsalves instructed Rego to send the Mughal fleet up to Sandwīp. Chittagong was then captured without any loss of life. It would be interesting to know whether this Gonsalves was the same Sebastião Gonsalves Tibau who had made himself Lord of Sandwīp. He came to India in 1607 and if he was, say about 25 years old then, he would be about 83 years old in 1665 and might have been living. But it is impossible that even till 1665 he could wield such power in Sandwīp and Chittagong as Manucci suggests. That the names of the two brothers are quite different is no evidence against the fact, because there are many instances in Portuguese history in which two brothers had no common names or surnames, the latter having been, perhaps, surpressed by the Portuguese historians.

† *J. A. S. B.*, June 1907, p. 425.

‡ Both Shiāb-ud-dīn Talish and the *Alamgīrnāma* refer to the Portuguese captain named "Moor". This is not a Portuguese name. Muhammadan historians have frightfully mutilated Portuguese names. Pedro Tavares has been converted into Partab Bar (*Vide* p. 52), and Rodolfo into Radif in the *Akbarnāmā*. The real name of captain Moor might have been Mourão or Moraes.

All the twelve months of the year we made our collection, [i.e. booty] without trouble. We had not to bother ourselves about *amlas* and *amīns*; nor had we to render accounts and balances to anybody. Passage over water was our [land] survey. We never slackened the enhancement of *our* rent viz. booty. For years we have left no arrears of [this] revenue. We have with us papers of the division of the booty village by village for the last forty years.' One can infer from this answer the condition of things and the weakness of the Governors of Bengal. The coming over of the Feringis gave composure to the hearts of the people of Bengal. Two thousand rupees were presented from the Nawwāb's own purse as reward to Captain Moor and the other Feringis who had come from Chatgaon and from the Imperial treasury a monthly stipend of Rs. 500 was settled on the Captain, and other comfortable salaries on others of the tribe."

The conquest of Chittagong by the Mughals and their mastery over the Sundarbans broke the power of the Portuguese adventurers and thenceforward they joined hands with the other Portuguese that were spread all over Bengal even after the siege of Hooghly, becoming peaceful civilians and merchants. They drove a peaceful trade and must have wielded much influence and power especially in Chittagong oven up to 1727, for Alexander Hamilton writes*: "The *Mogul* keeps a *Cadjee* or Judge in it (Chittagong) to administer Justice among *Pagan* and *Mahometan* Inhabitants but the Ofispring of those Portugueze that followed the fortune of *Sultan Sujah* when he was forced to quit *Bengal*, are the domineering Lords of it". There is an earlier account of the Feringhis of Chittagong by

* A *New Account of the East Indies*, Vol. II, Chap. 35. p.25. Bernier (*Travels* p. 109) also mentions that when Shāh Shuja was driven away from Bengal by Aurangzeb, he went to take refuge in Arakan in Galliasses manned by the Portuguese. He adds that the Portuguese robbed Shāh Shuja of his precious stones on the way. Hamilton betrays little knowledge about the origin of the Portuguese of Chittagong.

Fr. Barbier, a Jesuit missionary, who in 1723 describes in a letter to another Jesuit Father, an Episcopal Visitation by Rev. Fr. François Laines, Bishop of St. Thomé, Madras.* In a detailed description of the Feringhis and their customs, he says that they were divided into three colonies each having its Captain, its Church and its Missionary. They were held in great respect by the natives ; they carried arms and had military discipline and full liberty to celebrate the feasts in the same order and with the same solemnity as in Europe. The writer regrets, that Chittagong was not chosen in preference to Hooghly as the headquarters of the European (Portuguese), settlements. It is very interesting indeed to see that the Portuguese and their descendants had a sort of military discipline even in the eighteenth century. At this time, however, the Portuguese in Eastern Bengal were mere mercenaries. Even till 1786 when Chittagong District was invaded by the Arakanese under a Peguan general, against whom Major Ellerber was sent, the Arakan army contained 500 Portuguese mercenaries.†

* This letter appearing in the *Lettres Edifiantes et Curieuses* Vol. XIII, Paris 1781, has been translated by W. Firminger in *Bengal Past and Present*, 1910, Vol. VI, pp. 200-215.

† O'Malley, *Chittagong Gazetteer*, p. 39.

PART III

RELICS

OF THE

PORTUGUESE IN BENGAL.

CHAPTER XV

THE RELICS

Though the Portuguese Empire in the East has long fulfilled the grim destiny which rules the duration of nations and empires, they have left important vestiges that no time can erase. The Portuguese have long disappeared from Bengal, but everywhere can be seen their various relics, eloquent in their silence, of departed power and glory. How many scenes that appear so fresh to-day have been wistfully gazed upon by the old navigators? On how many ruins of their houses, have modern architects reared their proud edifices? And equally so, how many places alive with the hum of the Portuguese and busy with their industries are desolate to-day? It is not, however, the historical remains of the Portuguese, as much as the silent forces which they have left behind that, though generally unknown, are all the more striking.

General Outlines

The influence of the Portuguese in the East has not yet been adequately dealt with, though a lot has been written on the Portuguese navigators, their conquests and their heroic feats. The permanent Portuguese influence, largely working unkown, is felt in numerous walks of life in India. The Portuguese were the first to establish an intimate contact between the East and the West. The first impressions of the East about the West were largely such as the Portuguese created. These impressions were, therefore, more profound and lasting than it is generally recognized.

The Portuguese introduced in the East new methods of agriculture opened new industries, established new customs, taught a new religion and countenanced a policy of intermarriages between themselves and the natives. The results of each of their sphere of activities are manifest to-day. The latter European comers often modified or sometimes amplified the work of the Portuguese, but they have not removed the traces of the original influence. Dr. Heyligers* recognises this Portuguese influence in the Indian Archipelago as an absolutely singular force in its history and traces it under the headings : population, race, customs and language. This is equally true of Bengal as of India in general.

In Bengal, though there is a great tendency of self identification with the ruling nation, the Portuguese stamp can be discerned on whatever they came in contact with. Their names, their blood, their institutions, their churches, their language and their archæological remains, speak to-day of their domination in Bengal.

Portuguese Descendants or Luso-Indians

It was the principle laid down by the Portuguese from the time of Albuquerque that, in order to establish an affinity between Portugal and her dependencies, the Portuguese should give to the people under their influence the Portuguese names, the Portuguese religion, the Portuguese dress and even the Portuguese blood. Intermarriages between the Portuguese and Indians were also advocated by Albuquerque's successors. It must be said this privilege was considered a great honour and none but men of valour were allowed to marry Indian women of high families on their becoming Christian.†

There was generally neither promiscuous nor illegitimate union between the Portuguese and the Indians. There must have been certainly some abuses, and during the declining years

* *Traces de Portugais dans les principales langues des Indes Orientales Neerlandaises*, La Haye, 1889.

† *Commentaries of Affonso de Albuquerque*, Hakl. Ed., Vol. III, pp. 41-42.

this policy was not rigidly followed, especially in Bengal where the piratical section of the Portuguese recognized no law nor principles of morality. The number of marriages between the Portuguese and Indians was enormous throughout India. "For already at this time" say the *Commentaries** "there were in Goa about 450 married men, all servants of the King, Queen and of the Lords of Portugal and those who desired to marry, were so numerous that Afonso Dalboquerque could hardly grant their requests, for he did not give permission, except for the men of proved character, to marry."

It cannot be ascertained how extensively this policy was followed in Bengal. All that is certain is that marriages between the Portuguese and the Indians were very common and that the converts were given Portuguese names on their becoming Christians. They were also named after the Portuguese who became their sponsors. There was on the other hand a voluntary effort on the part of the Indians to identify themselves with the Portuguese. Lafitau mentions that many Hindus took Portuguese names like Albuquerque, only for the honour of it.† In Ceylon the pride of possessing Portuguese names is very remarkable. Emerson Tennent relates that while the Dutch feats in Ceylon have been buried in oblivion the chieftains of southern and western Ceylon perpetuate the Portuguese title of *Dom* and to their ancient patronymics prefix the sonorous names of the Portuguese.‡

There are numerous communities of the Portuguese descendants all over Bengal. Some have identified themselves with the natives of the place. Others preserve their traditions of Portuguese parentage. Many have changed their names

---

* *Commentaries of Afonso de Albuquerqne*, Hak Ed., Vol III, p. 41 *et seq.*

† Lafitau, *Histoire dés Découvertes des Portugais dans le Nouveau Monde.*

‡ Tennent, *Ceylon, an Account of the Island*, Vol. II, pp. 70-71.

and form part and parcel of the Anglo-Indian community. In the eighteenth century the community of the Portuguese descendants was a distinct one. They are all called Portuguese in the English records, in the accounts of the travellers in the Bengal Directories and by the historians. Many Indians who were given or took Portuguese names have been also called Portuguese. Hence much confusion has arisen in estimating the relative characters of the Portuguese race, those of their descendants and those of the Indians who identified themselves with the Portuguese. It is time, therefore, a proper denomination were given to the Portuguese descendants. They will be referred to in this work as Luso-Indians,* in contradistinction to Anglo-Indians, by which name the descendants of the English are now called.

The Portuguese Language

The Portuguese influence in the East can most remarkably be seen in the extent their language has affected the Asiatic languages. As Dr. Schuchardt says,† the history of the Portuguese discoveries and conquests is the history of the propagation of the Portuguese language. It was the *lingua franca* throughout the East not only among the Portuguese and their descendants but among the different indigenous races and, what is more, among the Europeans of other nationalities, who followed the first conquerors. It was spoken all along the coast of India, in Malasia, Pegu, Siam, Tonquin, Cochin-China, Basra, Meca, and,

---

* Lusitania is the classic name for Portugal. As first shown by Garcia de Menezes in the fifteenth century and then proved by Bernardo de Brito, Lusitania was the Roman province of the Iberian Peninsula, and was identical with Portugal. Bernardo de Brito, therefore, claimed the great Viriatus as a Portuguese hero. The Portuguese are called the Lusian people and Camões named his immortal Epic *Os Lusiadas*. Hence Luso-Indians would be a proper denomination for the Portuguese descendants.

† *Beitrage zur Kenntniss des kreolischen Romanisch Vol. V.* (Quoted by Mons. R. Dalgado).

in fine, wherever the Portuguese domination had extended.* "This they (the Portuguese) may justly claim" says Lockyer in 1711,† "they have established a kind of *Lingua Franca* in all the Sea-Ports in *India*, of great use to other *Europeans* who would find it difficult in many places to be well understood without it." Sixteen years later Alexander Hamilton found the Portuguese language still maintaining its hold in India. He writes, : "along the sea-coasts the *Portugueze* have left a Vestige of their Language tho' much corrupted, yet it is the Language that most *Europeans* learn first to qualify them for a general Converse with one another, as well as with different inhabitants of *India*."‡

What is still more remarkable is that the Portuguese language continued to be the medium of general converse long after the Portuguese power was extinguished. The Dutch also dominated great many eastern centres. But their language in the East disappeared with them and left no vestiges in the languages of the East. Emerson Tennent thus speaks of Ceylon,§ "Already the language of the Dutch which they sought to extend by penal enactments has ceased to be spoken even by their direct descendants, whilst a corrupted Portuguese is to the present day the vernacular of the middle classes in every town of importance." The reason why the Portuguese language exerted such an influence on the Asiatic languages was evidently that the Portuguese were the first Europeans who introduced new things in the East and along with them, the names which they called them by. Besides, they helped to bring about a better communication between the eastern trading centres, transmitting the eastern

---

* Cunha Rivara, *Grammatica de Lingua Concani.*

† *An Account of the Trade in India*, p. 286.

‡ *A New Account of the East Indies*, *Preface* p. xii.

§ Tennent, *op. cit.* Vol. II p. 70.

goods and customs from one place to the other. Thus one finds Chinese words like *Cha* (Tea) introduced in the Indian through the Portuguese language, and Arabic words like monsoon, typhoon in the Anglo-Indian vocabulary.

The influence of the Portuguese language on the languages of Bengal is very striking. The English,* the Bengali, the Hindustani, the Ooryia and the Assamese possess a vocabulary containing numerous Portuguese words. This is not, however, surprising as Portuguese was really at one time the *lingua franca* of Bengal, as will be seen in a separate chapter.

Portuguese Archæological Remains

The most vivid and apparent remains which bear testimony to the Missionary work of the Portuguese are their numerous Churches and Convents all over India. Excepting the doubtful remains of some Portuguese forts and factories, the Churches are practically the only archæological remains of the Portuguese in Bengal. The factories of the Portuguese merchants have long disappeared and even the sites on which they stood are forgotten. The rich houses and proud edifices of the Portuguese governors and grandees have crumbled into dust. But many of the Churches which the Portuguese Missionaries erected still exist in all their original grandeur commanding the respect and mystery of hoary antiquity. In Bengal, the old Portuguese Churches are not as numerous as in Western India. There was, however, scarcely any place of importance in Bengal where the Augustinians had not built their Churches. The oldest Christian Church existing, is in Bandel, Hooghly, and is still administered by the Portuguese Mission. Its origin dates back to 1599. There are various other Portuguese Churches in Bengal, which will be briefly

* The Anglo-Indian words now current in the English language are referred to.

dealt with in a separate chapter. As works of architecture, they compare very unfavourably with the majestic convents existing in Goa, which have been compared by foreigners with the best edifices of Europe.*

It is not only in the number and the architectural beauty of the Churches, that the magnitude of the Portuguese Missionaries can be seen. The vast number of Roman Catholics who existed in Bengal in the sixteenth and the seventeenth and even in the eighteenth centuries bear evidence to the missionary zeal of the Portuguese. The remains of these Roman Catholic communities still exist in many parts of Bengal.

Geographical Names

Many of the geographical names which the Portuguese gave to places in Bengal and were adopted by the later Europeans are no longer current. Porto Pequeno (Sātgāon and Hooghly), Porto Grande (Chittagong), Ilha de Gallos (at the mouth of the Hooghly) are names only of historical interest to-day. They were at one time in general use and were used by Cæsar Federici, Van Linschoten and even by the servants of the East India Company. Some geographical words such as Dom Manik Islands at the mouth of the Titulia in the Bākarganj District and Point Palmyras which is a headland on the Orissa coast, still survive. Feringhi Bunder in Chittagong and Feringhi Bazar in Dacca are also two places associated with the Portuguese. Bandel in Hooghly owes its name entirely to the Portuguese.† In a Portuguese Map in

---

* Mandelslo (*Voyages and Travels*), Careri (Churchill's *Voyages*) Dr. Buchanan (*Christian Researches in Asia*) Dr. Wilson (*Oriental Christian Spectator*) Dr. Fryer (*A New Account etc.*) and others speak highly of the Goa Convents.

† Bandel is a corrnption of *bandar*, a wharf The Portuguese termed several of their ports in the East, *Bandels*. Thus there is mention of *the Bandel* of Chittagong, the Bandel of Ormuz etc. Though *the Bandel* of Hooghly (*Ugolim*) was the original termination, the word *Bandel* gradually dissociated itself from *Hooghly*, and came to be regarded as a place or a town.

Thevenot* "Ilha de Martim Affonso de Mello" is marked on the coast of Arakan, and it was evidently so called in commemoration of the feats of the Portuguese Captain.† The denomination does not seem to have been made use of by other European writers, and was probably confined to the Portuguese.

Plants introduced by the Portuguese in Bengal

Among various things which owe their existence in Bengal to the Portuguese, may be mentioned a good deal of plants introduced by them throughout India. Directly or indirectly, they have found their way to Bengal. It is worthy of remark that the first Indian botanical names were given by a Portuguese named Garcia de Orta in his celebrated work *Colloquios* etc. printed in Goa in 1563. C. da Costa followed him with his *Tratado*, published in 1578.

---

* *Voyages Curieux*, Vol. I, map facing p. 128.

† *Vide* p. 31, *et seq.*

CHAPTER XVI

PORTUGUESE DESCENDANTS

(Luso-Indians)

Among the various relics which the Portuguese have left in Bengal, the most notable are their descendants. It is very remarkable, indeed, that no nation of Europe has less egotism of race and a greater tendency to identify themselves with the indigenous people than the Portuguese nation. It is not surprising, therefore, that all over Bengal, in Calcutta, Dacca, Hooghly, Chittagong, Noakhali, Assam and other places there are communities having some connection or other with the Portuguese and possessing their names if not always their blood. The quite characteristic names of the Portuguese are borne to-day by many, many families in Bengal. As it is in the eighteenth century that the history of the Portuguese merges into the history of their descendants the following list of Portuguese families in Bengal from 1700 to 1900 is compiled from old Bengal Directories, and especially from old Catholic Church Registers* of births, marriages and deaths. Many of these names are quire common to-day and appear in the latest registers and visitors' books. Some names, however, which were common between 1700 and 1800 have died out. These names as they are found to-day are not in all cases strictly spelt as the ones in the list below. The connection between them is, however, obvious. In many cases the

---

* The Registers of Bandel Church (Hooghly) do not date earlier than 1757 and those of Murgihatta Cathedral earlier than 1740. St. John's Church (Calcutta) Records also contain numerous Portuguese names which show that many Luso-Indians adopted the Protestant religion.

Portuguese names have been Anglified or sometimes entirely changed so as to remove all trace of their Portuguese origin.

The Goans or the Goanese

The Goans, or the Goanese as they are termed in Bengal, must be differentiated from the Luso-Indians. The Goans are immigrants from Goa (Portuguese India) and have found their way to Bengal roughly from the beginning of the nineteenth century. As Goa is not an agricultural and industrial place, the Goans, especially in the humbler walks of life, meet the economic necessities by immigrating to British India. There are about a thousand Goans in Bengal at present, most of them (about 800) being in Calcutta.* They are not, in general, descendants of the Portuguese but are pure christianized Indians with Portuguese names and European customs and manners. Brought up with a close association with the Portuguese and in an atmosphere of four centuries of European civilization, the Goans are on the same social level as the Portuguese. However, some habits and institutions, like the caste system, characteristic of the Indian race, still linger among the Goans. The Goans have the same ideals and spirit of nationality as the Portuguese and possess equal rights of free citizenship with the latter. The names of the Goans, which are the same as the names of the Luso-Indians, have not been included in the following list of Luso-Indian names.

* O'Malley's *Census Report of Calcutta of 1911* mentions 644, (619 males and 25 females), as being born in the Portuguese Settlements *i. e.* chiefly in Goa. Considering the number of Goans in Calcutta, who were born outside Goa, and the increase of their numbers since 1911, the figure 800 is approximately correct. In the *Census*, those who entered themselves as belonging to the Portuguese nationality were 254. Almost all of these were certainly Goans, because the Luso-Indians entered themselves as Eurasians or Anglo-Indians. Only 10 of them who gave Portugal as their birth-place may be said to have been European Portuguese, though one or two Goans may have also been born in Portugal. It may be remarked that only 53 entered themselves as Goans, though 298 mentioned Konkani (Goanese) as their language.

Common Luso-Indian Surnames in Bengal*

(1700—1900)

ABREU, D'ABREU
Affonso
AGOSTINHO
AGUIAR, DAGUIAR
ALCANTARA
Aleixo
Alerim
Alexandre
ALMEIDA
André
Argotte
Arnaldo

BAPTISTA
BARRETTO
Barros
BASTIAN, SEBASTIAO
Botelho

CABRAL
CARDOZO
Carneiro
Carnes
CARVALHO
Castellino
CASTRO
Cavella
Cenaculo
Colaco
Conceicão
Consolacão
CORNELIUS
CORREA
COSTA, DACOSTA
COSTELLO
Coutinho
COUTO
Couzo
CRUZ, DECRUZ
Curado

Dalgado
DANIEL
DIAS
DOMINGO
Dores
Duques
FARIA
FERNANDES
Fernando
Ferrão
Figueiredo
FONSECA
Frangos
FREITAS
Furtado

Gallis
GARRETT
GASPAR
Gill
Godinho
GOMES
GONSALVES
GOUVEA
GRACIAS
Gusmão

Henriques

Innocencia
Jesus
José

Leal
Leitão
Lobo

---

* The names printed in capital letters are quite common, at present, in Bengal. Some names like Alexander and Martins may not necessarily point to a Portuguese origin.

LOPES
Lovo
LUCAS
Luis

Machado
Malques
MANOEL
Marcos
Maria
Martins
MARTYRES
Mascarenhas
MELLO, DE MELLO
MENDES
MENEZES
Mercado
MESQUITA
Milheira
Miranda
Moira
MONTE
Monte Sinaes
Neves
NORONHA

Oliveira

PAIVA, DEPAIVA
Peicheiro
Penha
PEREIRA
Peres
Pessoa
Phillipe
PINHEIRO
Pinna
PINTO
Prazeres
Prezentina

Quadros

Ramos
REBEIRO
REBELLO
REMEDIOS
Robalo
Rocha
RODRIGUES
Roza
ROZARIO, DE ROZARIO

SA, DESA or DESSA
Salgado
Salvador
Santiago
Santos
Seixas
SEQUEIRA
Serrão
Soveral
SILVA, DE SILVA
SILVESTRE
Soares
SOUZA, DE SOUZA

Tavares
Teixeira

Urage

VALENTE
Vallis
Vás
Ventura
Verona
Viana
Victoria

Xavier

Common Luso-Indian Christian names in Bengal (1700 – 1900)

Agostinho
Alberto
Alexandre
Andre
Antonio
Assenço
Augusto

Bendito
Bernardinho
Bernardo
Boaventura
Bonifacio

Caitano
Candido
Carlos
Casimiro
Clemente
Constantino
Cornelio

Daniel
Diogo
Domingos

Estevam

Fernando
Florentino
Francisco
Gabriel
George
Guilherme

Henrique
Hilario

Ignacio

Jacob
Jeronimo
João
Joaquim
José
Juliano

Lazaro
Lourenço
Luis

Manoel
Mariano
Matheus
Michael

Miguel

Nicolau

Pascoal
Paulo
Pedro
Phillipe

Raphael
Raymundo
Ricardo
Roberto
Romaldo

Salvador
Santiago
Silvestre
Simão
Simplicio

Thomas
Timotheo

Valentino

Xavier

Female Names

Agnida
Agostinha

Albina
Amelia

Anastasia
Andreza

Anna	Eulalia	Paula
Antonia	Izabel	Phillipa
Angelica		Prezentina
Apolonia	Joanna	
Aurora		Rita
	Leonora	Rosa
Catarina	Luiza	Rozalina
Clara	Luzia	
		Tereza
Dominga	Margarida	
	Maria	Victoria
Elizabeth	Mariana	

Different Elements in the Luso-Indian Community

All those who bear Portuguese names are not, however, the real descendants of the Portuguese, but most of them are pure natives, some of whom in the evolution of time mixed with other races, sometimes changing their names sometimes retaining them. As to the pure Portuguese there are very few, and these have come recently as sailors or with some other occupations and have settled in Bengal The Census-Report of 1911 mentions only ten as being born in Portugal. In the *Calcutta Review*, Vol. LIII, 1871, H. Beverley* makes mention of a family of real Portuguese descent, residing in Chittagong. The Portuguese descendants were first known as Feringhis; indeed the Portuguese themselves were so called. This name was once applied to the Crusaders and was an honoured name but now it is used in derision. These Feringhis and the native Christians afterwards began to be known as *Topasses* (from *Topi*, a hat) especially in Eastern Bengal. At present, the Feringhis, the Native Christians and the heterogeneous

* *The Feringhees of Chittagong*, Cal Rev. 1871, Vol. LIII, p. 82.

mass of people living in the slums of Calcutta, are called *Kintalis* (from *Kintal*, an enclosure).

There are no reliable statistics in any of the Censuses or the Gazetteers with regard to this community. It is difficult to give any accurate statistical account, considering the heterogeneous elements this community is composed of. They are at present all classed as Eurasians or Anglo-Indians. It is almost impossible to differentiate the racial characteristics excepting where Mongolian blood has entered and a great part of these so-called "Anglo-Indians" is a promiscuous fusion of the Portuguese, English, Indians, East Indians, West Indians and Chinese. However, the section of the "Eurasians" associated with the Portuguese in some form or other may be divided into three main classes :—

(1) Pure Indians, who are converts and bear Portuguese names.

(2) True descendants of the Portuguese, who though they have freely mixed with other races, still maintain the Portuguese surnames if not the Christian names.

(3) True descendants of the Portuguese who intermarried to a greater extent with the English descendants and who having changed their names into English names, have apparently lost all relation with the Portuguese.

The bulk of the community consists of pure Indians who having been converted to Christianity were given Portuguese names and adopted the European dress. The change of religion brought to a large extent the change of customs and a gradual association with the Europeanised population, made them lose most of the characteristics of the natives of India. Of course there are many Indian Christians who wear the *dhoti*, though they have Portuguese names, but they are not entered in the classification of the mixed community, as their national dress differentiates them.

First group—Pure Indians with Portuguese names

When the Portuguese came to Bengal, the slave trade was very rampant and was sanctioned by the Hindu and Muhammadan law. The Portuguese possessed a large number of slaves who were given Portuguese names. Many of them took Portuguese names when their masters died. The Portuguese missionaries in Calcutta used to buy slaves who were packed in many vessels and shipped there, rather than see them bought by others and ill-treated. They used to baptise these slaves with Portuguese names and then sell them to Christian masters. Hence among the so-called Portuguese descendants, there was a vast majority of simple Indian converts or slaves converted to Christianity. These Indian Christians, who formed part and parcel of a mixed Portuguese community, talked in the Portuguese language just like the Portuguese or their descendants even up to the end of the eighteenth century, but towards the middle of the nineteenth century the English language began to be generally spoken though many Portuguese words still survive. Their complexion is obviously as that of the ordinary Indian, and among their customs can be seen the relics of their ancestors. There is no sharp line of distinction between this class and that of the true Luso-Indians because both these classes have intermixed and acted and reacted on each other. The arbitrary classification holds good in that the first group is mainly Indian in blood while the second has to a certain extent affinities of blood with the Portuguese. That the mixed Portuguese community is mainly Indian has been attested to by many authorities. Abbé Dubois remarks :* "Most of them (Christians called Portuguese) have no more relation by birth, or otherwise, to the Portuguese or to any other European nation than to the Tartar Calmucks. They are partly composed of half-castes, the illegitimate offspring of Europeans and a few descendants of the Portuguese ; whilst

* J. A. Dubois, *State of Christianity in India*, Lond. 1823, pp. 75-76.

the majority of them are the offspring of Hindoos of the lowest rank, who after learning some one of the European dialects put on a hat, boots and the European dress and endeavour to copy the European manners." It must be remarked that as to acquiring European manners, the conversion to Christianity contributes to it more than an effort to copy European and to wear a hat, boots and the European dress. Most of the customs that differentiate the Indian from the European have their origin in the difference of religious tenets that especially in the Hindu religion include social and hygienic principles. Once the bar is taken away the acquiring of European manners is natural, provided there are Europeans or Europeanised people to associate with.

Second Group—True Luso-Indians

There is no sharp line of demarcation between the pure Indian members of the Luso-Indian community and the descendants of the Portuguese. The two classes can scarcely be distinguished. Colour is no criterion because the Luso-Indians could have had a pure Portuguese parentage or a parentage closely related to the pure Portuguese, for only one or two generations about two centuries ago, that is, up to the end of the seventeenth century after which very few Portuguese came to Bengal. After this period of time, the generations that followed were largely a result of intermixture among other Indian races and hence they have in general the Indian colour. During the last half of the eighteenth century and onwards, the servants of the East Indian Company and other Englishmen freely married with the descendants of the Portuguese,* and the resulting race naturally turned comparatively fair and this colour had been generally maintained as long as the marriages took place between fairer descendants. The representatives of this race are partly the fairer portion of the Anglo-Indians, many

* St. John's Church (Calcutta) Marriage Records show many names of Portuguese or Luso-Indian ladies married to Englishmen.

of whom have some Portuguese blood in them though they have not the Portuguese names. It is a mistake to suppose, as it has been done, that the descendants of the Portuguese naturally turned out dark while the descendants of the English turned out generally fair. In fact the opposite seems to be true if one observes the descendants of the real Portuguese in Goa among whom one can scarcely see a man of a dark complexion. Bishop Heber remarks in 1826*: "The Portuguese natives form unions among themselves alone, or if they can, with Europeans yet the Portuguese have, during a three hundred years residence in India became as black as Caffres; surely this goes far to disprove the assertion which is made that climate alone is insufficient to account for the difference between the Negro and the European." He seemed to have forgotten that almost none of those he saw was a real Portuguese and that in almost all of them the original Portuguese parentage was reduced to an infinitesimal degree through succeeding generations.

The generality of the members of the mixed community had Portuguese names as well as surnames up to the middle of the last century, as can be seen from the tombs in the cemeteries of Bengal. Then gradually the Portuguese Christian names began to be substituted by English Christian names. In modern times the tendency is to work a complete transmutation of name into an English or Anglicised one. It is this metamorphosis of names that offers the greatest difficulty in preparing a statistical account.

Third Group—Luso-Indians with English names

As to the third group there is little definite that can be said. A good many Anglo-Indians who have English names and who seem to have nothing in common with the Portuguese have Portuguese blood in them, though generally they are not aware of it. English names have been adopted

* Bishop Heber, *Narrative of a Journey* etc. Vol. I, p. 54.

for a long time past. The Portuguese name, Correa has been changed into Currie; Leal changed into Lea by an easy dropping of the L; Silva into Silver; Souza into Sauseman; Gouvea into Govey and so on. Still more recently a radical change has been worked in the names and what was a Pereira is now a Johnson and what was Gomes is now a Fitz Patrick. The adoption of such names has probably followed either betterment of circumstances or the acquiring of a fairer complexion. On the other hand the change of name might have had some influence in bettering the circumstances. The adoption of English names has removed from many Anglo-Indians all trace of connection with the Portuguese. Besides Portuguese blood courses in the veins of some Anglo-Indians from the mothers' side, and of this no names, obviously, can give an indication.

Luso-Indian Merchants

The Luso-Indian trade, as distinguished from the Portuguese trade, roughly began with the dawn of the eighteenth century. The Luso-Indians held quite a a subordinate position in the commercial activities of Bengal in comparison with the Dutch and especially the English who were rising on the tide of fortune. S. C. Hill remarks* that in the middle of the eighteenth century the Portuguese (i.e. Luso-Indians) in Hooghly chiefly traded as native merchants. The statement is exaggerated and has no evidence in the collection of letters of the English factors, which Hill publishes. Watts and Collet, in fact, wrote that "if the Nawab (Sirāj-ud-daula) admitted the English into Calcutta, it would not be on better terms than the Portuguese and Prussians trade on."†

The following Luso-Indian merchants are mentioned in the Calcutta Annual Directory and Almanac for 1806:—

Joseph Barretto, & Co., Antonio Rebeiro Pereira de

---

* S. C. Hill, *Bengal in 1756-57*, Vol. I, p. XXXIV.

† *Ibidem*, Vol. I, p. 117.

Almeida, Philip and John Da Cruz, Joachim Joseph Mendes, John D'Abreu, Lawrence Picachy, James Robertson, Diego Pereira, Mark and A.Lackersteen, Philip Leal. It is worthy of note that L. Picachy, J. Robertson and the Lackersteens have no Portuguese names at all, yet the Directory mentions them as Portuguese. Similarly in a list of Portuguese militia in the same Directory, there are English names like John Bateman, and William Armstrong. This shows very clearly that early in the nineteenth century, and perhaps even long before, the Luso-Indians had begun adopting English names. It is probable they assumed the surnames of their mothers who happened to be English descendants. It is also possible that the English descendants went about as Portuguese—a much better denomination than a *half-caste*, which was a common expression at that time. This explains the remark of Dr. Carey who writing from Serampore in 1800 says that the children of the English, French, Dutch or Danes were all called Portuguese.*

The Barrettos

Barretto and Company, was a firm of renown until recently. The vast sums of money that the proprietors of the Company have left for different charities are well-known. The munificence of the Barrettos was, however, directed chiefly towards building Churches and endowing religious institutions. There is scarcely any old Church in or near Calcutta, which has not received some benefit from the Barrettos. Joseph Barretto was foremost among those who contributed to the enlarging of Murgihatta Church. The Dum Dum Chapel owes its origin to the Barrettos. When the artillery regiment was first stationed there the Catholic soldiers could not find a better place than a small hut of thatch and straw, lent by a kind widow, to assist their Sunday services. Though the artillery commandant raised a general subscription in his regiment to which the Protestants

* Smith's *Life of Carey* p. 152.

contributed freely, it fell short when Joseph Barretto came to the rescue. He, in fact, wanted exclusively to bear the cost of erecting the chapel. The first movement for building a Church in or near Boitakhana was initiated by Joseph Barretto. The Barretto family also built the Church of Santa Madre de Deus in Serampore. The Church of the Sacred Heart of Jesus, Dharamtala, owes its origin to Pascoa Barretto who had married Thomas deSouza. Many people in Calcutta are aware of the interesting legends concerning the erection of this Church founded on the fact of Louis deSouza, uncle of Sir Walter deSouza, having fought a duel from the judicial consequences of which he was saved. Mrs. deSouza (Pascoa Barretto) had really made a vow that should her son be acquitted she would build and endow a Church on her own land.

The deSouzas

The de Souzas were other Luso-Indian merchants whose opulence is within the memory of many Calcutta citizens. The original firm was established in Bombay and it carried on an extensive trade mainly in ivory, opium and Venetian beads. It had branches in China, France and Calcutta. The local firm was called Thomas de Souza and Company. The last representative of the firm was Sir Walter de Souza, whose intelligence allied to his munificence won for him laurels from various parts of the world. It must be mentioned his grandfather was born in Goa. Lawrence de Souza Junior, Sir Walter's half-brother, was no less famous for his charities, to which various educational institutions and Charity Homes still bear witness in Calcutta. Among other lesser charities in Calcutta, Lawrence de Souza Jr., who died in 1871, bequeathed Rs. 3,00,000 to the Doveton College, Rs. 25,000 to the Free School ; Rs. 10,000 to the Mayo Native Hospital ; Rs. 33,000 for a scholarship to enable East Indian lads to proceed to England to compete for the Indian Civil Service ; Rs. 15,000 for a scholarship in

English literature tenable at the Doveton, and Rs. 2,00,000 to found the Home for East Indian widows and orphans, which is seen in Dharamtala Street.

Luso-Indian Soldiers and Mercenaries in the Eighteenth Century

When in the seventeenth century the Portuguese power fell in Bengal, especially in Hooghly and in Chittagong, they and their numerous descendants either followed their profession of traders or employed themselves as mercenaries in the armies of the Bengal rulers. As a body, they do not seem to have engaged in military operations as they did during the memorable sack of Calcutta and Hooghly in 1756 in which they played an important though secondary part. In the East India Company Records, they are all called Portuguese though they were, mostly, Luso-Indians. It may be well to recapitulate the events of this period so as to bring out clearly the part played by the Luso-Indians.

On Nawāb Aliverdi Khān's death in April 1756, his grandson Sirāj-ud-daulā succeeded to the throne of Bengal. Scarcely twenty years old, profligate but strong-willed, he at once showed his hostility towards the English, by refusing to accept a present which they had sent him and appointing a spy Rajaram to watch their movements in Calcutta. Bent on ousting the Europeans from his kingdom he first directed his attention to the English. On the ground that the English had built some fortifications, that they had abused their privileges of trade and that they had protected the servants of his Government, whom he wished to be surrendered—grounds that were in a large measure true, he declared war against the English. He plundered the English factory of Cossimbazar taking all the English officers prisoners, among whom was Warren Hastings. At the head of 50,000 men he began his rapid march to Calcutta covering 160 miles in eleven days.*

* These facts are mainly based on the East India Company Records published in S. C. Hill's *Bengal in 1756-57*.

Strangely enough there were about 200 Luso-Indians in Sirāj-uddaulā's army as well as in the English garrisons. The Nawāb's artillery, consisting of Frenchmen and Luso-Indians, was commanded by a French renegade who styled himself Le Marquis de St. Jacques. The English militia under arms on the 8th June numbered 250. The letter of Watts and Collet to Council Fort George, and Drake's account say that out of the 250 men of the garrison 70 were English and a great part of the remaining 180 were Portuguese (Luso-Indians) and Armenians.* These were placed under the command of Captain Minchin and Lieutenant Bellamy. The English who most feared the attack of the Nawāb's artillery, consisting of Frenchmen and Luso-Indians, sent through some priests three letters asking them to desist from fighting on the side of a Moorish ruler but they replied they had no other choice.

Luso-Indians in the English and in the Nawāb's Armies

Sirāj-ud-daulā forced the Mahratta Ditch and on the 17th June was entering the town of Calcutta burning and pillaging everything before him. The English were seldom so panic-stricken as they were on this occasion. The Luso-Indian and the Armenian soldiers scarcely knew what they were about. Drake, Holwell and Baillie had great difficulty in persuading the British themselves to take up arms and, as Holwell says in his letter, among the European militia there were few "who knew the right from the wrong end of their pieces."† The British women were admitted in the Fort and as the Luso-Indians and the Armenians refused to fight unless their families were also safely lodged in the Fort, they were allowed to "crowd into

The Luso-Indians during the Capture of Calcutta and the Black Hole Tragedy

* S. C. Hill, *op. cit.*, Vol. I. p. lxviii and p. 129.

† S. C. Hill, *op. cit.*, Vol. II. p. 28.

it to the number of thousands." The women and children were eventually placed on board the English vessels which steered two miles down the river. Meanwhile the Nawāb had broken through the lines of defences surrounding the Fort. Drake, the Governor of the Fort and Captain Minchin jumped into the two boats that were remaining and basely deserted their comrades in the Fort. The angry soldiers and officers elected Holwell, a civilian, their leader and resolved to hold out to the last. There were 170 men capable of defence besides the Luso-Indians and the Armenians. But they could not hold out long. On June 20th the Fort capitulated. Holwell was brought to the Nawāb in bonds but the latter released him and promised him and the prisoners his protection. The joy of the prisoners was great but it was soon dispelled. The great tragedy of the Black Hole (doubted by some) was to close round them. Its description is irrelevant. What is of interest is that Holwell refers to the Portuguese (Luso-Indians) who were among those ghastly forms that perished in the Black Hole.* Captain Grant in his account, dated 13th July 1756 confirms Holwell and says : "They were put into the Black Hole, a place about 16 feet square, to the number of 200 Europeans, Portuguese and Armenians of which many were wounded."† The Luso-Indians who escaped took refuge in Chandernagore. A letter from Watts and Collet, dated 7th July 1756, says that the French Government and Council maintained in Chandernagore by charity 3,000 poor Portuguese men, women and children, who were inhabitants of Calcutta.‡ The names of the Luso-Indians who died in the Black Hole are not spared to posterity. However, in the Mayor's Court Proceedings, 3rd May 1757, it is said one

* S. C. Hill. *op. cit.*, Vol. III. p. 153.
† S. C. Hill, *op. cit.*, Vol. I. p. 88.
‡ S. C. Hill, *op. cit.*, Vol. I. p. 59.

Maria Cornelius died during the siege and in the western aisle of the Bandel Church there is a tombstone of one Elizabeth de Sylva, with a Latin inscription to say that she died on 21st November 1756, aged 22 years from the troubles and infirmity arising from the war of the Moors against the English.

The Sack of Hooghly, 1756

After driving the English from Calcutta and re-naming the town *Alinagar*, Nawāb Sirāj-ud-daulā marched on the 25th June against their settlement of Hooghly, and sacked the town. It was not only the English who suffered. He demanded twenty lakhs of rupees from the Dutch who had a settlement in Chinsura. Rather than pay this huge sum of money the Dutch prepared to abandon their town altogether. Through the intercession of Coja Wasjid the sum was reduced to 4½ lakhs but the Dutch being unable to pay even this amount the Seths, the famous merchants, advanced it to them. The French were forced to pay to the Nawāb 3½ lakhs of rupees, the Danes Rs. 25,000, and the Prussians, or Emdeners as they were called, Rs. 5,000. The Portuguese or the Luso-Indians of Bandel had also to pay their toll of Rs. 5,000.* The amounts of money paid by the different nations, evidently indicate their relative commercial prosperity and importance. Though the Luso-Indians paid the least yet it is clear that in spite of not enjoying any privileges as they had enjoyed before or as the Dutch, the English and the French enjoyed at the time, their commercial activities had not ceased in Bandel. After playing this terrible havoc among the European settlers, Sirāj-ud-daulā wrote to the Emperor of Delhi in glowing terms priding himself upon "the most glorious achievement in Indostan since the days of Tamerlane."† The reply to this message was given by the guns of Clive

---

* S. C. Hill, *op. cit.*, Vol. I, p. 306

† *Orme Mss.*, *India* Vol. II, p. 79.

who, it may be added, knew no Indian language, but could speak Portuguese fluently and commanded his native troops in the Portuguese language.

Luso-Indian Militia

Since Clive laid the foundation of the British Empire in India on the fields of Bengal, the Luso-Indians, numbered among the English forces. A Luso-Indian Militia (in the Directories called Portuguese Militia) was maintained in Calcutta even in the last century. The Calcutta Annual Directory and Almanac for 1806 gives the names of the Portuguese officers in the Portuguese Militia which corresponded to the present or rather the recent Volunteer Battalions and was created for the defence of Calcutta :—

Captains : John Bateman, William Jackson, Mathew Louis, Louis Barreto.

Lieutenants : Courtney Smith, William Armstrong, Lawrence Picachy, James Robertson, Mathew Mendes.

Ensigns : Charles Leal, John de Faria, Joseph Pereira, William Mendes, Charles Cornelius.

All these gentlemen got their commissions in 1799 except the first three who got them in 1788. It is strange to find such English or non-Portuguese names as John Bateman, William Jackson, Courtney Smith, Lawrence Picachy and James Robertson in the list of the officers in the Portuguese Militia. It cannot be said these men were Englishmen or Anglo-Indians attached to the Portuguese militia for the names of some of the same gentlemen (James Robertson, Lawrence Picachy) appear in the list of Portuguese Merchants in the same Directory. Obviously they were Portuguese, *i. e.*, Luso-Indians with English names.

Luso-Indian Life

The mode of living of the Luso-Indians in places like Calcutta does not differ from that of the Anglo-Indians, with whom they are often indistinguishably mixed. The well-to-do portion of the

Luso-Indians have all their habits in common with the well-to-do Anglo-Indians. The poorer classes of the Luso-Indians in common with the poorer classes of Anglo-Indians, of Europeans, of Native Christians and of many other races, live the slum life of Calcutta in hopeless misery and degradation. These inhabitants of the slums are called *Kintalis* (from *Quintal, Kintal,* an enclosure), as their dwelling places consist of a courtyard, round which is built a hut, divided into a number of rooms, each about eight feet square, in which a family drags out its melancholy existence.

It is worthy of note, however, that in the last century, especially in its earlier decades numerous Luso-Indians held important appointments in the public offices of Calcutta as can be seen from the old Bengal and Calcutta Directories. Even to-day many Luso-Indians hold important positions, but most of them do not bear any Portuguese names and are recognized as Anglo-Indians. Generally speaking, it cannot be said that as a class the Luso-Indians are faring much worse than the Anglo-Indians in the struggle for existence, because the Luso-Indians in flourishing circumstances have merged into the community of the Anglo-Indians. Excepting the "*Kintal*" people, the Luso-Indian mode of living is generally like that of the Anglo-Indian, that is to say, like that of the European, and requires no description.

In Eastern Bengal

The Feringhis of Eastern Bengal have in general distinct characteristics of their own.* They are entirely or chiefly Indian in blood and are known as *Kala Feringhis* or *Matti Feringhis.* H. Beverley thus described the appearance of the

* Most of the Feringhis of Eastern Bengal are not descendants of the Portuguese but are pure Indian Christians with Portuguese names. Hence I have not called them Luso-Indians. These Feringhis are descendants of about 30,000 Indian converts who were baptized by the Portuguese Missionaries in the seventeenth and the eighteenth centuries. (*Vide infra.*)

Feringhis of Eastern Bengal in 1871: "In appearance the Feringhee is darker than the Hindustani, his complexion having a brownish tint. His hair is black and shiny. The men are short, thin, flat-chested and generally ill-made. When industrious, they can get through twice as much work as a native but their industry cannot be depended on. The girls are occasionally handsome. At Christmas, Easter and other great feasts, they exhibit their fondness for dress in bright-coloured damask garments. The hideous effect, however, is partially atoned for by the graceful white veil which rests on the head and falls mantilla-fashion to the ground."* Some Feringhis of Chittagong hold appointments in the public offices. True to their ancient traditions some Feringhis follow the sea-faring life. Many can also be seen in agricultural occupations. Though they are Portuguese in name and Christian by religion, there are various native customs and pagan rites among them. Their baptism ceremonies include the performances of the *Shatuara*, just as well as the creating of a *Padrino* or a *Madrina* (god-father and god-mother). The child is christend not only with the Christian name but sometimes with the *Shatuara* name. Similarly in the marriage and funeral ceremonies, can be discerned the relics of their ancestral Hindu or Muhammadan origin. L. S. S. O'Malley summarizes some of the customs of the Chittagong Feringhis in his Bengal Census Report of 1911: "In Chittagong they form connections with Magh and Musalman women, but do not marry them unless they are baptized. The children inherit the names of their fathers, whether they are the offsprings of concubines or not; if illegitimate, public acknowledgment by the parents entitles them to aliment and recognition. In manners and habits they resemble natives, and they are even darker in colour. Their religion, dress and

---

* Beverley, *The Feringhees of Chittagong*, Cal. Rev. 1871 Vol. 53.

names are practically the only things that distinguish them from their neighbours. They adopt English Christian names but the surnames are still Portuguese, such as DeBarros, Fernandez, DeSouza, DeSilva, Rebeiro, DeCruz, DaCosta Gonsalvez etc."*

Most of the Feringhis residing in Noakhali are cultivators or domestics. Though there is very little Portuguese blood in them, they proudly retain their Portuguese names, though these have undergone many changes, a Fernandes having become Foran and a Manoel having become Manu.† Some of them however are known by Bengali names and do not know that they had Christian names, which causes many difficulties when their marriages are celebrated according to Christian rites. Beveridge gave a brief description of the Feringhis of Bākarganj forty years ago, which is no less true to-day. He says, "The Feringhies of Sibpúr, (Bākarganj District) as they are called, are less numerous and less prosperous than they were half a century ago. They support themselves chiefly by going about to Mahomedan marriages and firing off *feux de joie.* They are also employed by the villagers to kill pigs, and some hold appointments in the police. They are indisposed to agriculture or other regular industry, and they are about as ignorant and superstitious as their Bengali neighbours. The only thing for which I can heartily praise them is the great neatness and cleanliness of their homesteads. Probably, however, the want of cattle or agricultural implements has something to do with this. They have adopted the Eastern notions about the seclusion of women, and do not like to give their daughters any education."‡ In Bākarganj there have, however, been very flourishing Feringhis. One Domingo de Silva made a large fortune in the rice trade and

* L. S. S. O'Malley, *Bengal Census Report,* 1911 p. 218.

† Noakhali Gazetteer, p. 34.

‡ Beveridge, *the District of Bákarganj*, p. 110.

was one of the leading *talukdar* in Buzurgumedpur. He re-built the Shibpur Church which was originally built by one Pedro Gonsalves. Among other leading *talukdars* in Buzurgumedpur, Beveridge mentioned Bagdeshwar (Balthazar) Johannes and Thomas Gomes.

It will be seen from what has been said that in a city like Calcutta, civilization has levelled Luso-Indians and Anglo-Indians in general to the same social status with a chiefly European mode of living, while in Eastern Bengal the representatives of the Portuguese are the Feringhis, most of whom are pure Indian Christians with Portuguese names, having distinct characteristics as a whole, and exhibiting a mixed picture of the Indian and the European.

Luso-Indian Statistics, Calcutta

The materials for a statistical account of the Luso-Indians are scarce and sometimes unreliable as the accuracy of the Censuses that have been taken from time to time largely depended on the whims and the inclinations of the people, especially of mixed descent. The figures in the earlier Censuses may be considered to be approximately correct, as the identity of the Luso-Indians, spoken of as Portuguese, was not, as it is to-day, in a large measure lost in the process of the generalised miscegenation such as occurs in Calcutta.*

In F. W. Birch's Census of 1837 the number of Portuguese (*i. e.*, chiefly Luso-Indians) in Calcutta was given as 3,181. Besides these, 4,746 Eurasians were mentioned. Chick's

* The term *Luso-Indians* is not used here as synonymous with *Feringhis*, which is adopted by the Censuses and Gazetteers, and includes not only the descendants of the Portuguese but also pure Indian Christians with Portuguese names. The Feringhis of Eastern Bengal are almost entirely Indian Christians converted by the Portuguese missionaries and cannot be called Luso-Indians which is a term adopted in this work to denote the Portuguese descendants or a community having generally some Portuguese blood in them. It is true, however, that the line of demarcation is broad, and that there are some Luso-Indians among the Feringhis of Eastern Bengal just as there are Feringhis among the Luso-Indians of Calcutta.

Census of 1872 mentioned 252 European Portuguese as residing in Calcutta. The figure is evidently incorrect. Only four years after (1876) H. Beverley took a Census of Calcutta which was much more scrupulous and accurate. In this Census the Luso-Indians, or Indo-Portuguese, as Beverley called them, were differentiated into a separate community and not included among the Eurasians or Indo-Europeans as it was done in the succeeding Censuses. The number of the Luso-Indians given was 707, and only 5 Portuguese were mentioned as resident in Calcutta. The total of the Eurasians numbered 10,566. A curious fact in this Census is that one Smith and one Campbell entered themselves as Spaniards. That the number of the Luso-Indians, which was 3,181 in 1837, (Birch's Census) dwindled down to 707 in 1876, is explained by the fact that they identified themselves gradually with the Eurasians or Anglo-Indians of the present day. In 1881, H. Beverley took another Census of Calcutta and its Suburbs, in which 19 were mentioned as having been born in Portugal, 261 as speaking the Portuguese language and 55 (41 males 14 females) as being European Portuguese. The discrepancy between the figures is obvious. Only 19 who were born in Portugal and not 55 could have been European Portuguese unless this number included the descendants of the latter born in Calcutta. The difference between the two figures (36) gives most probably the number of the Goans, who returned themselves as Portuguese. The Goans are politically entitled to call themselves Portuguese and are officially recognised as such by the Portuguese Government. The majority of those who declared that Portuguese was their language must have also been Goans, and, in fact, they mentioned Goa as their birth-place. It would have been curious to know how many Luso-Indians, if at all, gave Portuguese as their language.

In his second Census Report (1881), H. Beverley gave up

the term Indo-Portuguese and classed all Luso-Indians among the Eurasians, whose number he gave as 9,410. The later Censuses of Calcutta do not throw much light on the community of Luso-Indians, for they are classed as Indo-Europeans or as Eurasians.

In the Calcutta Census Report, 1911, by O'Malley, which is the latest one and formed part of the general Census of India, there are palpable discrepancies regarding the "Portuguese." The Luso-Indians are all included among the Anglo-Indians. The number of those who declared themselves as belonging to Portuguese nationality and speaking the Portuguese language, was 254. Only 10, however, are mentioned as having been born in Portugal, and this may be taken as the number of European Portuguese in Calcutta. The rest are undoubtedly Goans. It is doubtful whether any Luso-Indians or Indian Christians with Portuguese names claimed Portuguese nationality.

All over Western Bengal, isolated numbers of Luso-Indians can be found. In the Hooghly District where lay the headquarters of the Portuguese, there are comparatively few Luso-Indians, for they have migrated to Calcutta. The Hooghly Gazetteer, 1912, mentions that there were 94 Eurasians, more than half of whom were Roman Catholics. It cannot be definitely said how many of these were Luso-Indians.

In Hooghly

Near Geonkhali in Midnapore District there is a community of Luso-Indians, who in 1911 numbered 129. They call themselves descendants of some Portuguese gunners whom the Raja of Mahisadal brought from Chittagong in the latter half of the eighteenth century to protect his property against Mahratta raids. These soldiers settled on some rent-free lands granted by the Raja and intermarried with the women of the place. Many of them seem, however, to be pure Indians and as the Census

In Midnapore

Report has "they bear both Bengali and Portuguese names such as DeCruz, Rosario and Lobo, but they are Bengalis in every thing but name and religion."* Most of them are Roman Catholics but some of them were converted to Protestantism by Rev. J. Bower, of the S. P. G. Mission, who visited them in 1838 and described them as "nominal Christians with scarcely any sign of Christianity except a few images of the Virgin Mary and saints, no public worship or prayer, no scriptures, no sacraments."

In Eastern Bengal

In Eastern Bengal the Portuguese descendants are very few compared with the Indian Christians who were converted in enormous numbers by the Portuguese Missionaries in the seventeenth and the eighteenth centuries and whose descendants still bear Portuguese names and are now called *Kala Feringhis.* According to the Augustinian accounts about thirty thousand people were converted in Eastern Bengal before 1680.† By 1750, the number of the Christians for Eastern Bengal was reduced to 8733, as it appears from the Relation of Frei Ambrosio de Santo Agostinho given to the Viceroy of Portuguese India.‡ What happened to the rest is a question that need not be discussed here. It is beyond doubt that a vast majority of those who bear Portuguese names in Eastern Bengal are the descendants of these Indian converts and not the descendants of pure Portuguese, who were more adventurers than settlers in Eastern Bengal. Hence in order to differentiate between the two communities they are called in this work Feringhis and not Luso-Indians.

---

* L. S. S. O'Malley, *Bengal Census Report*, 1911, p. 218.

† Letters of Frei Fernão Queiros (Oct. 7, 1678) and of others, preserved in one of the volumes of the Marsden Mss., Brit. Mus Add. Mss., 9855. Cf.Fr. H. Hosten's translations in the *Catholic Herald of India*, Aug. 29, 1917 and succeeding Nos.

‡ *O Chronista de Tissuari* Vol. II pp. 57-62. Cf Fr Hosten's Translation in *Catholic Herald of India*, Dec. 19, 1917 and succeeding Nos.

The earliest statistics of the Feringhis of Chittagong were published by H. Beverley in the *Calcutta Review*, 1871 Vol. 53.

Chittagong, Noakhali, Bākarganj, Dacca

In 1859 the Feringhis of Chittagong numbered 1,025, the males being 510, the females 515. In 1860, the number of the males decreased to 466, while that of the females rose to 519, on the whole there being a falling off of 40 persons. In 1866 the number further decreased to 865, of whom 424 were males, and 441 females. Besides those resident in Feringhi Bazar, Beverley ascertained the existence of some 322 Feringhis, of whom 85 were returned as adult males, 107 as adult females, 82 as boys and 48 as girls. From 1845 to 1865 the number of births among the Feringhis was 984 and the number of deaths from 1815 to 1866 was 1,082. The Chittagong Gazetteer, 1908, is not definite about the number of the Feringhis in Chittagong. It says that out of the 1,237 Christians that are found there, most belong to the Feringhi community. In the Bengal Census Report of 1911, the number of the Feringhis in the whole of the Eastern Bengal was given as 1,202, but the number must have been a much greater one. They were classed among the Eurasians and were mentioned as mostly residing in Bākarganj, Noakhali and Chittagong. According to the Bengal Census Report of 1901, in Noakhali alone there were about 490 Feringhis, almost all of whom were Roman Catholics and were classed among the Eurasians. In the Bākarganj Gazetteer (1918) a thousand Roman Catholics are mentioned out of whom 841 are the parishioners of the Portuguese Church of Shibpur or Padrishibpur. These numbers include also the native Christians but most of them bear Portuguese names and though really Indian in blood are called Feringhis or Portuguese. In 1876 Beveridge gave the number of the Feringhis in Bākarganj as 800*. Hence the Feringhis of Noakhali and Bākarganj would

* Beveridge, *the District of Bakarganj*, p. 110.

exceed in number the figure given by O'Malley for the whole of Eastern Bengal. In the absence of more accurate statistics, the present number of the Luso-Indians in Eastern Bengal may be roughly put down to about 10,000,—Dacca District accounting for about 6,000, Chittagong for about 1,000, Bākarganj District for 1,000, Noakhali for about 800, Assam, Tippera and other places for about 1020.*

The conclusion that can be arrived at from these statistics is that the number of the Luso-Indians and the Feringhis in Bengal is on the decline. In the case of the Feringhis of Eastern Bengal the reason is that they are not prolific, a fact already pointed out by H. Beverley in his article in the *Calcutta Review*.† In Calcutta a different factor has to be considered. The Luso-Indians in Calcutta gradually merge themselves into the Anglo-Indian community, either by intermarriages or by changing or modifying their names and thus lose all association with the Portuguese, while few Portuguese come and settle in Bengal and leave their descendants.

---

* These figures are chiefly based on the number of parishioners of the Portuguese and other Catholic Churches in Eastern Bengal. These parishioners generally bear Portuguese names, and those who do not, have been excluded.

† *The Feringhees of Chittagong*, Cal. Rev. 1871 Vol. 53.

CHAPTER XVII

PORTUGUESE LANGUAGE

The Portuguese language was, in the seventeenth and even in the eighteenth centuries, a *lingua franca* in Bengal. It was the medium of converse not only among the Portuguese and their descendants, but also among the Indians and later on among the English, the Dutch, the French and the other settlers who came to Bengal. Only in the native Courts the Persian language was used. Long after the Portuguese power was extinguished their language was freely spoken in Bengal as in other parts of India The Portuguese language was not confined to Hooghly and Chittagong only, but it was generalized throughout the country for as already stated the Portuguese had small settlements all over the banks of the Ganges and on the lower parts of the Brahmaputra and of the various rivers that flow into them. Outside their homes the people of Bengal came either for commercial purposes or for litigations and were forced to adopt the language of the Portuguese who knew no Bengali. Hence enormous number of Portuguese words have found their way in the Bengali language.

In Calcutta, Hooghly, Balasore and other settlements the East India Company employees made themselves understood only in Portuguese ; even their servants spoke no other language but Portuguese. Marshman well summarises the important part which the Portuguese language played at one time in Bengal. He says : "Portuguese language came in with the Portuguse power two centuries and a half before, and survived its extinction. It was the lingua franca of all foreign settlements and was the ordinary medium of conversation between the

Europeans and their domestics; while Persian was the language of intercourse with the Native Courts. Even in Calcutta Portuguese was more commonly used by the servants of the company and the settlers than the language of the country. The Charter granted to the East India Company, at the beginning of the 18th century contained a provision that they should maintain one Minister at each of their garrisons and superior factories and that he should be bound to acquire the Portuguese language within a twelve-month of reaching India. Clive who was never able to give an order in any native language, spoke Portuguese with fluency. The use of this language has since died out in Bengal so completely that the descendants of the Portuguese now speak Bengali from their cradle. Yet down to so late a period as 1828, the Governor of Cri Rāmapur, a Norwegian, received the daily report of his little garrison of 30 sepoys from the Native commandant, a native of Oudh, in Portuguese."

Kiernander the first Prostestant missionary in Bengal preached in 1780 in the old Mission Church in the Portuguese language ; Clarke another missionary who came to Calcutta studied the Portuguese language to preach to the native congregations. Ringletanha did the same in 1797. A writer in the Quaterly Review of 1814 asserts "If in the eventual triumph of Christianianity in India a Romish Church should be formed, Portuguese will be the language of that Church wherever it stands". As a matter of fact, up to 1811 Portuguese was used in all the Christian Churches in Calcutta whether under the direction of the Portuguese or not.

In connection with the missionary labours it is an interesting fact that the first three printed books in the Bengali language (though in Roman characters) were printed by the Portuguese in Lisbon in 1743. These books on religious ins-

* Marshman, *History of Cri Rāmapur Mission*, Vol. I. pp. 21-22.

truction were arranged for the press by an Augustinian, Frei Manuel Assumpção, who was in Nagori near Dacca. One of these books can be seen in the Library of the Asiatic Society of Bengal, Calcutta.

To-Day the Portuguese language is not spoken among the descendants of the Portuguese or their converts. In a few families a corrupted form of Portuguese is spoken largely intermingled with English words. Only a few years ago a parish priest of the Portuguese Mission in Calcutta confessed a Luso-Indian lady in a broken but comprehensibe Portuguese. Many descendants as Marshman remarked, speak nothing but Bengali. In general, the English language is spoken with a peculiar soft accent and a modulation of voice suggestive of Portuguese. They use however, some Portuguese phrases and words, which very curiously refer to religious ceremonies, to greetings and to the dinner-table.

The following are some of the words that have survived in the English, which the some Portuguese descendants and some Feringhis speak, and which are peculiar to them. Besides these words, they use other Portuguese words or their derivations which have passed into the English language in general, and which are called Anglo-Indian words. H. Beverley noticed many of these Luso-Indian words being in use in Eastern Bengal.*

Luso-Indian and Feringhi Words

Greetings	Movit-obrigad (Muito obrigado)	Thank you
	Filiz nuevo an (feliz novo anno)	Happy new year
	Filiz Natal (feliz natal)	Merry Christmas
	Bon di (Bom dia)	Good Day
	Ba nite (boa noite)	Good night

* *The Feringhees of Chittagong*, Cal. Rev. 1871 Vol. 53.

Days of the week	Dooming (domingo)	Sunday
	Sagund-fer (Segunda-feira	Monday
	Ters fer (tersa-feira)	Tuesday
	Kart fer (Quarta-feira)	Wednesday
	Quint fer (Quinta-feira)	Thursday
	Sext fer (Sexta-feira)	Friday
	Sabbaddoo (Sabado)	Saturday
Words associated with religious ceremonies	Quaresma (Quaresma)	Lent
	Resuresam (Resurreição)	Resurrection
	Fillad (Filhado)	God-son
	Fillad (Filhada)	God-daughter
	Padrin (Padrinho)	God-father
	Madrin (Madrinha)	God-mother
	Compadre (compadre)	God-father
	Comadre (Comadre)	God-mother
Words associated with the Dinner table	Janto (Janter)	Dinner
	Cer (cear)	Supper
	Almusso (almoco)	Break-fast
	Bindaloo (Vinho de alho)	Dishes
	Foogath (fogado)	
	Pantifrith (pente-frito)	
	Bol-comaro (bolo-comadre)	
	Mel-de-rose (Mel de rosa)	
	Temperado	

Anglo-Indian Words of Portuguese Origin

Many Portuguese words, directly or indirectly, have found their way in the Anglo-Indian vocabulary, and thence into the English language. Some Anglo-Indian colloquialisms, such as *goglet*, *gram*, *plantain*, *muster*, *caste*, *peon*, *padre*, *mistry*, *almyra*, *aya*, *cobra*, *mosquito*, *pomfret*, *cameez*, *palmyra* are distinctly Portuguese in origin. Words such as *palanquin*, *mandarin*, *mangelin*, *monsoon*, *typhoon*, *mango*, *mangosteen*, *jack-fruit*, *batta*, *curry*, *chop*, *cangee*, *coir*, *cutch*, *catamaran*, *cassanar*, *nabob*, *avadaval*, *betel*, *areca*, *benzoin*, *corge*, *copra*, are native in origin but have found their way into the Anglo-Indian vocabulary through the Portuguese.*

Most of the words, which the early Englishmen in India used, are now obsolete. Yet it is not likely that Portuguese words like caste and cobra will be ever deleted from the English Dictionary. The following Anglo-Indian words are mentioned on the authority of Yule and Burnell (*Hobson-Jobson*) and Mons. R. Dalgado (*Influencia do Vocabulario Português em Linguas Asiaticas*). For details and controversial points the readers are referred to those learned works.

Portuguese	*English* (*Anglo-Indian*)
Abada	Abada (rhynoceros)
Achar	Achar (pickles)
Aia	Ayah
Albacora	Albacore (a species of fish)
Alcatifa	Alcatif (carpet)
Alcatraz	Albatross
Aldeia	Aldea (a village)
Aljófar	Aljofar (a jewel, pearl)
Ama	Amah (wet-nurse)
Amargosa	Margosa (*neem* tree)
Ananás	Ananas (Pine-apple)
Anil	Anile, Neel (indigo)
Apa	Ap, appas,
Areca	Areca (betel-nut)
Armário	Almyrah (wardrobe)
Arraca	Arrack, Rack (distilled spirit)
Arrátel	Rattle, rottle (pound weight)
Azagaia	Assegay (spear)
Bailadeira	Bayadere (dancing-girl)

* *Vide* Yule-Burnell, *Hobson-Jobson*, Intro. p. xix. Though it is not strictly correct, the Anglo-Indian words are mentioned under the heading "English," for the term "Anglo-Indian" has lost its former significance.

Portuguese	*English*
Balchão	Balachong, balichaw.
Balde	Balty (bucket)
Bambu	Bambu
Bandeja	Bandejah (a tray)
Bangue	Bang (hemp)
Basta	Bus (enough)
Bata	Batta (rations)
Batão	Batta (difference in exchange)
Bate	Batty, paddy
Batel	Batel, botilla (a boat)
Bazaruco	Budgrook (coin)
Beijoim	Benzoin
Beringela	Brinjaul
Bétele	Betel (betel-nut)
Bicho do mar	Beech-de-Mer (sea slug)
Bilimbim	Blimbee, (fruit of *Averrhoa B.*)
Bói	Boy (servant)
Bonito	Bonito (a fish)
Bonzo	Bonze (budhist priest)
Botica	Boutique (shop)
Botiqueiro	Botickeer (shop-keeper)
Brava	Brab (Palmyra tree)
Bufalo	Buffalo
Cabouco	Cabook (Laterite)
Cafre	Caffre
Cairo	Coir
Caixa (molda)	Cash (coins)
Caju	Kaju, Cashew (tree or fruit)
Calabaça	Calabash
Calafate	Calputee (caulker)
Calaluz	Calaluz (rowing vessel)
Camara	Cumra (chamber)

Portuguese	*English*
Camisa	Cammeeze (shirt)
Campo	Campoo (camp)
Canja	Congee, canjee (rice preparation)
Carambola	Carambola (fruit)
Caravela	Caravel (sailing vessel)
Caril	Curry
Casta	Caste
Castiço	Castees (Portuguese born in India)
Catanar	Cattanar, cassanar (Syrian priest)
Cate	Catechu, cutch
Catur	Catur, cutter (boat)
Cavala	Cavally (a fish)
Chá	Chaw (tea)
Chapa	Chop (a seal-impression)
Chave	Chabee (key)
Chuname	Chunam (prepared lime)
Cipai	Seepoy
Cobra	Cobra (snake)
Cobra de capelo	Cobra capella (a snake)
Cobra manila	Cobra manilla (a snake)
Côco	Cocoa, coco-nut
Côco do mar	Coco-de-Mer (double coco-nut)
Comprador	Compradore, compadare (a purchaser)
Copra	Coprah (dried kernel of coco-nut)
Corja	Corge, coorge (a score)
Cornaca	Cornac (elephant driver)
Cotonia	Cuttanee (a kind of piece-goods)

Portuguese	*English*
Côvado	Covid (a measure)
Curral	Corral (enclosure)
Cuspidor	Cuspadore (spittoon)
Doirado	Dorado (fish)
Emprestimo	Imprest (advance money)
Escrivão	Scrivan (clerk, writer)
Estivador	Stevedore (one who stows and unloads cargo of a ship)
Fazendeiro	Fazendar (proprietor)
Feitor	Factor
Feitoria	Factory
Fogaça	Fogass (a cake baked in embers)
Foros	Foras lands (lands reclaimed from the sea)
Fulano	Falaun (somebody, so-and-so)
Galeão	Galleon
Gentio	Gentoo (a gentile)
Gergelim	Gingelly (*till* Hind.)
Gorgoleta	Goglet
Grão	Gram
Guarda	Guard
Gudão	Godown
Holandes	Hollander
Horta	Oart (coco-nut garden)
Hortulana	Ortolan (a lark)
Igreja	Girja (church)
Jaca	Jack fruit
Jagra	Joggree
Janela	Jillmill (window-shutters)
Jangada	Jangar (a raft)
Lagarto	Alligator
Lascarim	Lascar (a sailor)

Portuguese	*English*
Leilão	Leelam, neelam (auction)
Lima	Lime (fruit, *citrus medica*)
Lingua	Linguist (interpreter)
Louvado	Lawad (arbitrator)
Machila	Muncheel, Manjeeb (a kind of palanquin)
Mandador	Mandadore (one who commands)
Mandarim	Mandarin (a counsellor, officer)
Manga	Mango
Mangelim	Mangelin (weight)
Mangostão	Mangosteen
Manguço	Mongoose
Manilha	Manilla-man (a dealer in corals or gems)
Mão	Maund (weight)
Martelo	Martil, martol (a hammer)
Mesquita	Mosque
Mestiço	Mustees, mestiz(a half-caste)
Mestre	Mistry, mestri (a workman)
Monção	Monsoon
Mordexim	Mort-de-chien (cholera)
Mosquito	Mosquito
Mostra	Muster (a pattern)
Mouro	Moor (a Muhammadan)
Mura	Moorah (a measure)
Nababo	Nabob, nawab
Naique	Naik (o corporal)
Naire	Nair (a caste in Malabar)
Negro	Nigger
Ola	Ollah (palm-leaf)
Padre	Padree

Portuguese	*English*
Pagode	Pagoda
Palanquim	Palanquin
Palmeira	Palmyra (a palm-tree)
Pampano	Pomfret (fish)
Papaia	Papaya
Pataca	Pataca (a coin)
Patacão	Patacoon (a coin)
Paulista	Paulist (a Jesuit)
Peão	Peon (an orderly)
Peres	Pairie (a variety of mango)
Pertenças	Pertenças (appurtenances)
Picota	Picotta (a contrivance to draw water)
Pintada	Pintado (a painted cloth)
Pintado	Pintado (a kind of pigeon)
Poial	Paial, pial (a raised platform)
Quintal	Kintal, kintalis (a mixed class of people in Calcutta)
Quita-sol	Kitty-sol (an umbrella)
Recibo	Reseed (receipt)
Rial	Reas, rees (coin)
Rolão	Rolong (flour)
Sagu	Sago
Sagüeiro	Sagwire (a variety of palm)
Sumatra	Sumatra (Geog.)
Sombreiro	Sombrero, summerhead (umbrella, broad brimmed hat)
Talapõi	Talapoin (Budhist priest)
Tambaca	Tomback (alloy)
Topaz	Topass (a half-caste, Indian christian)
Tronco	Trunk of a tree
Tufão	Typhoon

Portuguese	*English*
Tutanaga	Tootnague (chinese zinc)
Valado	Walade (a property by the river-side)
Varanda	Verandah
Verdura	Verdure (vegetables)

Bengali Words of Portuguese Origin

Lists of Portuguese words in the Bengali language have appeared now and then in modern writings. But these lists are not only incomplete but often faulty. Mons. R. Dalgado's work on "*The Influence of the Portuguese Vocabulary on the Asiatic Languages*," has supplied a long-felt deficiency. Mons. Dalgado mentions about a hundred and seventy Portuguese words current in the Bengali Language, but the author has been able to add more to the list. It is doubtful, however, whether some Bengali words, marked with interrogation marks, are derived from Sanskrit or other languages. For a discussion on controversial points Monsenhor Dalgado's work should be consulted. The words marked with asterisks are either religious terms or are chiefly current among Bengali Christians.

Bengali	*Portuguese*	*English*
Bāphādú	Abafado	A dish
Kābár	Acabar	Finish, Last day of the month
*Ag-bent	Agua benta	Holy water
Aiyà	Aia	Ayah
*Alamp	Alampada	Lamp, lantern

Bengali	*Portuguese*	*English*
Alkātrà	Alcatrão	Pitch, Tar
Alpinêt, Alpín	Alfinete	Pin
Almús	Almoço	Breakfast
*Altàr	Altar	Altar
*Alva	Alva	Alb, an ecclesiastical vestment.
Ambar	Ambar	Amber
*Amen	Amen	Amen
Anārasí	Ananàs	Pine-apple
Nona,	Anona	A fruit (*Anona Reticulata*)
*Apostôl	Apóstolo	Apostle
Almārí	Armàrio	Almyrah
Atá	Ata	Custard-apple
*Avemārí	Ave Maria	Hail Mary
*Avó	Avó	Grandfather
Bàsan	Bacia	Plate
? Bhàp, bāspô	Bafo	Vapour, breath
Bajrá	Baixel	Barque
Balcham'	Balchão	Balachong
Bāldí, Bāltí	Balde	Bucket
Bànk	Banco	Bench
Bāvtijmà	Baptismo	Baptism
*Bentút	Bençāo	Benediction
Biskut	Biscoito	Biscuit
*Bispa	Bispo	Bishop
*Bovasnoiti	Boas noites	Good night
*Bovás tardiyà	Boas tardes	Good evening
Bayá	Bóia	Buoy
Boyám'	Boião	An earthen vessal
*Bolinos	Bolinho	A little cake
Bomá	Bomba	Hydraulic machine
Bomsdiyá	Bons dias	Good day

Bengali	*Portuguese*	*English*
Botam'	Botão	Button
? Botal, botal	Botelha	Bottle
Kaderá, kadārá	Cadeira	Chair
? Káphi	Café	Coffee
Kāphirí	Cafre	Caffre
Kāju	Caju	Cashew
Kakatua	Catatua	Parrot
Kālāpātí	Calafate	Calker
Kāldó	Caldo	Broth, grevy
•Kális	Calís	Chalice
Kamíj	Camisa	Shirt
Kāmán	Canhão	Cannon
Kāppa	Capa	Overcoat
Káj	Casa (de botão)	Button-hole
Kasūl	Casula	Chasuble, an ecclesiastical vestment
•Kātekísma	Catecismo	Catechism
Katholika	Católico	Catholic
*Semeterí	Cemitério	Cemetery
Chá	Chá	Tea
? Cháp chhāp	Chapa	Seal, type, stamp
Chābi, chábi sābí	Chave	Key
Kôch	Coche	Palanquin, sofa
*Komādrí	Comadre	God mother
Komedorí	Comedoria	Eatables
*Kompādrí	Compadre	God-father
? Kampás	Compasso	Compass
*Komuniyāñ	Comunhão	Communion
*Komphisañ	Confissão	Confession
•Konsuvādá	Consoada	A light supper
Karnel	Coronel corporal	Colonel
Kobi, kobíxak	Couve	Cabbage
Karābu	Cravo	Nail, also cloves

Bengali	*Portuguese*	*English*
*Krisma	Crisma	Chrism
Kristáñ	Cristão	Christian
Krux, kruxācriti	Cruz	Cross
Koindú	Cunhado	Brother-in-law
*Dalmatíc	Dalmatica	Dalmatic
Damás	Damasco	Damask
*Devus	Deus	God
*Anjeūl	Em joelhos	Kneeling down
*Entrudú	Entrudo	Shrove-tide, carnival
*Ejmolá	Esmola	Alms
Ispát	Espada	Sword
*Spiritú, Sāntú	Espirito Santo	Holy Ghost
Spanj	Esponja	Sponge
Stāntí	Estante	Desk
Istrí	Estirar	To iron
Estól	Estola	Ecclesiastical vestment
Fāltár	Faltar	To fail, to want
Festà	Festa	Feast
Fitá	Fita	Ribbon
Formā	Forma	Form
Funnel	Funil	Funnel
Garādiyá	Gráde	A grate partition with bars
Gūdam'	Gudão	Godown
Abdú	Habíto	Sutaine
*Isopa	Hissope	A brush to sprinkle holy water
*Osti	Hóstia	Host
Girjá, Girjjá	Igreja	Church
*Insensú	Incenso	Incense
Ingláj	Inglês	English
Irmáñ	Irmão	Brother

Bengali	*Portuguese*	*English*
Julāp	Jalapa	Jalap
Jānālá, Janāla	Janela	Window
(Juá, Juva-Khelá)	Jogar	Play
Lantará	Lanterna	Lantern
Nilám', Nilām, Nilāmá	Leilão	Auction
Lebu	Limão	Lemon
Madí	Madrinha	Godmother
Māldisán	Maldição	Malediction
*Maná	Mana	Sister
*Maná	Mana'	Manna
*Mānú	Mano	Brother
Mārtel	Martelo	Hammer
Mástūl	Mastro	Mast
Mej	Mesa	Table
*Misán	Missão	Mission
*Misiyonár	Missionario	Missionary
*Muita mercê	Muita mercê	To your health
*Nātál	Natal	Christmas
*Novená	Novena	Novena
*Ol	Oleo (santo)	Holy oil
Opa'	Opa	A kind of mantle without sleeves
Orgán	Orgão	Organ
Pādrí	Padre	Priest
*Pādrovādú	Padroado	*Padroado*
Pādú	Padrinho	God father
Paum	Pão	Bread
*Pāpá	Papa	Pope
Papayá	Papaia	Papaya fruit
*Pāskuvá	Páscoa	Easter
*Particul	Partícula	Particle
Páti-hams	Pato	Goose

Bengali	*Portuguese*	*English*
Pená	Pena	Penalty, punishment
? Pilurí,	Pelouro	Pillory, iron-ball
Perú, Piyará	Pera	Pear
Perú	Peru	Turkey
Piyá	Pia	Holy water basin
Pipá, Pipe, Pimpa	Pipa	Pipe (of wine)
Pirij	Pires	Saucer
Pistol	Pistola	Pistol
*Pobrí	Pobre	Poor, a servant of the church
Perek	Prego	Nail
*Provijor	Provisor	Purveyor, Provisor
*Purgātorí	Purgatório	Purgatory
*Kárūbím	Querubim	Cherub
Kintál	Quintal	Compound
*Korjmu	Quaresma	Lent
Rêndá	Renda	Lace, rent
Reytor	Reitor	Rector
Resto	Resto	Fund, remainder
*Rituál	Ritual	Ritual
Sābán, sābānbat	Sabão	Soap
Sākrāmentú	Sacramento	Sacrament
Sacrár	Sacrário	Tabernacle
Sankristán	Sacristão	Sacriston
Chhāyá	Saia	Gown
Saláta	Salada	Salad
Sāvudí	Saude	Health
Siyor	Senhor	Sir
Surtti	Sorte	Fate, luck
Sobrpêlíz	Sobrepeliz	Eclesistical vestment

Bengali	*Portuguese*	*English*
Tamák, tāmák, tamáku, tāmakú, tamrakú	Tabaco	Tobacco
? Tití	Tia	Aunt
? Tív	Tio	Uncle
*Tersú	Terco	Rosary
Tocā	Toca	To note down
Toyále	Toalha	Towel
? Tuphán	Tufão	Typhoon
Tumbá	Tumba	Tomb, coffin
*Turibúl	Turíbulo	Censer
? Bārāndá	Varanda	Verandah
*Berdí	Verde	Green
Boroga	Verga	Rod, rafter
Burmá	Verruma	Tendril, gimlet
Vévu	Véu	Veil
Biyala	Viola	Viola, guitar

Assamese Words of Portuguese Origin

As the Assamese and the Oorya languages are spoken in the Bengal Presidency (Assam and Orissa), lists of Portuguese words in those languages will not be out of place. These words are mostly the same as the ones current in the Bengali language*.

Assamese	*Portuguese*	*English*
Achár	Achar	Pickle
Aiyá	Aia	Ayah
Alpin	Alfinete	Pin
Almārí, ālmāirá	Armário	Almyrah

* There are Portuguese words current also in the *Garo* and the *Khassi* languages, spoken in the southern part of Assam. For the list of these words, Mons. Dalgado's work should be consulted.

Assamese	*Portuguese*	*English*
Atlas	Ata	Custard-apple
Bájan	Bacia	Basin
? Báp	Bafo	Vapour, Breath
Bhoyám'	Boião	An earthen vessel
Boma-gola	Bomba	Hydraulic machine
Káphi	Café	Cofee
Káphri	Cafre	Caffre
Cháh, chái	Chá	Tea
? Cháp and derivatives	Chapa	Stamp, impress
Chábi, sábi	Chave	Key
Kampás	Compasso	Compass
Istrí	Estirar	To iron
Phitá	Fita	Ribbon
Phataká	Foguete	A cracker
Gūdam'	Gudão	Go-down
Girjá	Igreja	Church
Ingráji	Inglês	English
Jalangani	Janela	Window
Juá and derivatives	Jôgo	Play
Lilám'	Leilão	Auction
Nemú	Limão	Lemon
Mastúl	Mastro	Mast
Mej	Mesa	Table
Mistrí	Mestre	Master
Pāti-hámh	Pato	Goose
Perú	Peru	Turkey
Pipá	Pipa	Pipe (of wine)
Piris	Pires	Saucer
Rachita	Recibo	Receipt
Sában, Chaban	Sabão	Soap
Sāyá	Saia	Gown, Petticoat

Assamese.	*Portuguese.*	***English.***
Tambaru, Tamburu	Tambor	Drum
Barandá	Varanda	Verandah

Oorya Words of Portuguese Origin

Ooriya	*Portuguese*	*English*
Achár	Achar	Pickle
Aiyá	Aia	Ayah
Anáras	Ananás	Pine-apple
At	Ata	Custard-apple
Bájan	Bacia	Plate, Basin
? Bháp, Bhámp	Bafo	Vapour, breath
Botal	Botelha	Bottle
Kāphí	Café	Cofee
Kalāpātí	Calafate	Calker
Kam'rá	Câmara	Chamber
Chá	Chá	Tea
Chháp, Chhāpá	Chapa	Stamp, impress
Chābí	Chave	Key
Kobi	Couve	Cabbage
Istrí	Estirar	To iron, Stretch
Phitá	Fita	Ribbon
Falána	Fulano	So-and-so
Gudáma	Gudão	Go-down
Girjá	Igreja	Church
Juá and Derivatives	Jôgo	Play
Nīlám	Leilão	Auction
? Lemu, Nemu, Nimu	Limão	Lemon
Mástul	Mastro	Mast
Mej	Mesa	Table
Papayá	Papaia	Papaya
Páti-hams	Pato	Goose

Uriya.	*Portuguese.*	*Euglish.*
Perú	Peru	Turkey
Rasíd	Recibo	Receipt
Sábun, Xābiní	Sabão	Soap
Sāgú	Sagu	Sago
Sapát	Sapato	Shoe
Surti	Sorte	Fate, luck
Tamákhu	Tabaco	Tobacco
? Tuphán	Tufão	Typhoon

Hindustani words of Portuguese Origin

Hindustani, whether an independent language or a dialact of Hindi and Urdu, is the *lingua franca* of India and is spoken in Bengal. Many Portuguese words are current in Hindustani and some have passed through its medium into other languages.

Hindustani	*Portuguese*	*English*
Achár	Achar	Pickle
Ayá	Aia	Ayah
Alpin, Alpín	Alfinete	Pin
Amá	Ama	Wet-Nurse
Ambar	Ambar	Amber
Amín	Amen	Amen
Ananás	Ananás	Pine-apple
? Anīsún	Anis	Anise
Almārí	Armário	Almyrah
Ratal	Arrátel	Pound (weight)
At, Atá	Ata	Custard apple
Basan, Bójan	Bacia, Bacio	Plate
Báph	Bafo	Vapour, breath
Bajrá, Bujrá	Baixel	Arabic barque
Baldí, Baltí	Balde	Bucket

Hindustani	*Portuguese*	*English*
Balsán	Balsamo	Balsam
Baptismá	Baptismo	Baptism
Bas	Basta	Enough
Bāolá	Baú	Trunk
Berinjal	Beringela	Brinjaul
Bilet	Bilhete	Ticket
Bilambú	Bilimbim	A fruit
Biskut	Biscoito	Biscuit
Boyam'	Boião	An earthen vessel
Bam'kágulá	Bomba	Pump
Bótám'	Botão	Button
?Botal, Bottal	Botelha	Bottle
Kalpatti, Kalāpatiyá	Calafate	Calker
Kāmará, Kamará, Kamera, Kam'rá	Câmara	Chamber
Qamis, Qamíj	Camisa	Shirt
Kampú	Campo	Field
Qandil	Candil	Kandi (weight)
Kaptán	Capitão	Captain
Karābín	Carabina	Rifle
Kārtús	Cartucho	Bullet
Káj	Casa	House
Chá, cháh, Cháy, Cháe	Chá	Tea
Chháp and derivatives	Chapa	Press, imprint
Chāví, Chābí, Chábhí	Chave	Key
Kochbán	Cocheiro	Driver, Coachman
Kampás	Compasso	Compass
Kurdham'	Cordão	Chain
Kobí	Couve	Cabbage

Hindustani	*Portuguese*	*English*
Kuñya, Kuñiyáñ, Koniya	Cunha	Wedge
Ispát	Espada	Sword
Istrí	Estirar	To iron
Phá1tu	Falto	Excess
Fitá, Fītá, Phītá	Fita	Ribbon
? Phatakhá	Foguete	Cracker
Farmá	Forma	Form, Mould
? Fulán, Fulaná	Fulano	So and So
Jinjalí	Gergelim	*Til*-oil
Garādiyá	Grade	Grate partition
Garnál	Granada	Grenade
Garandil	Granadeiro	Grenadier
Gārad	Guarda	Guard
Godám'	Gudão	Go-down
Girjá	Igreja	Church
Angrezí	Inglês	English
Juláb, Julláb	Jalapa	Jalap
Jhilmil	Janela	Window
Jakêt	Jaqueta	Jacquet
Juákhelná and derivatives	Jogar	To play
Lamp	Lampada	Lamp
Nilám'	Leilão	Auction
Līmú, Lemú, Nīmbú	Limão	Lemon
Langūchá	Linguiça	Sausage
Man	Maná	Manna
Marmar, Marmarí	Mármore	Marble
Mārtil, Martol, Martol, Martaul	Martelo	Hammer
Mastúl	Mastro	Mast

Hindustani	*Portuguese*	*English*
Mājkabár	Mês (acabar)	End of month
Mej, Mez	Mesa	Table
Mastisa	Mestiço	Half-caste
Mistrí	Mestre	Master, workman
Mūsikí, Mūsígí, Mūsīgīdán	Música	Music
? Naul, Nuval, Naul ká mál	Naulo	Freight
Argan, Arghanúm	Orgão	Organ
Pādrí	Padre	Priest
Pagár	Paga	Pay
Pasún	Pagina	Page
Pamvrotí, Pao-rotí	Pão	Bread
Papayá	Papaia	Papaya
Piyará	Pera	Pear, Guava
Perú	Peru	Turkey
Pirich	Pires	Saucer
Pīpá	Pipa	Pipe (of wine)
Pistol, Pistaul	Pistola	Pistol
Polís	Polícia	Police
Parātí, Parát	Prato	Plate
Preg, Pareg	Prego	Nail
Kārūbím	Querubim	Cherub
Rasíd	Recibo	Receipt
Sābun, Saban, Sābún	Sabão	Soap
? Sāgú	Sagu	Sago
Sāyá	Saia	Gown
Saláta, Salútih, Salítih	Salada	Salad
Sufa	Sofá	Sofa
Shartí	Sorte	Fate

Bengali	*Portuguese*	*English*
Sepát	Sapato	Shoe
Tambākú, Tamākú, Tamakú	Tabaco	Tobacco
Tambúr	Tambor	Drum
Tauliyá	Toalha	Towel
Turanj	Toronja	Pommelo
Toróp	Tropa	Troops
? Tūfán	Tufão	Storm
Barāmada	Varanda	Verandah
Barmá	Verruma	Gimlet, tendril
Bindālú	Vinha de alhos	Bindalu*

* The alphabetical order is followed in the columns of Portuguese words. In cases where Portuguese words have passed into other languages with complete or slight changes of meaning, the English meanings of the words thus changed and not those of the Portuguese words, are given. It must be mentioned that some of the Bengali words of Portuguese origin, given above, are not common everywhere in Bengal but are confined to certain divisions or places.

CHAPTER XVIII

PORTUGUESE CHURCHES

The Bandel Convent, Hooghly

Barely twenty miles away from Calcutta lies this grey and hoary building—the Augustinian Convent and Church of Bandel, Hooghly.* It is the oldest Christian Convent and Church in Bengal, being founded in 1599, the year when Manoel Tavares in virtue of a *farman* of Akbar established the great Portuguese settlement in Hooghly.† According to Manrique the foundation stone was laid on the day of the feast of our Lady of Assumption, that is on the 15th of August.‡ The Convent was dedicated to the Augustinian saint, St. Nicholas of Tolentino and the attached Church to

* There are some vague ideas current as to whether the Bandel Convent was a Nunnery or a Convent or a Church. I have been told by the present Prior of the Bandel Convent that some visitors inquire after the nuns in the belief that a Convent always harbours Nuns. The Bandel Convent was really a monastery of Friars, called *convento* in Portuguese, and a Church dedicated to O. L. of Rosary was attached to it. At present there are no friars in the Convent but one priest who ministers there, is still called a Prior because he is the head of the Convent at the same time that he is the Vicar of the Church.

† That the Convent was founded about the same year that Tavares founded the Settlement of Hooghly, *i.e.* in 1599, is asserted by Manrique. Cf. Fr. Cardon's Trans. of the *Itinerario* in *Bengal Past and Present* 1916, Vol. XII, p. 290. Above the eastern gate of the Convent there is a copper plate with the inscription: Founded 1599; and on the western gate there is a stone bearing the same date. D. G. Crawford (*A brief History of the Hughli District*) and L. S. S. O'Malley, (*Hooghly Gazetteer*) evidently relying upon him, state that this stone was the key-stone of the original building. The former says it was set up at the eastern (should be western) gate when the Convent was re-built by Gomez de Soto in 1660. Whether this stone is the key-stone or not there is no doubt the Convent was founded in 1599.

‡ "On the day of the triumphant entrance into heaven of the Heavenly Empress." Vide *Itinerario*, Fr. Cardon's Trans. *Bengal Past and Present*, *ut supra*.

Our Lady of Rosary. This Convent was, however, burnt down during the siege of Hooghly in 1632, by the Portuguese themselves while retreating.* For a time all commercial hopes of the Portuguese merchants and the religious enterprises of the Portuguese Missionaries seemed destined to be at an end in Hooghly. But the Portuguese managed to obtain a new *farman* from Shāh Jahān and returned to Hooghly before July of the following year.†

After their return the Portuguese established their settlement not on the site of the former one in Hooghly but a little to the north, the present Bandel. Hence the present Convent cannot be standing on the same site as the original one. Fr. Hosten, however, supposes that the Augustinians and the Jesuits must have insisted on getting back the sites of their former establishments for "it would have saved the expense of buying new ground, and would have made it possible to utilize the foundations and old materials of the earlier buildings; moreover the sanctity attaching to the spot where their Church had stood and where many of the faithful and of the Missionaries must have been buried made it desirable that they should return to the same place."‡ These suppositions do not warrant any definite conclusion and for an

---

* *Vide* Fr. Cabral's letter from Ceylon, Fr. Besse's Trans. in the *Catholic Herald of India*, 27 Feb. 1918, p. 166.

† The popular tradition recorded in various modern writings is that the *farman* was obtained as a consequence of a miracle worked by Frei João de Cruz in Agra before Shāh Jahān. The question has been discussed on p. 145 *et seq*. It remains to be said that George Germain (*Vide Addenda II*) remarks that the Portuguese returned to Hooghly through the influence of Frei da Cruz but makes no mention of the miracle. He asserts that the *farman* was signed by Shāh Jahān. That twenty Portuguese persons returned to Hooghly in 1633 with the *farman* of Shāh Jahān is also evident from John Poule's (Powell's) letter written from Harishpur, Orissa, to Cartwright of Balasore on July 17, 1633. Cf. p. 141 *et seq*.

‡ *A Week at the Bandel Convent*, *Bengal Past and Present*, 1915, Vol. X, pp. 45-46.

archæologist there is a vast field within the narrow limits of Hooghly.

The date of re-erection of the Convent forms a controversial point. In an inscription to John Gomes de Soto, which Asiaticus published in 1803, but is no longer existing, it was mentioned that the Convent of Bandel was rebuilt by him or his relatives, the last words of the inscription being ANNO **1661**.* Fr. Hosten remarks that from this inscription the Rev. Long,† appears to have concluded that the Church was built in 1660. Crawford,‡ O'Malley § and others have repeated the Rev. Long's statement. However, from this inscription it is plain to a Portuguese archæologist that the date does not signify the date of the erection of the Church but the date when the inscription was put. It is more likely that the Rev. Long's date 1660 is a misprint for 1640, which was the date assigned by Asiaticus to the re-erection of the Church, and with which the Rev. Long was acquainted. Else, he would have given the date 1661 according to the inscription. Asiaticus does not give any evidence in support of his date but it may be taken as correct for he had good access to all the documents of the Church. Yet, it is strange that the Augustinians took seven (1633-1640) years

---

* Asiaticus, *Ecclesiastical Chronology and Historical Sketches respecting Bengal, Calcutta, 1803.* The inscription was the following :—

ESTE CARNERO MAND-	S ONDE ESTAM SVAS
OV FASER IOM GOM	FILHAS SOGRA E CV
ES DE SOTO E SUA MO-	NHADO. OS QVAIS MA
LLER PERA ELES E S	NDARAM FAZER EST
EVS DESSENDENTE	A IGREJA ANNO **1661**.

Translation :—Jom (Joam or João) Gomes de Soto and his wife ordered to make for them and their descendants this tomb, where lie their daughters, mother-in-law and brother-in-law, who ordered to build this Church : Year 1661.

† *The Portuguese in North India*, Cal. Rev., 1846, Vol. V. p. 260.

‡ *A Brief History of the Hughly District*, p. 8.

§ *Hooghly Gazetteer*, p. 265.

before they re-erected their Convent, considering they were in such favourable circumstances and that their chief ambition must have been to have their temple again.

Privileges of the Convent

The *farman* of Shāh Jahān, which allowed the Portuguese to return to Hooghly in 1633 and which was confirmed in 1646 by Shāh Shuja, granted the Prior of Bandel the right of administration of justice to its inhabitants in all offences excepting those punishable with death.* This right the Prior exercised till 1797, when the English Government took it away though the Prior of Bandel protested to Sir John Shore, afterwards Lord Teignmouth, that since the time of the grant of 777 *bighas* of land, he had exercised civil and criminal jurisdiction over the *raiyats* of the Bandel lands ; that this grant was confirmed in 1646 by a new *farman* ; that the Bandel lands were distinct and were not included in the Sarkar of Sātgāon ; that a letter from William Cowper, dated 17th July, 1787, showed that the Collector was prohibited from exercising any civil or criminal jurisdiction over the inhabitants of Bandel. The Government decided that no claims could be admitted, but that there was no objection to the Prior's "continuing to arbitrate and settle the disputes of the Christian inhabitants of Bandel as heretofore, whenever it may be agreeable to the parties to refer to him for the purpose," but that "the inhabitants of Bandel are subject to the jurisdiction of the Courts equally with other inhabitants of the Company's provinces".† Even till the death of the last Augustinian friar, Frei José de S. Agostinho Gomes in 1869, the Prior was like a petty Governor, having a police force of his own. At present the Convent has none of the privileges which the Mughal Government

---

* For other privileges granted by the *farman* see p. 143 *et seq.*

† G. Toynbee, *Sketch of the Administration of the Hooghly District*, p. 6.

had given to it and out of the 777 *bighas* of land there remain only 380 *bighas* yielding a rent of Rs. 1,240 per annum the rest being lost through carelessness and litigations.*

Bowrey remarks that in 1676 the Portuguese pulled down their Church and began to re-build it, but that when it was one-fourth finished the Moors stopped the work only for the sake of demanding a sum of money.† Now Bowrey is not definite at all where this Church was, but L. S. S. O'Malley and Fr. Hosten believe it must have been in Hooghly. The story itself is doubtful and Sir R. C. Temple, acknowledges that he could not find any confirmation either in the printed or Manuscript records of the period available. ‡ Fr. Hosten argues that the Church referred to by Bowrey was the Bandel Convent built by John Gomes de Soto in 1640. § The statement of Bowrey as referring to the Augustinian Convent, is at best a conjecture. If it be a fact, then it is probable, as Fr. Hosten supposes, that the old Church must have been too small to accommodate the vast number of Portuguese who flocked to Hooghly from their other places taken by the Dutch, and that it was necessary by 1676 to replace it by a new one.

When Sirāj-ud-daulā marched on Hooghly in 1756 and levied a toll of Rs. 5000 on the Portuguese he pillaged the Bandel Convent and ransacked all
1757 documents. Hence the Convent possesses

---

* Toynbee *op. cit.* p. 6 and O' Malley, *Hooghly Gazetteer* p. 267. Frei J. ão de S. Nicolau said in 1785 that more than two-thirds of the 777 *bighas* were lost, which means that less than 260 *bighas* remained to the Convent. In 1784 George Germain said that only 270 *bighas* were remaining, *Vide Addenda II.*

† *Countries round the Bay of Bengal*, pp. 194-95.

‡ Temple's note to Bowrey's *Countries Round the Bay of Bengal* p. 195.

§ *A Week at the Bandel Convent*, *Bengal Past and Present*, 1915, Vol. X, pp. 52-53.

no registers previous to that date. He did not however destroy the building. During the taking of Hooghly by the English in 1757, the Bandel Convent was a scene of military activities. On Wednesday morning, 12th January, 1757, Lieutenants Morgan, Lutwich and Hayter, 150 seamen and 10 boats landed at the Bandel Convent, where they were joined by Captain (afterwards Sir) Eyre Coote with 100 battalion men and 100 sepoys.* From the tower of the Church the English made a survey and discovered that three to four thousand of the enemy were encamped two miles away. Bandel was full of provisions for Sirāj-ud-daulā's army. The English drew up "abreast of the Portuguese Church", hoping to give battle but the enemy avoided it, till the Nawāb's camp was attacked.†

In 1897 another accident befell the convent. The memorable earthquake of that year completely destroyed the tower that was at the south entrance of the Church ; the statue of Our Lady of Happy Voyage was badly damaged and the walls of the Church and the Convent were considerably cracked. The Prior, Father P. M. da Silva, collected a subscription of Rs. 1000 and with "wonderful rapidity" erected a new tower with architectural improvements.‡ The Church, the Augustinian Hall, the cloysters and the Statue of Our Lady of Happy Voyage were quickly repaired, and there this wonderful Church stands after the vicissitudes of more than four centuries, as stately and admirable as it ever was.

What scenes has this Church not witnessed since its original foundation in 1599 ! Who could read in those

---

* *Vide* Remarks on board His Majesty's ship *Bridgwater* in Hill's *Bengal in 1756-57*. Vol. III pp. 13-16 and the Journal of Captain Eyre Coote, entry Jan. 12th, *Ibid.* p. 43.

† The English must have drawn up along the southern side of the Bandel Convent, as they saw a forest to the right.

‡ *Indo-European Correspondence*, Calcutta, June 23, Sept. 15 and Nov. 17, 1897.

mouldering stones around that Church the tale of so many races, of so many nations that strove for supremacy in that narrow area! The Muhammadan, the Afghan and the Mughal power, pomp and pride are all buried in the dust around it. The efforts of the Danes, the French, the Flemish, the Dutch and the Prussians who all sailed up the Hooghly with their goods are all a matter of history. And where is the Portuguese power that once was so great? It has long vanished but that old antiquity-aureoled Church is a living monument to the martial valour and the religious zeal of Portugal.

Public Faith and Traditions

Thousands of people of every race and caste, flock to this Convent with costly offerings, fulfilling their vows and praying for more favours. Wonderful stories are told of the miracles worked in that Church by Our Lady of Happy Voyage, whose very statue is associated, in public faith with miraculous facts. Let a tradition be recorded, which though unhistorical in some points counts so much in the piety and faith of hundreds of pilgrims that resort there every year. It is supposed that the statue of Our Lady of Happy Voyage was in the Military Chapel attached to the Portuguese factory destroyed in the siege of Hooghly. A pious Portuguese merchant who had special devotion to the Blessed Virgin Mary caught this statue and jumped into the river in order to save it from the sack of the Muhammadans, but was heard of no more. When the Bandel Church was being rebuilt (how long after?) the river Hooghly burst into a furious storm and one night Frei João da Cruz who was roused from his sleep heard the voice of the Portuguese merchant who had gone down in the river with the statue crying out: *Salve! Salve, a nossa Senhora de Boa Viagem que deu nos esta victoria. Levante, levante, oh padre e orai por todos nos!**

*Hail, hail. Our Lady of Happy Voyage, who has given us this victory. Arise, arise, Oh Father and pray for us all.

The holy friar thought it was a dream and slept again. But next morning some pagans were bustling around the Church shouting that *Guru Má* (Blessed Virgin Mary) had come. Frei João da Cruz found the statue on the bank of the river near the Church where a ghat still visible was built in commemoration of the event. This image with a pompous ceremony was placed on the tower facing the river and was afterwards transferred to the place it now occupies. This is not all.

Every visitor (and it may be said, by the way, Sir John Woodburn, Sir Andrew Fraser, Sir Edward Baker, Lord and Lady Minto with a big party and many other distinguished persons have been visitors) is struck by the sight of a mast standing before the main door in the piazza of the Church. This mast is supposed to be the offering of a Portuguese captain, whose ship was miraculously saved by a vow to Our Lady of Happy Voyage. The tradition is that this occurred during the life time of Frei João da Cruz who died in 1638 and Lt. Col. Crawford says that the mast was offered in 1655 by a Portuguese Captain as a thank-offering for a miraculous escape from storm.*

A Nunnery

The Rev. Long asserted in 1848, that there was a Nunnery in Bandel.† Taking this on trust, others have repeated the statement. Asiaticus had, in fact, suggested in 1803 or rather insinuated in a flippant language that the Bandel Convent itself was a mixed convent of Friars and Nuns. "When I had gratified my curiosity," he writes "in examining the Convent, Imagination pointed to me sequestered Nymphs in the cloysters : I sought what Fancy represented but alas ! I sought in vain :—No speaking eye—no panting bosom—no graceful form appeared to rivet my soul to Bandel ? *Pure Holy, but solitary Bandell*—

* *A Brief History of the Hughli District*, p. 11.

† *The Portuguese in North India*, Cal. Rev. 1846, Vol. V. P. 260.

I wished to have imbibed religious admonitions from the rosy lips of Beauty—How strongly impressed must they have been when delivered in a Cloyster!"* There are no records yet found in the archives of Goa or Mylapore referring to the erection of a Nunnery in Bandel. Fr. Hosten S. J. who has investigated the question very deeply, says that a Nunnery was probably contemplated in Hooghly.† Mannuci refers in 1707 to an Augustinian hospice with a sisterhood in Mylapore, Madras,‡ and it would not be strange if something of the kind was attempted at Hooghly, which was under the jurisdiction of Mylapore. In 1714 the Augustinians of Bandel did actually declare before Don F. Laines, Ordinary of Mylapore, that a widow named Izabel de Jesus was a professed Religious of their Order and claimed exemption for her from his authority. They confessed, however, that she had never lived in a monastery, such being the distance from Bengal to Goa (*sic*); but they contended that this was not an essential condition. They said they had the power to admit her to the profession, and that she depended from the *nearest* convent, St. Monica's of Goa.§ It is beyond doubt that there was no Nunnery in Bandel. Izabel de Jesus may, however, be said, though not quite strictly, to have been the first nun in Bengal.

Immorality in Bandel?

The power of creating nuns which the Augustinian friars claimed though there was no canonical nunnery, added probably to other scandals, has given rise to many allegations against their morality. It is easily conceivable that the Augustinian friars, having no proper discipline and having a Superior who was far away in Mylapore had for a time degenerated in their morals. Captain

* *Ecclesiastical Chronology*, etc., p. 48.

† *The Catholic Examiner*, 1913, p. 349.

‡ *Storia, de Mogor*, Vol. IV. p. 68.

§ *The Cath. Exam. ut supra.*

Alexander Hamilton describing Bandel, as he saw it in about 1710, writes: "The *Bandel* at present deals in no Sort of Commodities, but what are in Request at the Court of *Venus*, and they have a Church where the Owners of such Goods and Merchandize are to be met with, and the Buyer may be conducted to proper Shops, where the Commodities may be seen and felt, and a priest to be Security for the Soundness of the Goods."* These remarks have served to inflame the religious prejudices of writers like the Rev. Long and prompted Asiaticus to write: "The lascivious damsels of this once gay city slumber under its ruins. When Pomp withdrew from thence, Debauchery vanished. Poverty now stalks over the ground where once beguiling Priests led the unwary stranger in the morning to the altar of God and in the evening to the chamber of riot: regardless of their sacerdotal robes here Priests for gold were the Factors of Pleasure."† It is possible that there were serious abuses in Bandel on the part of the priests but it is clear that imagination has been unduly strained in the descriptions and generalized statements about Bandel, even if they could be applied in 1710. Writers who visited Bandel shortly before A. Hamilton and after him, have nothing to say about the immorality of the priests of Bandel. Charpentier Cossigny who has used bitter Voltairian sarcasm against the Bandel Church which he visited in 1798 (7th year of the Republic) has nothing to say about the immorality of Bandel and only describes it as a poverty-ridden place, with a few huts and barracks of the Portuguese.‡ It is possible, however that during his time debauchery had yielded place to poverty. But yet the very next year Sir Robert Chambers, Judge of the Supreme Court, went to spend the vacation at the "pleasant

* *A New Account of the East Indies*, Vol. II, p. 21.

† *Eccl. Chron.*, p. 44.

‡ *Voyage au Bengale*, Paris 1798, Vol. I, pp. 94—97.

and healthy settlement of Bandel."* He calls the Bandel Church a huge barn (*grange*), describes the Portuguese descendants as spending their lives in begging, stealing and saying *Paternosters* (Lord's Prayer) ; the Prior of Bandel, whom he calls the Governor of the town, as employing his days and nights in drinking and fighting with his subordinates, and gives a sarcastic account of the Procession of the Lady of Bandel, which he saw being attended by Catholics, Lutherans, Calvinists, Muhammadans, Hindus and others.

The Bandel Church is administered by the Portuguese Mission in Bengal which maintains there a Prior. It is under the Diocese of Mylapore. Four solemnities are held every year in the Church :—The feast of Our Lady of Happy Voyage in the month of May ; the feast of Our Lady of Rosary in November ; the feast of St. Augustine in August and the feast of Domingo da Cruz on the first Sunday in Lent (February or March), when a solemn procession is held representing the journey of Jesus Christ to the Calvary.

THE ROMAN CATHOLIC CATHEDRAL.

Murghihatta, Calcutta.

Though this Church is no longer under the Portuguese Mission, its history deserves a place in this chapter as it was the chief and the oldest Portuguese Church in Calcutta, and as its past is entirely or almost entirely associated with the Portuguese. It was referred to by Cottineau de Kloguen as the "richest in all India" and considering the legacies that have been kept for it, is still one of the richest in India.†

---

* *Calcutta Gazette*, 3rd September, 1799.

† C. de Kloguen, *An Historical Sketch of Goa*, p. 123.

Its origin dates back to 1690, when Job Charnock gave the Roman Catholics who followed him to Calcutta a plot of ground at the site of the Old Fort ten *bighas* in area for the purpose of erecting a Chapel.* The Augustinians at once erected a temporary chapel of wooden and mud walls covering it with mats and straw. This little temple can be said to be the oldest place in Calcutta, where Christian worship was performed. In 1693, however, the Chapel was pulled down by order of Sir John Goldsborough who arrived at Sūtanūtī on the 12th of August of that year as Commissary-General and Chief Governor of the Company's settlements. His immediate attempts were directed towards correcting the abuses of the Company. In a long account which he has kept, he states that he found the merchants and factors of the Company marrying black wives who were Roman Catholics and that they were too much under the influence of the Augustinian friars. He, therefore, turned all friars out of Sūtanūtī and ordered the destruction of the Chapel which he called the "Mass-house."† After the lapse of hardly three months, Sir John Goldsborough died in Sūtanūtī and ceased to be worried over the Company's abuses and the Augustinian "Mass-houses."

Foundation, 1690

The Portuguese friars replaced the Chapel in 1700 by a brick-built one, further away from their old Chapel, in Murghihatta where now the Cathedral Church stands.‡

---

* Rev. Long, *Portuguese in North India*, Cal. Rev. 1846, Vol. V. pp. 251-52. Also Cf. *Bengal Catholic Herald*, Jan. 1. 1842, pp. 2-3.

† Hyde, *Parochial Annals of Bengal*, p. 21 ; Cf. also Wilson's *Early Annals of the English in Bengal*, Vol. I, p. 143.

‡ How this quarter came to be known as Murghihatta (*Murghi*, a fowl ; *hat*, a bazar) is explained in the *Census of India 1901*. vol. VIII, pt. 1 p. 89. "With the growth of a heterogeneous population came the necessity of allotting particular areas to particular races. Thus shortly after the English came, the Portuguese who were the only people who kept fowls, the rest of the inhabitants being Hindus to whom fowls are forbidden, were allotted a quarter which came to be designated as Murghihatta and the Armenians a *tola* or division which was named Armanitola."

The expenses of the erection were defrayed by Mrs. Margaret Tench whose tomb may be seen in the Churchyard, and by other Roman Catholics who contributed to it. In 1720 the Chapel was enlarged by Mrs. Sebastian Shaw under the direction of the Vicar Frei Francisco d'Assumpção. This Chapel was however ransacked and the records destroyed in 1756 during the sack of Calcutta by Sirāj-ud-daulā. The Chapel escaped destruction.

Protestant Worship in the Church

On the return of the English to Calcutta in 1757 they took possession of the Church and made use of it for Prostestant worship for four years, and Roman Catholic religion was interdicted in the Church. The Council in Fort William reported this action to the Court of Directors at Home in its letter dated January 31st, 1757. The letter runs : "The inconvenience we experienced at the siege of Calcutta from the prodigious numbers of Portuguese women who were admitted for security into the Fort, the very little or no service which that race of people are of to the settlement, added to the prospect we had of a war with France in which case we had reason to suppose they would refuse to take up arms against an enemy of their own religion (should we be attacked) induced us upon our return to interdict the public exercise of the Roman Catholic religion and to forbid the residence of their priests in our bounds".*

The high-handedness of the Governor met with the disapprobation of the Court of Directors. In the letter of the 3rd March 1758, they said " we cannot approve of your so generally interdicting the exercise of the Roman Catholic religion within the whole bounds, as such a step may be attended with many inconveniences. But if any priest is troublesome or suspected of doing anything prejudicial to our

* Hyde, *Parochial Annals of Bengal*, p. 116.

affairs, we would have such an one immediately dismissed and not permitted to reside any where within the bounds. As to Fort William itself it will be a prudent measure so long as the French War subsists not to suffer any person professing the Roman Catholic religion, priests or others, to reside therein, and this you are strictly to observe".*

After Frei Caitano de Madre de Deus, the Vicar, was expelled from the Church, Rev. Richard Cobbe officiated as the Chaplain and conducted the English services. He was succeeded by Rev. Thomas Northcotte who put the Church in repairs. He having complained to the Council that "it be entered and Captain Brohier do put the church and churchyard in proper repair; and that the Secretary do acquaint Mr. Northcotte he may appoint his own clerk, sexton and undertaker."† Rev. Henry Butler was next appointed Chaplain by Governor Drake. It was this chaplain who, in the ministry of the Murghihatta Church, first entertained the Rev. John Zachary Kiernander, the founder of the Old Mission Church. Rev. Butler seems to have done some more repairs to the Church for on the 10th September he wrote to the Council asking that, "as the roof of the Church was much decayed and in danger of falling, Mr. Plaisted may be ordered to survey and examine the same."‡ Soon after, two other Missionaries Rev. John Moore and John Cape were sent out from England.

Meanwhile the English community discontented with the religious affairs as they were going on, and possibly resenting that the services should be held in a misappropriated Church, appealed to the Council for a new Church. On the 24th March

* Hyde, *Parochial Annals of Bengal, p. 116.*

† Hyde, *op. cit.*, p. 117.

‡ Hyde, *op. cit.*, p. 120.

1760 the Council decided: "Taking into consideration the unwholesomeness and dampness of the church now in use, as well as the injustice of detaining it from the Portuguese—*Ordered* the surveyor to examine the remains of the gateway in the Old Fort, and report to us what it will cost to put it in tolerable repair and make it fit for a chapel till such time as the chapel designed to be erected."* On July 17th the surveyor having reported to the Council that the Chapel ordered to be built was ready "agreed that the Church belonging to the Portuguese be restored to them and that the secretary do advise Padre Caitan the head priest, of our resolution." Thus the Portuguese got back the Murghihatta Church. The Chapel which the English built was called St. John's Chapel, the predecessor of St. John's Church.

The Erection of the Present Building

Towards the end of the eighteenth century the Catholic Community in Calcutta was growing in numbers and a need was felt for a bigger Church which could accommodate the Catholic population. Two philanthropic brothers, Joseph and Louis Barretto, initiated the movement and at a general meeting of the Catholics it was decided to build the Church which is now known as the Murghihatta Church. The first stone of the Church was laid on the 12th March, 1797, by the Augustinian Vicar Frei Joaquim de Santa Rita assisted by his wardens Louis Barretto, Gabriel Vrignon, Antonio de Coito and Diogo Pereira. On the 21st of November, it was consecrated by the Rev. Francisco de Santa Maria and dedicated to Our Lady of Rosary. The architect was Thomas Syars Driver who having died before completion, the work was carried on by Monsieur Hemo of the Chief Engineer's office. The building cost 90,000 Sicca rupees, 30,000 of which were collected from the revenues of the Church and the remain-

---

* Hyde *op. cit.*, p. 120.

ing from subscriptions which having fallen short, the Barrettos made up the deficiencies.

Many endowments have been made to this Church especially by the Barrettoes, Count John Lackersteen and two ladies, Mrs. Rita Griffiths and Mrs. Philadelphia Bonfield. Over some legacies kept for this Church and over the management of its affairs many lawsuits have taken place in the Supreme Court of Judicature, Calcutta, and Joseph Barretto as a warden of the Church took active part in some of them.

On either side of the high altar of the Cathedral are the tomb-stones to the memory of Mrs. M. Tench and Mrs. E. Shaw. There are many monuments in the Church some of them dating as early as 1712. The tomb stones of most of the members of the Barretto family are in this Church. Archbishop Patrick Carew and Archbishop Goethals have also been buried in the Church.

CHURCH OF OUR LADY OF DOLOURS

Boitakhana, Calcutta

The Portuguese, their descendants and their converts first settled in Murghihatta and then dispersed to other parts of Calcutta, as the population increased and especially when the Maharatta ditch was filled up and the Circular Road was constructed off Boitakhana.* Along with the English and the

* *Boitakhana* was so called from a tree, under which pedestrians were wont to sit on account of the shady rest it afforded. It was a *pipal* tree, standing at the junction of Bow Bazar Street and Lower Circular Road. Captain Alexander Hamilton (*New Acct. of East Indies*) wrote that Job Charnock chose Calcutta on account of a large shady tree and in Tekchand Thakur's *Alaley Gharer Dulál* (Ch. 7) it is mentioned : "Job Charnock was often passing and repassing by the place of Bothukhaná; there was an immense tree there, and sitting at the foot of it, he would rest and smoke tobacco; at that place many merchants would meet. He had so much affection for the shade of that tree that he resolved to fix his factory there." Cf. *Bengal Past and Present* Vol. VIII, 1914, p. 137.

English descendants they occupied the locality between Dharamtala and Bow Bazar Streets. This locality was once the fashionable quarter of Calcutta and was called the European quarter of Calcutta. The Catholics who settled near Boitakhana, felt the necessity of having another Church for divine worship as the Murghihatta Church was far away from them. Louis Barretto was the first to take steps to found a Church near Boitakhana. In 1804 he obtained permission from the Marquis of Wellesley to do so, but he died soon after and the project was not carried out. The idea was taken up by an Indian Christian lady, Mrs. Grace Elizabeth, who with the help of four Portuguese gentlemen Diogo Pereira, Jesoph Pereira, Philip Leal and Charles Cornelius, founded the Church of Our Lady of Dolours at Boitakhana. The foundation stone was laid on the 13th June, 1809. The foundress bought the plot of ground (2 bighas, 4 cottas and 12 chattacks) from an Indian firm of goldsmiths ; she offered in addition Rs. 20,000 for building expenses and then again 10,000 as a fund for defraying current expenses and lastly 2,000 more on completion of the work. The Church was consecrated by the Rev. Frei Francisco dos Prazeres on the 30th June, 1810, and dedicated to *Nossa Senhora de Dores*. The foundress made over the Church to the Portuguese Augustinian Mission but reserved for herself the right of presentation of the Vicar. The first Vicar was an Augustinian named Frei Antonio de Padua. This Church still belongs to the Portuguese Mission and is under the diocese of Mylapore. During the *Padroado* question attempts were made by the English Mission to take over the Church. Bishop St. Leger interdicted the Church in 1835, and the wardens of the Murghihatta Church erected a Chapel for religious worship in the burial ground at Boitakhana. By virtue of the Concordat between the Holy See and the King of Portugal in 1887, this Church came under the Jurisdiction of the Portuguese Bishop of Mylapore.

CHURCH OF THE SACRED HEART OF JESUS

Dharamtala Street, Calcutta

This Church was founded by Mrs. Pascoa Barretto e Souza, the grand-mother of Sir Walter de Souza, in fulfilment of a vow. Louis de Souza had in 1821 been tried by the Supreme Court for causing grievous hurt to a Mr. Joseph Gonsalves, by shooting at him in a buggy, when returning one night from the Old Chowringhi Theatre—not wounding him in a duel as is generally believed—and Mrs. de Souza made a vow that should her son be acquitted she would build and endow a Church on her own land. The foundation stone was laid by the foundress on the 12th February 1832, the ceremony being performed by the Rev. Frei Simão de Conceição, then Vicar of the Boitakhana Church. On Easter Sunday, the 30th March 1834, Frei A. Antonio Assumpção, Provisor of the Bishop of Mylapore, consecrated it, dedicating it to the Sacred Heart of Jesus. One Mrs. Sheriff erected the building and all the costs including those of the purchase of the ground, organ bells, vestments, ornaments, furniture and the erection of a cemetery in Entally for the poor, amounted to more than 200,000 *sicca* rupees which Mrs. Pascoa Barreto e Souza paid.

The Church is now under the ministration of the Jesuit Mission and not of the Portuguese Mission.

THE CHURCH OF JESUS, MARIA, JOSE

Chinsura

This is one of the three Churches that belong to the Portuguese Mission in Western Bengal, the other two being the Bandel Convent and the Boitakhana Church. The funds for the erection of the Church were left by Mrs. Sebastian Shaw on her demise—the same lady who in 1720 enlarged the

Murghihatta Church. The Chapel was built in 1740, but according to Asiaticus, there was a Chapel of mats and straw in Chinsura before 1740. The two-storied building attached to the Chapel was called the Hermitage of the Infant Jesus as the Augustinian friars were dwelling there. The Church is under the care of the Prior of Bandel.

CHURCH OF SANTA MADRE DE DEUS

Serampore

This Church owes its existence to the Barretto Family. It is a beautiful edifice situated on the Strand. It was consecrated in 1783 and dedicated to Santa Madre de Deus. (Holy Mother of God). The erection of the Church cost Rs. 14,000, part of which (Rs. 600) was contributed by the Hon'ble Colonel Bie, the Danish Governor of that Settlement. It is no longer under the Portuguese Mission.

ST. PATRICK'S CHURCH

Dum-Dum

When Dum-Dum became the head-quarters of an artillery regiment, the Catholic soldiers had no means of attending divine service except in a hut which a pious Indian lady, Mrs. Moran, lent to a Portuguese priest for the purpose of saying mass on Sundays. This humble practise continued till 1822, when Joseph Barretto learning the state of affairs offered to erect a Chapel at his own expense and obtained from the Government a plot of ground for the purpose. Major-General Hardwick, the commandant of the artillery regiment, was unwilling that Barretto alone should bear the cost and proposed that the regiment itself should raise the necessay funds. He himself subscribed Rs. 100, but though even the Protestant soldiers subscribed, the amount realised was only Rs 3,000. The

Catholics of Calcutta, among whom Joseph Barretto was most conspicuous, raised a subscription and Rs. 11,000 was realised. The foundation stone was laid in Feb. 1822, and Major General Hardwick and the regimental officers attended the ceremony. The erection of the Chapel had not extended far, when the architect, Mr. Goss managed to run away with a considerable part of the funds. Another subscription was raised in Calcutta and the work was completed. The Chapel was consecrated on Good Friday in 1823 and dedicated to St. Patrick. The Rev. Misquita was appointed the first Chaplain. This Chapel now belongs to the Jesuit Mission.

CHURCH OF ST. NICHOLAS OF TOLENTINO

Nagori, Dacca

The Church of Nagori had its origin in the Mission of San Nicolau de Tolentino, that first started in Coxabanga (?) in the lands of the King of Busna (Faridpur ?), and then spread all over Eastern Bengal.* In the conversion of Eastern Bengal Christians, the figure of a layman, D. Antonio de Rozario the son of the King of Busna, stands pre-eminent above all others. In 1663 he was taken prisoner by the Maghs and carried to Arakan, where an Augustinian Friar, Manoel de Rozario, bought him and tried to convert him in vain, until St. Anthony is said to have miraculously appeared to him in a dream and beckoned him to embrace the Christian religion. Having thus become a Christian, he began to convert others with a fervour and zeal, that eclipses that of the Missionaries themselves. He composed dialogues and canticles, argued and preached in public about the faiths of the Christian religion, extended the field of his Mission to the whole of Eastern

* Relation of Frei Ambrosio de Santo Agostinho, in *O Chronista de Tissuari*, Vol. II. 1867 pp. 57-62 or Fr. Hosten's trans. in *The Catholic Herald of India* Dec. 19, 1917 and succeeding Nos.

Bengal, and is credited with having performed miracles and converted thirty to forty thousand souls.

According to the Madras Catholic Directory (1912) the Church of Nagori was built in 1664. But according to the *Relation* which the Father Provincial of the Congregation of St. Augustine of Goa, Frei Ambrosio de Santo Agostinho, gave to the Viceroy of Portuguese India in 1750, the *Aldea* (village) of Nagori was not acquired until 1695, when Frei Luis dos Anjos bought it, because the Christians of the place were subjected to vexations by other landlords. Nagori, eventually became the head of the Mission of St. Nicholas of Tolentino in Eastern Bengal and the Church of Nagori was dedicated to the patron of the Mission, St. Nicholas of Tolentino.

From Frei Ambrosio de Santo Agostinho's *Relation*, it appears that the Church of Nagori in 1750 was a big thatched building with mud walls. There were in that year in Nagori 600 Christians grown to an age of confession, besides a large number of children. There was a school attached to the Church, which was frequented by 150 boys. Hence Nagori was known as a Rectorate. Besides, there were about 9,000 occult Christians who, though really Christians, would not openly avow their religion for fear of losing their caste. Frei Ambrosio also mentions that the Mission counted among its members 1500 public Christians, 8,000 occult ones and 9,733 Christians who dressed like Europeans.

The Church was accidentally burnt almost completely on the 8th of April, 1881. The present Nagori Church was built in 1888 on a site about 150 yards away from the place where the old one stood. Its foundations were blessed on the 24th August, 1885, the Church itself being consecrated on the 22nd February, 1889. Its parishioners number 2,185. It has a confraternity of the Apostleship of Prayer. It maintains a dispensary in which free medical advice and medicines are given. There are many schools under its direction—St. Nicholas'

School for boys; St. Joseph's School for boys and girls at Culon; St. Anthony's School for boys and girls at Doripara; St. Anthony's Convent School for girls; Sunday School for boys; Sunday School for girls; Eleven Cathechism Schools in eleven villages. It also maintains Homes for the poor and the destitute such as St. Joseph's Cathechumenate for women St. Anthony's Cathechumenate for women and a Home for widows.

CHURCH OF OUR LADY OF ROSARY

Tesgaon, Dacca

This Church, dedicated to our Lady of Rosary, was built in 1679. The Madras Catholic Directory however gives the date of erection as 1714. This is evidently wrong as there is an inscription in the Church bearing the date 1706 and as early as 1682 its parishioners are recorded to have been 700, exclusive of the Portuguese and their families.* The Church was re-built in 1779, in its present form. The stone floor is full of inscriptions to the memory of those who are buried beneath it. The present congregation of the Church is 309. The Church was for a time the mother Church of many Churches in Bengal including those of Nagori and Chandernagore.

CHURCH OF OUR LADY OF ROSARY

Hasnabad, Dacca

The original Church of Hasnabād was built in 1777, but it was broken down and the present one erected in 1888. In some old papers of the Church it is recorded that the first Missionary came to Hasnabād as early as 300 years ago. The Zemindar of the place, enraged at his success amongst his

---

* *The Catholic Herald of India*, Oct. 17, 1917, p. 697, n. 25.

tenants, ordered the priest to be bound hand and foot and thrown into a well. But the priest having survived this treatment, the Zemindar taken by surprize made him the grant of land for erecting a Church.* It is scarcely possible to make out how much truth and how much fiction lie in such traditions. The Catholic population is 3,146. The Church maintains St. John's School for boys ; Our Lady of Rosary's School for girls, Sunday School for boys and girls. It has a Confraternity and three Sodalities.

CHURCH OF THE HOLY GHOST

Tuital, Dacca

The Church of Tuital was built in 1894 and is comparitively modern. The villages of Old Tuital, New Tuital and Sonabazar were under the religious ministration of the Church of Hosnabād. But as these villages were distant from the Church of Hosnabād it was difficult both for the people to attend their religious duties and for the parish priest of Hosnabād to minister to their religious welfare. Hence by the decree of the 25th May 1894, the Bishop of Mylapore, Dom Henrique de Silva had the Church of Tuital erected.

Its parishioners number 920 and it maintains St. Thomas' School for boys, Our Lady of Lourdes' School for girls and a Sunday School for boys and girls.

CHURCH OF OUR LADY OF PIETY

Dacca

The Church was built in 1815. Its parishioners number 125. It has a Confraternity of the Apostleship of prayer.

---

* Allen, *Dacca Gazetteer*, p. 69.

CHURCH OF OUR LADY OF GUIDANCE

Shibpur, Bakarganj District

The Portuguese Missionaries acquired the *taluk* of Shibpur in 1764, the lease being granted to Frey Raphael dos Anjos on or previous to the 9th Phalgun 1171 B. S. by Rajah Raj Ballab Sein. In the decision of Sadr Diwani Adâlat, dated 18th April 1856, it is mentioned that the lease was granted by Rajah Pitambar Singh (Sein), Zemindar of Arangabad, who was the grandson of Rajah Raj Ballab. But Beveridge remarks that the date of the lease bears out the tradition that it was Rajah Raj Ballab who granted the lease. Pitambar Sein only confirmed the lease. "The tradition is," says Beveridge,* "that he (Raj Ballab) wanted to coerce his tenantry, who were inclined to be disobedient to him, and that he judged that Christians would be well fitted for the purpose, as mere contact with them would be sufficient to destroy the ryots' caste and that the latter would therefore gladly come to terms in order to avoid the visits of the Christian servants. He accordingly applied to the Portuguese Mission at Bandel for some Christians, and four were sent to him. They afterwards applied to him for a priest, in order to perform their religious ceremonies. He procured one from Bandel and assigned him four pieces of land or howalas for his maintenance. The four Christians were put in charge of the property, but in consequence of their dissensions the howalas were formed into a taluq, and made over to the priest in trust for the mission." This priest was Frei Raphael dos Anjos. The *taluk* at present yields an income of about Rs. 800.

The original Church in Shibpur was built by one Pedro Gonsalves, but in 1823 Manoel de Silva pulled it down and

Beveridge, *The District of Bákarganj*, pp. 106-107.

constructed the present enlarged building with the funds left by his father Domingo de Silva

Till 1836 the Portuguese Mission administered the Church in peace, but in that year, disputes arose between the Portuguese and English Missions. St. Leger, the Vicar Apostolic of Bengal, attempted to bring the Church under his jurisdiction and dismissed the Vicar, Frey José das Neves, appointing Ignatius Xavier Mascarenhas to be the incumbent in Shibpur. Beveridge supposes that the parishioners of Shibpur, owing to their quarrels with the Vicar, placed themselves under the protection of Dr. St. Leger.* The Augustinians sued for recovery of their Church and lands and for twenty-one years litigation followed. Longman, the Judge of Bākarganj, being a Roman Catholic, desired that the suit be transferred to the court of the Judge of the Twenty-four Pargannas. This Judge, Robert Torrens, as well as the Sadr Diwani Adâlat decided the suit in favour of the Portuguese priests who in 1857 not only recovered the possession of their Church and lands but obtained a decree for mesne profits.

The parishioners of the Church number a thousand. It maintains a dispensary where free medical advice and medicines, are given and has under it, St. Anthony's School for boys, St. Joseph's School for girls and a Sunday School for boys and girls.

* *The District of Bákarganj*, p. 108.

ADDENDA

Some Plants Introduced by the Portuguese in Bengal*

The Portuguese not only brought to India new kind of goods, a new language and new creeds, but also added very much to the flora of India. The following is a brief list of some of the plants which Bengal owe to the Portuguese. Some of them were introduced directly and others found their way to Bengal from other parts of India where the Portuguese had introduced them. The list is, however, far from being complete as there are many plants which were not known in India before the arrival of the Portuguese and may have been introduced by them though there is no record of the fact. On the other hand, a few of the plants mentioned below have a doubtfut origin and it is only by botanical and not written evidence that it is ascertained that they owe their introduction in India to the Portuguese. Though in this line of enquiry much has been done, much has still to be done. Not only did the Portuguese bring new plants to India but they carried Indian plants to Europe, America, and Africa. Some kind of canes carried by the Portuguese from Bengal and used in the Portuguese army were called *Bengalas* and still the word is a common application to any sort of cane.

1 **Achras Sapota** (*Sapotaceæ*)—Beng. *Sapota*, English, *Sapodill plum.*

This tree originally a native of America is cultivated in Bengal and on the Western Coast, its fruit being in great demand in the markets of Calcutta and Bombay. It is sold in Calcutta under the name of *Mangosteen* which it resembles.

2. **Agave Americana** (*Amaryllideæ*)—Beng. *Jungli or bilati ánanásh, banskeora, bilatipát, koyan* incorrectly called *murga murji.* English, *The American aloe, the century plant, the carata.*

The plant was originally a native of America, and is supposed to have been introduced in India by the Portuguese. *Vide* Watt, *Dict. Econ. Prod. of India.*

---

* The chief works consulted in the preparation of this list of plants, are Garcia d'Orta's *Colloquios dos Simples e Drogas e Cousas Medicinaes da India* ; Watt's *The Dictionary of the Economical Products of India*, Dymock's (and others) *Pharmacographia Indica*, G. Dalgado's, *Flora de Goa and Savantvadi.* I am also indebted to the articles on the subject of Mariano de Saldanha in the *Oriente Português*, Nova Goa, vols. V and VI, 1908, and 1909.

3. **Allamanda Cathartica** (*Apocynaceæ*)—Vernacular, *Jahari sontakka, pivli kanher.*

This plant was introduced from Brazil by the Portuguese (Dymock *Pharm. Ind.*) It is a common creeper in Indian gardens.

4. **Anacardium Occidentale** (*Anacardiaceæ*)—English, *Cashew nut*, Beng. *Hijli badam, kaju.*

This plant originaly introduced from South America is well established in the forests of Chittagong and all over the coast forests of India and Ceylon. Its name *Bádám-i-farangi* among the Muhammadans and *Boa Farangi* in Amboyna (Rumphius) point to its being introduced by the Portuguese.

5. **Ananas Sativa** (*Bromeliaceæ*)—Eng. *Pine apple.* Beng. *Anánash anarási.*

Introduced in Bengal by the Portuguese in 1594 from Brazil. This fruit was daily served at the table of Akbar each costing 4 *dams* ($\frac{1}{10}$ of a rupee).

6. **Anona Squamosa** (*Anoneceæ*)—Eng. *Custard-apple.* Beng. *Ata, lúna.*

The plant is well naturalized in Bengal. General Cunningham held that there is an exact representation of the plant in the Bhárut Scriptures and also in the Scriptures of Ajanta caves, indicating that the plant was cultivated in India long before the Portuguese came. Watt, however, states that Botanical evidence is against Cunningham's contention. For other details, *vide* Watt and *Hobson-Jobson* s. v. Custard-Apple.

7. **Anona Reticulata** (*Anonaceæ*)—Eng. *The Bullock's heart.* **Beng.** *nóna.* What is said of the Custard Apple applies to this plant.

8. **Arachis Hypogaea** (*Leguminosæ*),—Eng. The *Ground-nut, Earth nut* or *Pea nut.* Beng. *Mát Kalai, chinar bádám, bilati mung.*

Introduced from Africa and America. Dymock thinks that the Ground nut reached India through China. Its Konkani name *Mosbimchim biknam* shows that in Western India the Portuguese must have introduced it from Moçambique, Africa.

9. **Argemone Mexicana** (*Papaveraceæ*)—Eng. *The Mexican or Prickly poppy.* Beng. *Baro-shiál kánta, sial-kántá.*

The plant is common in Bengal and in fact in the whole of India. Valued for its oil and medicinal properties. "Its use as an external application in conjunctivitis was probably introduced into this country with the plant by the Portuguese", Dymock, *Pharm. Ind.*

10. **Artemisia Sieversiana** (*Compositæ*)—The plant forms one of

the kinds of Afsantin sold in Indian Bazars. The plants "were no doubt introduced into the country by the Portuguese", Dymock, *Pharm. Ind.*

11. **Averrhoa Bilimbi** (*Geraniaceæ*)—Eng. *Bilimbi tree.* Beng. *Blimbi.*

Introduced by the Portuguese in India probably from Moluccas. Cf. Dymock *Pharm. Ind.* Completely naturalized in India. In the courtyard of the Portuguese Church of Bandel there can be seen some of these plants, having been long ago planted by the friars.

12. **Averrhoa Carambola** (*Geraniaceæ*)—Eng. *Carambola tree.* Beng. *Kâmrângá, kamarak.* In the Sunderbunds the wood of the plant is used for building purposes and for furniture. Its apples are very palatable when stewed.

13. **Capsicum frutescens** (*Solanaceæ*)—Eng. *Spur pepper, Cayenne chillies.* Beng. *Lál or gach murich, lal lanka murich.*

Cultivated all over India and especially in Bengal Orissa and Madras. It is one of the chief condiments in India dietary. The Portuguese brought the plant to India from Pernambuco according to Clusius (quoted by Dymock).

14. **Carica Papaya** (*Passifloræ*)—English, *The Papaya tree,* Beng. *Pappayá, papeyá.*

This common plant in India was not known before the Portuguese came and Atkinson (quoted by Watt) affirms it was introduced by the Portuguese.

15. **Cereus Pentagonus** (*Cacteæ*)—English, *Cactus.*

This plant was probably introduced from Brazil by the Portuguese. Cf. G. Dalgado, *Flora de Goa e Savantvadi.*

16. **Citrus Aurantium** (*Rutaceæ*)—Eng. *Sweet orange, Portugal orange.* Beng. *Kamlá nembu nárengí, nárengá.*

The controversy about the introduction of the orange-tree in India is a long one. It is admitted by most writers that there were orange trees in India as well as in Portugal long before the Portuguese came to India. It is more likely that the Portuguese introduced the plant in Europe. Watt says that the names *Portogalls* (Ital.) *Protokhal* (Alb.) and *Portogal* (Kurdish) "indicate the intimate relation which the Portuguese bore to the diffusion of the plant." There is no doubt the Portuguese spread the orange trees in India even though they were to be found before the arrival of the Portuguese.

17. **Curcuma Zedoaria** (*Scitamineæ*)—Eng. *Zedoary.* Beng. *Sati, shorí, kachura.*

This plant cannot be said to have been introduced by the Portuguese in Bengal for it seems to be a native of Chittagong but they spread it in other parts of India especially, as Dymock thinks, in Bombay.

18. **Durio Zibethinns** (*Malvaceæ*)—Eng. *Durian.*

According to G. d'Orta the Portuguese brought these plants to India from Malacca.

19. **Engenia Malaccensis** (*Myrtaceæ*)—Eng. *Malay apple* Beng. *Malaca jamrul.*

This tree was brought to India from Malaca by the Portuguese. G. d'Orta says he himself planted some in his own garden.

20. **Garcinia Mangostana** (*Guttiferæ*)—Eng. *The Mangosteen.* Beng. *Mangustán.*

In Bengal the plant does not grow so well as in Burma and Madras. The plant unknown to India before the arrival of the Portuguese came from Malaca and G. d'Orta says he had planted some of them which shows the Portuguese were the first to introduce them in India.

21. **Indigofera Anil** (*Leguminosæ*)—Eng. *Indigo plant* (not the commercial variety) Beng. *Nil.*

Of this variety of Indigo plant, Watt says, "It nowhere exists in a wild state in India and was probably introduced during the period of Portuguese ascendancy in the Western and Southern Presidencies."

22. **Ipomeœa Batatas** (*Convolvulaceæ*)—Eng. *Sweet potato* Beng. *Ranga-alú, lal-álu* (the red form) *Chine álu* (the white form).

All forms of sweet potato are not native of India but have been introduce from Africa or Brazil probably by the Portuguese. Watt remarks that the Batatas mentioned by Linschoten were a form of *Dioscorea* (Yams).

23. **Jathorrhiza Calumba** (*Menispermaceæ*)—Eng. *Calumba.*

"The drug appears to have been first introduce into India by the Portuguese......Flückiger and Hanbury's researches have traced its introduction into Europe to the Portuguese as far back as 1671." (Dymock *Pharm. Ind.*)

24. **Jatropha Curcas** (*Euphorbiacæ*)—Eng. *Physic Nut.* Beng. *Bághrénda, bágh-bherenda.*

This plant is said to have been introduced from Brazil by the Portuguese", Dymock *Pharm. Ind.*

25. **Jatropha Multifada** (*Enphorbiacæ*)—Eng. *Coral tree.*

"The plant appears to have been introduced by the Portuguese from Brazil", Dymock, *Pharm. Ind.*

26. **Mirabilis Jalapa** (*Nyctagineæ*)—Eng. *Marvel of Peru.* Beng. *Krishna-keli*, *grélá-bás.*

"Five varieties of this plant with red, white, yellow, red and white, and red and yellow flowers were introduced from the West Indies in 1596 and must have been carried by the Portuguese to the East shortly afterwards, as the plant is said to have been introduced into Persia in the reign of Shah Abbas the first and was established on the Malabar Coast in the time of Van Rheede," Dymock *Pharm Ind.*

27. **Nicotiana Tabacum** (*Solanaceæ*)—Eng. *Tobacco.* Beng. *Tamák.*

From the *Maúsir-i-ralumi* and the *Darashikohi* we learn that Tobacco was introduced into the Deccan by the Portuguese about A. H. 914 (A. D. 1508) and that it began to be smoked about 1605 towards the end of the reign of Sultán Jaláleddeen Akbar.". Dymock, *Pharm. Ind.* Watt also admits that the Portuguese introduced the Tobacco plant in India.

28. **Opuntia Dillenii** (*Cacteæ*)—Eng. *The prickly pear.* Beng. *Samar.*

" It is most probable that it was introduced by the Portuguese", Watt. " This plant is a native of Mexico and Central America, and was introduced into India by the Portuguese, doubtless with the object of feeding the cochineal insect upon it, but it is uncertain whether they ever carried out their intention.". Dymock, *Pharm. Ind.*

29. **Smilax Glabra** (*Liliacæ*)—Eng. *China root.* Beng. *Harina-shuck-china.*

The shrub is abundant in Eastern Bengal, Sylhet and the Garo and Khasia hills. Garcia d'Orta says that the plant was first introduced by the Portuguese into Goa from China about 1535. Dymock adds "The Portuguese however, appear to have lost no time in carrying it to their factories in Persia, as it was mentioned, a few years after its introduction into Goa, by Mir Imad-ed-din Mahmud of Shiraz Mirza Kazi of Yezd and Mir Muhamad Hashim of Teheran".

30. **Phemeria Acutifolia** (*Apocynaceæ*)—Eng. *Jasmin tree.* Beng. *Gorur-champa.*

"It appears to have been introduced into India by the Portuguese from Brazil, as it is usually planted in the churchyards of the native christians in order that it may deck the graves with its white deciduos flowers, which are produced almost all the year round." Dymock *Pharm. Ind.* C. T. Peters says that the plant is known as *Dalana phula* in Northern Bengal, where its milky juice has been found to be an effectual purgative (Quoted by Watt)

31. **Psydium Guyava** (*Myrtaceæ*)—Eng. *Guava* Beng. *Peyara*, *piyará.*

The guava-tree which is common in Bengal as everywhere in India, was introduced by the Portuguese from America (Royle). Cf. Watt *Dict. of Econ. Prod.*

32. **Spillanthes Acmella** (*Compositæ*)—Eng. *Para cress.*

This plant cultivated thoughout India is "supposed to have been introduced into India form Brazil by the Portuguese" Dymock *Pharm. Ind.*

33. **Strychnos Ignatii** (*Loganiaceæ*)—Eng. *Nux-vomica* or *Strychnine tree.* Beng. *Kuchilá thalkesur.*

This plant very valuable for preparation of strychnine was introduced in India by the Portuguese Jesuit Missionaries Dymock *Pharm. Ind.* The plant is rather rare in Bengal, but common in Madras and Tenasserim.

34. **Tagetes Erecta** (*Compositæ*)—Eng. The *French and African marigolds.* Beng.—*Genda.*

"Rojia the name current in Western India perhaps denotes the introduction of the plant by the Portuguese with whom it appears to represent the *Rosa do ouro* or golden rosa, which the Pope usually blesses at Mass on Sunday in Lent" Dymock *Pharm. Ind.*

35. **Zea Mays** (*Gramineæ*)—Eng. *Maize, Indian corn.* Beng. *Janar, bhutta, Jonár.*

It is probable that this important plant was introduced in India by the Portuguese. Cf. Watt's lenghty discussion (*Dict. of Econ. Prod.*)

II

Appeal of a Portuguese from Calcutta to Queen D. Maria I. of Portugal (1784)

I give below a translation of an important document which was found by J. E. de Souza Vellozo in the archives of the great archæologist Filippe Nery Xavier in Goa, and was registered in one of the volumes in the office of the *Ouvidor* of the City of Santo Nome de Deus in Macau. This document is published by Mr. Souza Velloso in *O Oriente Português*, Nova Goa, 1906, Vol. III pp. 129-134. It is an appeal made to Dona Maria I, Queen of Portugal, by a Portuguese from Calcutta on the 31st of December 1784, regarding the rights and possessions of the Portuguese nation in Bandel, Hooghly. (For the attempts of the Portuguese Government to recover Bandel, *Vide* p. 148 *et seq.*)

[P. 129] Your Majesty !

With due and most profound respect, your most obedient vassal appeals to your Majesty, representing through your Chamber of Commerce, the possessions and privileges which the Mughals of Delhi, conceded to the Portuguese nation in Bengal, and which are now forgotten; and [showing] how by obtaining them considerable benefit might result to the commerce of the vassals of your Majesty, and how these might be exempted from the burden which weighs on them, as they are obliged to deal in commerce with the English (nation) in their port of Calcutta, if your Majesty causes to examine through your Chamber of Commerce what I propose in my letter, so as to grant it according to your Royal pleasure (*agrado*). I wish that this little demonstration may affirm (*comprove*) before your Majesty my submission and obedience and respect, which with the greatest credit and honour of the faithful, humble and obedient vassal he professes to your Majesty.

Calcutta 31st of December 1784—George Germain.

[P. 130.] Knowing through a long experience the trade of the whole of India and particularly the disadvantages which, through their commercial non-equality, the Portuguese are labouring under in Calcutta because they do not know their ancient possessions in Bengal I resolve, through my love for my country and nation, to expose through this narrative, what these possessions are.

The Portuguese possessed in the year 1632 by means of a *farman* of the Mogor *i.e.* the Mughal Emperor on the borders of the river Hooghly in Bengal above Chinsura, the Dutch factory, the lands of Hooghly (*Ugoly*) which they peopled and called the city of Hooghly and [also possessed] the Bandel with 777 *bighas* of land contiguous and in a square, containing the villages of Christians, Hindus and Moors. They enjoyed through these possessions various immunities, exemptions, faculties privileges and different *parvanas*, also conceded by the Mogor, such as of tobacco areca and salt.

At this time the Mogor maintained a seraglio in the city of Hooghly and the Europeans who were there under one Correa the last Captain-in-chief* infringed upon the liberty of this seraglio and without attention or satisfaction, they continued in this behaviour, till at last the Mogor escandalized, sent troops from Agra, which rushed on the city of Hooghly and Bandel and put to the sword all the Europeans and Christians, who resisted, and the remaining they took prisonere before the Mogor.

* According to Fr. Cabral the last Captain of the Portuguese in Hooghly was Manoel d'Azavedo. *Vide* Chap. XII.

With them (prisoners) went Frei João da Cruz, Religious of St. Augustine and Vicar in Hooghly. This man was of an exemplary life and habits and of an affable behaviour and at his instance the Mogor pardoned all the Portuguese and conceded liberty to the Portuguese to return to Bandel. He confirmed the possession of 777 *bighas* of land conceding them the same immunities, exemptions, faculties and privileges as before, by a new *farman* signed by his own hand in 1633, only with the reservation that they should not convert the Moors to Christianity, and punish with death the subjects of the land without handing them over for the purpose, to the *Faujdar* at Hooghly, of the [P. 131] Nawab of Bengal, to whom only the right of such knowledge belonged.

According to this, the Portuguese re-established themselves in the Bandel and as the Europeans (European Portuguese) went on dying, and there was no more attention paid to it (conditions of re-establishment) the Augustinians who had there a Parochial Church which they called a Convent, took charge of the land and of the Christians, who still are sub-ministered by the Prior. He and the other Religious, thinking they were masters of the possessions, lost the *farman* of the Mogor as I shall presently tell, and after the English Company took possession of Bengal, and govern (now) with the title of Nawab, they (the English Company) arranged with the Prior and made him remain content with keeping for him in Bandel only 270 *bighas* of land,* telling that this was for the oil of the lamps, and gave him a document (*papel*) for this.

The Priors subjected themselves to this, I do not know why, when other European nations which were in Bengal, at this time, did not suffer anything, neither the English usurped their factories ; and the 60 *bighas* of land which each of them have, they maintain in virtue of the respective *farmans* of the Mughal Emperor, their ports being protected and their commerce being indisputable.

The Dutch then extended their factories to Patna on account of opium which they export, prohibiting this trade, especially to the English in their ports in Asia.

The French imitated them in commerce and both of these nations with their meagre (*tenues*) possessions to negotiate in the land, without privileges, exemptions and prerogatives (*regalias*) as those of the Portuguese nation, always gave trouble to the English after they (the English) possessed Bengal.

The *farman* of Mogor was lost by Frei José d'Apresentação in the year 1740 when he was prior of Bandel and the reason was this : An

* *Vide* p. 232.

Englishman whose name I do not know, happened to die. This man was rich, brought there all his wealth and possessions and died without a will and heirs. In such matters the Nawab considering himself inheritor in places under his jurisdiction, the *Faujdar* inferred that it was Bandel, and consequently took possesslon of what belonged to the Englishman.

The Prior being frightened, applied to the Nawab to give satisfaction through one Antonio George, native christian, who was a favourite of the Nawab of Cuttack (*Cataque*). This Nawab was at this time Nawab of Bengal, to whom the Prior sent the *farman* through the said Antonio George, instead of a copy. The Nawab in view of the *farman* at once ordered the *Faujdar* of Hooghly to deliver, as he indeed did, all the goods of the Englishman to the Prior. But Antonio George refused to give it back and then died in his place near Dacca, the *farman* remaining in the possession of his family which denied it. There is a man, sixty years old, in Hooghly, named Ignacio Correa, who they say is a natural descendant of a European named Correa, the last Captain-in-chief of Hooghly, who has in his possession various *parvanas* of the powers and the privileges which the Mughals granted to the Portuguese.

In the Convent of Bandel also, there are various papers of immunities, exemptions and privileges conceded by the Mughals to the Portuguese, which the Priests do not understand being in Persian and if they had understood, they would know their value (*soberião se lhes fazia conta*). The privilege of salt, according to the minutest (*bem particular*) information which I can have on everything, was sold by a Religious to an American for ten thousand rupees, who utilized it as long as he could till the English arrogated to themselves this contract.

And the rights of tobacco, and areca nut are also forgotten, though they may be among the papers of the Convent and among the ones of Ignacio Correa.

This well shows how all the papers are scattered.

It is however the politics and the custom of the Mughals to keep always a general register in their court, in which everything is registered without failing (*sem falencia*), besides many others (registers) in all its dominions; there are near Hooghly certain brahmins of authority, who keep one of these registers [p. 133] with great care, so that the English might not destroy it, which they sometimes fear (*atrapalha*) very much and in it can be found all the information which is wanted. And there is no public or even private success (successful event) that may take place among the English which does not appear in the gazettes which are scattered almost always from the court of Delhi in Calcutta in the Persian language and thus one can infer that all the grants of the Mughals to the Portuguese are registered in all these registers and in the general register, which shall serve for all times whenever any document (*papel*) may be wanting.

Considering that all these possessions and privileges (*titulos*) can be recovered, even though they are in a notable oblivion, provided that this is ordered and that there are faculties (*disposições*) for it, [and the fact of] there being no person with power and authority who may take cognizance of every thing, using caution and precaution with all, particularly, with the Religious [Priests] the investigation will be more arduous ; but I shall do what I can to take copies of the originals, titles, faculties privileges, if I succeed in getting them from the Religious when I see this raises no suspicion ; for if it is raised they would deny and burn all the papers, before there is one who can seize them by force, and compel them to give all satisfaction which may be necessary.

Thus foreseeing all these circumstances, if I manage to get the originals so as to copy them in Persian and in Portuguese, I shall send them at the first occasion to the Chamber of Commerce in order to lay them before Your Majesty ; but I cannot guarantee this, as I am only a private individual in these matters, which depend upon the facility (faculty ?) of the Religious. But as the possessions and rights of the Portuguese nation in Bengal are for such a long time consigned to oblivion through the fault of the Priors of Bandel, who accommodated themselves to [the will of] the English without informing the Governor of Goa, [in spite of] having the *farman* and the other papers and titles at this time, which the Mogor never so far revogued and which still less the English had dared to infringe, it seems, with all due [P. 134] respect to be necessary that the commerce (commercial men) above all should implore the benign favour and grace of your Majesty, so that being, pleased (*servindo-se*) to grant it, you may order your Government to interfere in the matter before the Mogor and that the latter may in attention to the distinguished request, renew by a new *farman* the ancient possessions, immunities, exemptions, faculties and privileges, by refering to its general register of all these concessions, if any papers or titles be wanting, with more faculties for whatever more may be considered to be necessary to obtain, according to the proposal of the Plenipotentiary who may be entrusted with the orders of the Estate in this respect.

(Done in) Calcutta on the 31st of December 1784.

[Signed] GEORGE GERMAIN

HENRY LOUIS VIVIAN DEROZIO.

III

Henry Louis Vivian Derozio

A Luso-Indian Poet

It is a memorable fact in the history of the Luso-Indians that, in general, they have never attained to any literary or scientific merit. From the surrounding gloom, there emerges, however, one illustrious and brilliant name, worthy to be inscribed in the Pantheon of the World's Poets—Henry Louis Vivian Derozio, who blazed in the skies of the realms of poetry like a meteor and as quickly disappeared. An account of his life is a record of the achievements of only 23 years of existence. Yet this brief span of life sheds an undying lustre on the whole Luso-Indian community.

Henry Louis Vivian Derozio, the son of Francis Derozio was born in 1809. The house in which he was born is still in existence. It is a large two storied building in Lower Circular Road facing the new St. Teresa's Roman Catholic Church. This house is distinctly shown as "Mr. Derozio's house" in Major J. A. Schalch's Plan of Calcutta and its Environs (1825). That Henry Derozio was a Luso-Indian is beyond doubt because his grand-father Michael is mentioned in the *Bengal Directory of 1795* as "a Portuguese Merchant and Agent" in Calcutta. But E. W. Madge has pointed out that in St. John's Baptismal Register 1789 he is called a "Native Protestant."

When a lad of scarcely eighteen summers, he published his first book of poems, which unlike the destiny of budding poets, met with immediate success. The poems were spoken of in the London press, and Dr. John Grant to whom the work was dedicated managed to give him an appointment as sub-editor of the *India Gazette* in 1826 and soon after that of a professor in the Hindu College, now Presidency College. As a professor, Derozio was remarkably successful. He taught literatare, history and philosophy and "possessed the rare power of weaving interest around any subject that he taught." He started an Academic Association, which was a sort of a debating club. Its meetings were attended by the *elite* of Calcutta, including Deputy Governor of Bengal, Chief Justice, Private Secretary to the Governor and others.

Beloved as he was by his pupils many of whom, like Peary Chand Mitra, became very distinguished men of Bengal, Derozio, played the role of a reformer. He worked for the emancipation of Hindu society and instilled into his pupils the ideas of liberalism. and taught them to think for themselves. But orthodox Hinduism revolted. Derozio was publicly denounced as having denied the existence of God, having taught that obedience to parents does not form any part of moral philosophy and even that marriages between brothers and sisters were permissable. But these were base calumnies, to which Derozio emphatically replied, "Not guilty." In a letter to Dr. H. H. Wilson he refutes what he calls " the infamous fabrications." An inquiry was instituted and though the charges against Derozio were proved to be unfounded, he was compelled to resign. His pupils, however, frequented his house where he taught just as he did in the school. As Edwards says, "the gifted Eurasian teacher philosopher and poet, during the short period of his connection with the Hindu College did more to arouse, quicken and impel the thought of Young India than any man then living or since dead." He indeed, was the oracle of Young Bengal, as he is called.

Derozio's journalistic career was remarkable. Under the pseudonym *Juvenis* he contributed to the Calcutta press when a young lad at Baghalpur. He helped his pupils to run a magazine called *The Enquirer*. He was sub-editor of the *India Gazette* which afterwards appeared as the *Bengal Hurkaru* and is now the *Indian Daily News*. He also conducted the *Hesperus*. His chief journalistic achievement was the *The East Indian*, a daily paper which he founded and edited till his death.

Derozio was very tender and affectionate towards his friends and relations. He was lively and humourous in his conversation. He was an eloquent orator, as it was evidenced in the Town Hall meeting of March 28th, 1831, when, he made his great speech on the occasion of the return of J. W. Rickets who had gone to England with the East-Indians' petition to the Parliament.

The fame of Derozio now chiefly rests on his poems. During his short life Derozio poured forth his heart in sweet lyrics, which though cannot be said to rise to the highest order yet betoken a poetic genius which in maturer years, might have greatly enriched the English literature. His poems are chiefly influenced by Byron, and like him. his feelings, his hopes and his disappointments constantly recur in his poems. He had all the pathos and depth of feeling of a poet. Music rings in his strains. Ornament and rich colouring abound in his stanzas. But there is lack of form and originality. In his only long poem *Fakir of Jungheera* which runs into two Cantos there is a wealth of Eastern imagery and the scenes breathe an oriental atmosphere. It has all the charm of Byron's *Childe Harold* or Scott's *Marmion*. D. L. Richardson included Derozio's poems in his *Selections from the British Poets*. Toru Dutt,

(*Bengal Magazine*, December 1874), W. T. Webb (*The Indian Review*, December 1883), R. W. Frazer (*The Literary History of India*), have high encomiums for Derozio's poetry. References to Derozio are even found in Kipling's and Max Muller's works.

As in the case of Keats, fate was unusually cruel to Arts. Death singled out the great Luso-Indian poet, philosopher and reformer, in the midst of his ambitions still unrealized and at a time when his genius was blossoming forth in the fairest flowers of the maymorn of his life. A victim to cholera, Derozio departed from the world on December 26th, 1831, in the 23rd year of his life.

A LIST OF AUTHORITIES FOR THE BIOGRAPHY OF DEROZIO

Calcutta Literary Gazette, Nov. 10, 1833.
Oriental Magazine, Oct. 1843, Vol. I, No. 10.
Calcutta Review, Vol. XIII No. 25, 1850.
" " Vol. XVII No. 34, 1852.
T. P. Manuel, • *The Poetry of our Indian Poets*, 1861.
T. B. Lawrence, *English Poetry in India*, 1869.
Peary Chand Mitra, *Biographical Sketch of David Hare*, 1877.
W. T. Webb, *Anglo Indian Verse*, *Indian Review* Dec. 1883.
T. Edwards, *Henry Derozio, the Eurasian Poet, Teacher and Journalist*, 1884.
H. A. Stark and E. W. Madge, *East Indian Worthies* 1892.
E. W. Madge, *Forgotten Anglo Indian Bards*, A lecture 1896.
C. E. Buckland, *Bengal under the Lieutenant-Governors* 1902.
Reis and Rayyet, June 28, 1902, Article by Saroda P. Dey.
Henry Derozio, *Eurasian poet and Reformer*, Lecture by E. W. Madge 1905.
B. B. Shah, *The Poetical Works of Henry Louis Vivian Derozio*, 1907, Calcutta.

IV

Feringhi Kali, Calcutta

At 244, Bowbazar Street, Calcutta, there is a temple of Kali known, very curiously, as Feringhi Kali. It is a little building in which the Kali stands on a white figure representing a dead male. This temple was built by a Feringhi (probably a Bengali Christian) named Antonio at the desire of a Brahmin widow, both of whom lived as husband and wife, though they were not married.* This Antonio had amassed immense wealth by trade and dwelt in Ghereti near Chandernagore, where the remains of his house can still be seen. Though he was a Christian he did not interfere with the religious views of the Brahmin lady and in fact joined in the Hindu ceremonies that were performed in his house. During the Hindu festivals his house was a resort of *Kaviwallas* who were a kind minstrels, consisting of men and women who went about singing songs and composing extempore verses on the highest religious subjects as well as on the lowest incidents of human life. He knew the Bengali language well and soon outrivalled the *Kaviwallas* in the composition of extempore verses. Leaving aside his coat and trousers he would wear the *chadar* and the *dhoti* and sing Bengali songs on the stage or in praise of the Goddess Kali. He indeed founded a party of *Kaviwallas* who excelled all others in satirical extempore compositions.†

Wilson has another story about the foundation of the Feringhi Kali. He says,‡ "The kali was established by one Srimanta Dom§ of very low caste who himself used to perform the duties of the priest for a period of not less than 70 years to this goddess up to the time of his death. The Dom used to treat the people of this quarter suffering from small pox and for this reason an idol of Sítalá is kept adjacent to that of Káli. In this way the Dom became popular among the Eurasian residents of this quarter thankful for cure from this particular disease. Hence the goddess has earned the name of Firinghi Kálí"

V

Early Indian Christians of Eastern Bengal

The following excerpts from the Relation which the Father Provincial of the Congregation of St. Augustine of Goa, Frei Ambrosio de Santo Agostinho, gave to the Viceroy of India and which is preserved in the *Livro das Monções No. 125, fol. 391* and published by J. H. da Cunha Rivara in *O Chronista de Tissuari* Vol. II, 1867, throw much light on the method of conversions of the Eastern Bengal Christians and the social conditions prevailing among then in 1750. I have followed the translation of Fr. Hosten in *The Catholic Herald of India*, Dec. 19, 1917 and succeeding Nos.

* Dinesh Chandra Sen, *History of Bengali Literature*, p. 707.

† For some of his satires Cf. Dinesh Chandra Sen, *op. cit.* p. 708 *et seq.*

‡ *List of Ancient Monuments in Bengal* 1896, Calcutta, p. 106.

§ The *doms* are a caste of a very low type in Bengal. But *Dom* is also a honourable Portuguese title prefixed before a name, and many Indian Christians were at one time given this title.

"The Christians of this particular Mission are all husbandmen (*homems lavradores*) who do not understand a word of Portuguese and they are and were all of them freemen, so that neither they, nor their fathers and grandfathers, were ever bondsmen (*captivos*)...

Here I must remark that our Christians of Bengala, whether those who dress after the fashion of the country or those who dress like Europeans, were all of them equal once they become Christians (*alias que carão Christãos*); they eat and drink and intermarry without minding the castes to which they belonged in heathenism—a thing which does not happen in other Missions where the converts keep the castes they had; and as they loose their castes all at once so too do they give up their heathenish belief, all of which is due to the good education our Religious Missionaries gave them from the beginning...

The occult Christians of whom a greater number are converted, are the best christianity, because they are people living in the fields and having no intercourse whatever with the towns, and also because they have not learnt and understood much of the accursed sect of Mahomed (*Mafoma*). These men are easy and docile to convert not the Gentios who are hard and wedded to their idolatries and their castes, so much so that it is very rare for one of them to embrace the law of Jesus Christ from really spiritual motives; those of them who come over are those who first lost their caste; their relatives refuse to receive them, and then they are obliged to become Christians; for instance those who fall into captivity (slavery?) those who wish to marry a Christian girl; but those who belonged to the law of (*Mahomed*) are converted for truly spiritual motives. They are occult because they have not the permission from the Great Mogor to make use of their liberty for changing their religion, nor are we allowed under pain of death for us and them, to admit them to the Law of Jesus Christ...

We have many Catechists who serve us without receiving any payment from us because we have not the means; their disciples both neophytes and catechumens maintain them. They call them masters (*mestres*) and treat them with every respect; catechising has now become for them an occupation and a means of living...

This is the way they are catechised. They begin to sing some canticles which they have, of the Mysteries of the Rosary. Dom Antonio composed them. And as the people collect to hear them and put some questions about their meaning the occasion arises for conversion. These canticles are very pious and very devout and all the Christians of the mission, public and occult, know them and they are the Psalms with which they praise God both in the Church and outside it, according to the time of day (*segundo os tempos*)...

Martyrs killed in hatred of the Faith there are none because the Moors of Bengala are not enemies of the Christians; they esteem them rather. Until now there never was any persecution in Bengala except when I was Rector, when there was a beginning of one, but it did not take effect, because the Moor would not...

The Christians of Bengala are brought up in such a way that they are free from all error, or heathenish ceremony; they are brought up like the Christians in Portugal and all the ceremonies of the Church are observed in the administration of the Sacraments. If we were to bring them up as they do the Christians of Malavar, we might have a greater number of Christians than we have; but they (the Fathers) understood it was better to have few and good ones than to have many and bad ones. There are at present in this Mission 1,500 public Christians, and 8,000 occult ones or 9,500 all together; the Christians who dress like Europeans are 8,733 which with the 9,500 of the Mission makes 18,233 a little more or less..."

VI

The Dominicans in Bengal

Among the Portuguese Religious Orders that worked in Bengal, the Dominicans remain to be mentiond. The Franciscans confined themselves to Burma and Arakan. But the Dominicans who had convents and houses in Goa, in other parts in Western India, in Ceylon, Cochim, Mylapore and Negapatam, also made Bengal for a time the scene of their activities. At the request of some Portuguese from Chittagong, Frey Gaspar d' Assumpção and Frei Belchior da Luz came to Dianga in 1601 and raised a Hermitage with a Church, which were however soon after burnt down and sacked by the King of Arakan during his war on the Portuguese.* The Jesuits also suffered during this year and one of the eyes of Fr. F. Fernandes S. J. was nearly torn out (*vide p.* 102) The King however made peace with the Portuguese and desired the Friars to remain in his kingdom and even built a new Home and Church for the Dominicans at his own expense. The Dominicans however

* *Vide* Frey Luis de Cacegas *Historia de S. Domingos* 1767, Vol. III, Liv. chap. XI or Fr. Hosten's Translation in the *Bengal Past and Present* Jul.—Sept. 1914, pp. 1—5.

did not remain long in Chittagong on account of the "danger and treacherous wars menacing their residence and the little protection it afforded."

VII

A Governor of Chittagong Slain by the Portuguese

The following account of Caesar de Federici regarding the Portuguese of Chittagong in 1569 is interesting. Cf. *Hakluytus Posthumus Purchas, His Pilgrimes* by Samuel Purchas Vol. X pp. 137—138, Glasgow, M C M V.):—

"This Iland is called Sondiva belonging to the Kingdome of Bengala, distant one hundred and twentie miles from Chatigan, to which place we were bound. The people are Moores, and the King a very good man of a Moore King, for if he had bin a Tyrant as others bee, he might have robbed us of all because the Portugall Captaine of Chatigan was in armes against the Retor of that place, and every day there were some slaine, at which newes wee rested there with no small feare, keeping good watch and ward aboord every night as the use is, but the Governour of the Towne did comfort us, and bad us that we should feare nothing, but that we should repose our selves securely without any danger, although the Portugals of Chatigan had slaine the Governour of that Citie, and said that we were not culpable in that fact; and moreover he did us every day what pleasure he could, which was a thing contrarie to our expectations considering that they and the people of Chatigan were both subjects to one King."

VIII

Luso-Indian Names

To the Luso-Indian surnames mentioned on pp. 179-180, the following may be added :—

Coelho, Cunha or D'Cunha, Gabriel, Joaquim, Luz or DeLuz, Rangel, Rego, Sanches or Sanges, Vieyra.

INDEX

D

E

F

N

O

T